# Transaction Economics of John R. Commons

Takahashi reconstructs the key blocks of one of the founders of the institutional school, John R. Commons' theories of the evolution of capitalism and of institutional change by taking the concept of transaction as a central point of departure.

Commons' theories continue to influence modern economics, and in this book, Takahashi scrutinizes his construction of transaction and its features and offers a reinterpretation of Commons' institutional economics and transaction economics. He then explores how Commons' analysis of going concerns (e.g., firms) has broader and deeper applications that extend to monetary policy, labor policy, and the business cycle. Takahashi examines how Commons' and Veblen's dynamic theories share cumulative causation. He closes by positing that Commons' transaction economics seeks "reasonable capitalism" through a virtuous cycle of reasonable value and generation of good business ethics.

This book will be attractive to researchers of institutional economics, political economy, heterodox economics, as well as the history of economic thought, law, and ethics.

**Shingo Takahashi** is a professor at the Tokyo College of Transport Studies, Toshima, Tokyo, Japan. He has taught economics and the history of economic thought and studied the institutional economics of Commons for more than 20 years.

## Routledge Studies in the History of Economics

**Adam Smith's Theory of Value and Distribution**
Economics as a Moral Science Once Again
*Jeffrey T. Young*

**Arthur Spiethoff and the German Historical School**
Continuities and Discontinuities
*Vitantonio Gioia*

**The Economic Thought of Hilaire Belloc**
A Christian alternative to the Servile State
*Alfonso Díaz Vera*

**Schumpeter's General Theory of Capitalism**
*Tristan Velardo*
*Translated by Katya Long*

**Slavery and Colonialism in the History of Economic Thought**
The Cases of France and Great Britain
*Simona Pisanelli*

**Hegel on Ethics, the State and Public Policy**
Comparisons with Immanuel Kant and Utilitarianism
*Samuel Hollander*

**Transaction Economics of John R. Commons**
Towards Reasonable Capitalism
*Shingo Takahashi*

For more information about this series, please visit: www.routledge.com/series/SE0341

# Transaction Economics of John R. Commons

## Towards Reasonable Capitalism

Shingo Takahashi

Routledge
Taylor & Francis Group
LONDON AND NEW YORK

First published 2025
by Routledge
4 Park Square, Milton Park, Abingdon, Oxon OX14 4RN

and by Routledge
605 Third Avenue, New York, NY 10158

*Routledge is an imprint of the Taylor & Francis Group, an informa business*



*British Library Cataloguing-in-Publication Data*
A catalogue record for this book is available from the British Library

*Library of Congress Cataloging-in-Publication Data*
Names: Takahashi, Shingo (Economist), author.
Title: Transaction economics of John R. Commons : towards reasonable capitalism / Shingo Takahashi.
Description: Abingdon, Oxon ; New York, NY : Routledge, 2025. | Series: Routledge studies in the history of economics | Includes bibliographical references and index.
Identifiers: LCCN 2024027679 | ISBN 9781032701387 (hardback) | ISBN 9781032701400 (paperback) | ISBN 9781032701394 (ebook)
Subjects: LCSH: Commons, John R. (John Rogers), 1862–1945. | Institutional economics. | Capitalism.
Classification: LCC HB119.C58 T35 2025 | DDC 330.15/52—dc23
LC record available at https://lccn.loc.gov/2024027679

ISBN: 978-1-032-70138-7 (hbk)
ISBN: 978-1-032-70140-0 (pbk)
ISBN: 978-1-032-70139-4 (ebk)

DOI: 10.4324/9781032701394

Typeset in ITC Galliard Pro
by Apex CoVantage, LLC

# Contents

# Acknowledgments

In writing this book, I received assistance from many people. I am indebted to Hiroyuki Uni, our project leader of a Japanese Grants-in-Aid for Scientific Research, for his academic ideas in distinguishing between "reasonable price" and "reasonable value" of Commons and the evolution of the transaction concept through manuscript analysis in *Institutional Economics* of Commons. Kiichiro Yagi, my advisor in graduate school, has been a great help through his comments on my report at the Japan Association for Evolutionary Economics (JAFEE) and for his specific advice on the English publication of this book. Tetsuo Taka, one of the pioneers of the study of institutional economics in Japan, gave me comments on my reports at the Japanese Society for the History of Economic Thought (JSHET) and shared his academic ideas on the interpretation of the reasonable value of Commons. Yukihiro Ikeda, my undergraduate advisor, has advised me on writing articles and books since he guided me in my undergraduate thesis. In addition, anonymous reviewers gave me specific advice on improving this book. Some of their advice are reflected in Chapters 8 and 9. I am grateful to the reviewers for making this book broad and deep. Finally, I am thankful to Japanese and international Commons scholars for their academic advice and inspiration at academic conferences, especially at JAFEE, JSHET, and Association for Evolutionary Economics (AFEE). I refer to their works in the chapters that follow. Although I have benefited from the advice of these individuals, I take full responsibility for any errors in the content of this book.

The following chapters of this book consist of partially modified or added material from my previous publications. I have written this book, with permission to reprint these papers.

### Chapter 1

Takahashi, Shingo. (2006). "J. R. Commons no 'Torihiki' Keizaigaku: Hō-teki Gainen ni yoru Seido Keizaigaku" (J. R. Commons's 'Transaction Economics': Institutional Economic Theory by Legal Concepts) (in Japanese), *Keizai-gakushi Kenkyū* (The History of Economic Thought), 48 (1), 16–31.

## Chapter 2

Takahashi, Shingo. (2010). "J. R. Commons no Gōingu-konsān Ron" (J. R. Commons' Theory of a Going Concern) (in Japanese), *Hitotsubashi-daigaku Shakai-kagaku Koten-shiryō-sentā Nenpō* (Hitotsubashi University Bulletin of the Center for Historical Social Science), 30, 19–31.

## Chapter 3

Takahashi, Shingo. (2020a). "Toward Reasonable Capitalism: The Role of John R. Commons's Price and Business Cycle Theories," *Journal of Economic Issues*, 54 (2), 420–427.

## Chapter 4

Takahashi, Shingo. (2020b). "J. R. Commons' Business Cycle Theory," *Journal of Economic Issues*, 54 (4), 907–917.

## Chapter 5

Takahashi, Shingo. (2008). "J. R. Commons no Kinyū Seisaku Ron" (J. R. Commons' Monetary Policy) (in Japanese), *Keizai Ronsō* (Kyoto University), 182 (5–6), 536–559.
Takahashi, Shingo. (2015). "J. R. Commons no Seido Keizaigaku ni okeru Shōraisei 1" (Futurity on J. R. Commons' Institutional Economics 1) (in Japanese), *Tokyo Kōtsū Tanki-daigaku Kenkyū Kiyō* (Tokyo College of Transport Studies), 20, 43–54.
Takahashi, Shingo. (2016). "J. R. Commons no Seido Keizaigaku ni okeru Shōraisei 2" (Futurity on J. R. Commons' Institutional Economics 2) (in Japanese), *Tokyo Kōtsū Tanki-daigaku Kenkyū Kiyō* (Tokyo College of Transport Studies), 21, 61–76.

## Chapter 6

Takahashi, Shingo. (2023). "Rōsai-hoshō to Shitsugyō-hoshō kara Umidasareru Kachi: J. R. Commons no Rōdō Seisaku Ron to Seido Keizaigaku" (Reasonable Value Generated from Accident Compensation and Unemployment Compensation: J. R. Commons' Theory of Labor Policy and Institutional Economics) (in Japanese), *Tokyo Kōtsū Tanki-daigaku Kenkyū Kiyō* (Tokyo College of Transport Studies), 28, 202–212.

## Chapter 8

Takahashi, Shingo. (2014). "J. R. Commons no 'Hō to Keizaigaku' " (J. R. Commons on 'Law and Economics') (in Japanese), *Tokyo Kōtsū Tanki-daigaku Kenkyū Kiyō* (Tokyo College of Transport Studies), 19, 63–72.
Takahashi, Shingo. (2022). "Seido no Shinka to Keizai Hatten: D. C. North to J. R. Commons no Seido Shinka Ron no Hikaku" (Institutional Evolution and Economic Development: The Comparison between D. C. North and J. R. Commons' Theory of Institutional Evolution) (in Japanese), *Tokyo Kōtsū Tanki-daigaku Kenkyū Kiyō* (Tokyo College of Transport Studies), 27, 93–102.

I thank JSHET, Hitotsubashi University: the Center for Historical Social Science Literature, Taylor & Francis, Kyoto University Economic Society, and Tokyo College of Transport Studies Research Committee for granting permission to reproduce this book. This publication was also supported by JSPS KAKENHI Grant Number JP21K01418.

# Introduction

This book describes the institutional economics of John Rogers Commons (1862–1945) and his theoretical system through the concept of "transactions." The full scope of Commons' institutional economics is complex and poorly understood. This understanding is because of the following reasons.

1. It is based on Commons' own various experiences (labor–management negotiations, social security policymaking, etc.).
2. It uses interdisciplinary terminology with mixed legal and ethical elements.
3. It explains economic society through a legal approach.

For these reasons, compared to his high reputation as the founder of the Wisconsin School in the study of labor history, his reputation as an institutional economist, especially as a theorist, is low. Indeed, Lafayette G. Harter, Jr, who wrote a detailed review of Commons, wrote, "While his works on general economics gather dust, his *History of Labor* remains a classic often quoted in its field" (Harter, 1962, p. 163). Ronald H. Coase also noted in *The American Economic Review* that:

> John R. Commons, Wesley Mitchell, and those associated with them were men of great intellectual stature, but they were anti-theoretical, and without a theory to bind together their collection of facts, they had very little that they were able to pass on.
>
> (Coase, 1998, p. 72)

Recently, Geoffrey M. Hodgson also said,

> No less important are the original American institutionalists, particularly Thorstein Veblen and John R. Commons. Although they lacked a comprehensive theory, they enhanced our understanding of the institutional and legal foundations of capitalism and also emphasized the role of technology in revolutionizing social life.
>
> (Hodgson, 2015, p. 7)

DOI: 10.4324/9781032701394-1

Hodgson notes the importance of Veblen and Commons but judges that "they lacked a comprehensive theory." Is the theory of institutional economics of Commons really useless, anti-theoretical, and not comprehensive? This is the main issue in this book.

The second issue is whether labor theory and institutional economics of Commons can be theoretically connected. John D. Chasse, in *A Worker's Economist*, praises Commons' work as a labor historian or labor lawmaker, stating that "The *Principle of Labor Legislation* (hereafter the Principles) may have been John R.'s most successful book" (Chasse, 2017, p. 155). Moreover, he states,

> The *Principle of Labor Legislation* is largely ignored today. Scholars interested in John R.'s thought generally pay more attention to the *Legal Foundations of Capitalism, Institutional Economics*, and perhaps *Myself*. But the *Principles* probably exercised a greater influence over his students Commons.
>
> (Chasse, 2017, p. 219)

emphasizing the importance of the *Principle of Labor Legislation*. Chasse and most Commons scholars treat the labor history research part and the institutional economics theory as separate. Should the two, especially labor theory and institutional economic theory, be understood separately? This is the second issue. In order to consider this issue, this book will take the labor theory that Commons wrote alone and compare it with institutional economic theory rather than the *Principle of Labor Legislation*, which he wrote with his student Andrews.

The third issue is the characteristics and possibilities shown if we view the institutional economics of Commons as "transaction economics" centered on the transaction concept. In particular, what can we say if we analyze his theory from the beginning to end using the transaction concept? The focus on the "transaction" concept is not new, as Commons emphasized in *Institutional Economics* (Commons, 1934a). However, Commons explained his theory in part, not whole, with the transaction concept. Even in previous studies, some have partially explained his view with transactions, but none have described his entire theoretical system by sticking to the "transaction" concept from the beginning to end. Therefore, with these understandings, we would like to grasp what features emerge in the transaction economics of Commons compared to new institutional economics of economists such as Oliver E. Williamson and Douglass C. North and then understand what implications for real capitalist society can be obtained through the transaction concept and discuss its potential. These are the three main topics of this book.

This book is structured to address these issues. First, as an "Institution," Part I will discuss the transaction concept and its characteristics as the basis of the transaction theory in Chapter 1 and explain how to view the institutional economic theory of Commons as transaction economics based on this concept. Chapter 2 deals with the going concern theory based on the transaction concept. This is a Commons-style analysis of markets and organizations. In this context, I will explain how transactions function.

Part II, "Basis of cumulative causation: markets and business organizations," will capture the connection between markets and business organizations. Chapter 3 discusses pricing theory and uses diagrams to examine how transactions and pricing are connected and how going concerns and pricing are connected. Chapter 4 will then deal with Commons' business cycle theory and confirm that the series of connections up to this point can be understood as a cumulative causation.

Part III deals with the role of the state and policy theory as "Stabilization policy: role of the state." Chapter 5 deals with monetary policy, examining the concept of "futurity" for Commons and his view of money. Chapter 6 deals with labor theory and labor policy. Since labor issues are the area in which Commons has devoted the most effort, this chapter is larger than the other chapters, including an overview of his labor history research. The critical point is how Commons' labor policy connects to cumulative causation, including transaction concepts.

Part IV, "Reasonable capitalism," deals with the relations between the theory of reasonable value and transaction economics. First, Chapter 7 will examine what Commons sees as "reasonable value." We will consider what interpretation is necessary to capture the core of reasonable value and attempt to understand this value using this book's unique interpretation. Chapter 8 will compare the transaction economics of Commons with the theory of new institutional economics and clarify the commonalities and differences between the two. After highlighting the characteristics of transaction economics through this comparison, we explain its potential in Chapter 9, using cumulative legal causation as a critical concept. Finally, in the Conclusion, we summarize what we have done in this book.[1]

This book extensively uses diagrams to illustrate the overall theoretical picture of transaction economics. I believe using diagrams to intuitively understand the theory of Commons is extremely important because of its uniqueness and complexity. We can understand the overall transaction economics of Commons using the diagrams in the chapters, especially the connections between each one.

Finally, I will mention the relationship between my study and previous studies. Currently, Commons is being reevaluated by Charles J. Whalen and other American Association for Evolutionary Economics (AFEE) members in the United States. Many researchers are paying attention to Commons in Japan, especially in the Japan Association for Evolutionary Economics (JAFEE).[2] Furthermore, in Europe, some regulation theorists, led by Bruno Théret of France, are paying attention to Commons. These studies have greatly influenced this book. Of course, this book has also been influenced by classic institutionalist researchers such as Joseph Dorfman and Allan G. Gruchy, as well as by Malcolm Rutherford, Yngve Ramstad, Warren J. Samuels, and others since mainly the 1990s. These and other previous studies will be introduced in subsequent chapters as needed.

## Notes

1 This book is primarily concerned with elucidating the essence of the institutional economic theory of Commons, focusing on transaction concepts. Therefore, it does not include philosophical analysis, especially reflections on pragmatism. Historical analysis and autobiographical studies are also limited to the extent necessary. For autobiographical reflections, see Commons' *Myself* (Commons, 1934b), Harter (1962), and Chasse (2017).

2 In order to show the achievements of Japanese researchers, this book introduces references in Japanese as well as English. Note that Tetsuo Taka and Toshihiro Tanaka pioneered the study of Commons in Japan. In particular, Taka (1998) discusses the difference between the transaction concept of Commons and that of new institutional economics. In recent years, JSPS KAKENHI projects led by Hiroyuki Uni, including the author, have produced research results using newly discovered manuscripts of *Institutional Economics.* One is Hiroyuki Uni (ed.), *Contemporary Meanings of John R. Commons's Institutional Economics; An Analysis Using a Newly Discovered Manuscript* (2017). Among the members of this group, Hiroyuki Uni studied detailed discussions of reasonable value from a manuscript analysis, as well as the evolution of rationing transactions and cumulative causation (Uni, 2014, 2019, 2022). Kota Kitagawa discussed a cumulative causation in the study on reasonable value and sovereignty (Kitagawa, 2014, 2017). In addition, Takayuki Nakahara has researched the fusion of Commons' institutional economic theory with the regulation theory (Nakahara, 2018). Akiyoshi Sakaguchi has also studied the money theory of Commons and the regulation theory from the perspective of monetary institutional theory (Sakaguchi, 2020). Meanwhile, Tokutaro Shibata published a Japanese book summarizing the institutional economics of Commons, focusing on the business cycle and stabilization theory of Commons (Shibata, 2021). Ken Kato has long studied Commons' labor relations theory and produced results on goodwill, workers' compensation, and unemployment compensation (Kato, 2006, 2009). Ryuichiro Terakawa has studied early Commons' money reform plans based on a detailed analysis of Commons (Terakawa, 2019), and Akihiro Abe has studied the relations between pragmatism and Commons (Abe, 2018).

## References

### *English*

Chasse, John D. (2017). *A Worker's Economist: John R. Commons and His Legacy from Progressivism to the War on Poverty.* New York: Routledge.
Coase, Ronald H. (1998). "The New Institutional Economics," *American Economic Review*, 88 (May), 72–74.
Commons, John R. (1934a). *Institutional Economics: Its Place in Political Economy.* New York: Macmillan.
———. (1934b). *Myself.* New York: Macmillan.
Harter, Lafayette G., Jr. (1962). *John R. Commons: His Assault on Laissez-Faire.* Corvallis, OR: Oregon State University Press.
Hodgson, Geoffrey M. (2015). *Conceptualizing Capitalism: Institutions, Evolution, Future.* Chicago and London: University of Chicago Press.
Kitagawa, Kota. (2017). "Two Methods of Institutional Reform in the *Institutional Economics* of John R. Commons," in Uni (2017), 73–98.

Nakahara, Takayuki. (2018). "Rethinking John R. Commons's Theory of Collective Action: The Viewpoint of Regulation and Convention," *Journal of Economic Issues*, 52 (2), 405–412.

Uni, Hiroyuki. (Ed.). (2017). *Contemporary Meanings of John R. Commons's Institutional Economics: An Analysis Using a Newly Discovered Manuscript.* Singapore: Springer.

### *Japanese*

Abe, Akihiro. (2018). "Keizaigaku no Tetsugakuteki Kisoduke no Kokoromi: Peirce teki Pragmatism no Ōyō wo Tsūjite" (An Attempt at a Philosophical Foundation for Economics: Through the Application of Peirce-like Pragmatism) [Doctoral thesis, University of Tokyo]. University of Tokyo Repository. https://repository.dl.itc.u-tokyo.ac.jp/records/50388.

Kato, Ken. (2006). "J. R. Commons ni okeru Koyō Mondai to Rōshi kan no Goodwill" (J. R. Commons on the Problem of Employment and Industrial Goodwill), *Keizai-gakushi Kenkyū* (The History of Economic Thought), 48 (1), 32–45.

———. (2009). "America 1910 nendai ni okeru Shitsugyō Hoken no Kōsō: Commons, Andrews, Rubinow" (American Unemployment Insurance Schemes of the 1910s: J. R. Commons, J. B. Andrews, and I. M. Rubinow), *Keizai-gakushi Kenkyū* (The History of Economic Thought), 50 (2), 38–55.

Kitagawa, Kota. (2014). "J. R. Commons *Seido-Keizaigaku* ni okeru Tekisei-na Kachi to Shuken" (Reasonable Value and Sovereignty in *Institutional Economics* on J. R. Commons) [Doctoral thesis, Kyoto University]. Kyoto University Repository. https://repository.kulib.kyoto-u.ac.jp/dspace/bitstream/2433/199050/1/ykeik00505.pdf

Sakaguchi, Akiyoshi. (2020). "J. R. Commons no Kahei Seido Setsu to Sono Shatei: B. Théret no Commons Kaishaku wo Chūshin ni" (J. R. Commons' Institutional Theory of Money: Based on B. Théret's Interpretation), *Senshū-University Shakai-Kagaku-Kenkyū-Nenpō*, 54, 57–71.

Shibata, Tokutaro. (2021). *J. R. Commons no Seido-teki Keizaigaku* (Institutional Economics of J. R. Commons). Tokyo: Nihon-Keizai-Hyōronsha.

Taka, Tetsuo. (1998). "Commons ni okeru 'Hō to Keizaigaku' to Seido-shugi" ('Law and Economics' and Institutionalism on Commons), *Keizaigaku-Ronkyū* (The Journal of Economics of Kwansei Gakuin University), 52 (1), 65–84.

Terakawa, Ryuichiro. (2019). "Shoki Commons no Tsūka Seido Kaikaku Kōsō" (John R. Commons' Early Monetary Reform), *Keizai-gakushi Kenkyū* (The History of Economic Thought), 60 (2), 20–41.

Uni, Hiroyuki. (2014). "J. R. Commons no Ruisekiteki Inga Renkan Ron: *Seido Keizaigaku* to 1927 nen Sōko no Hikaku Bunseki" (J. R. Commons' Theory of Cumulative Causation: A Comparative Analysis of *Institutional Economics* and Its Manuscript in 1927), *Kikan-Keizai-Riron* (Political Economy Quarterly), 51 (2), 77–88.

———. (2019). "J. R. Commons no Wicksell Rishi Riron Hihan: R. G. Hawtrey no Eikyō wo Chūshin ni" (John. R. Commons' Criticism of Wicksell's Theory of Interest: Focusing on an Influence of R. G. Hawtrey), *Keizai-Ronso* (The Economic Review), 193 (1), 85–105.

———. (2022). "J. R. Commons no Tekisei Kakaku Ron to Tekisei Kachi Ron" (John. R. Commons's Reasonable Price and Reasonable Value), *Kikan-Keizai-Riron* (Political Economy Quarterly), 59 (3), 84–95.

# Part I

# Institution

# 1 Theory of transactions

## The base of transaction economics of John R. Commons

This chapter aims to systematically view Commons' institutional economics as "transaction economics." To this end, we will focus on Commons' original conceptual device of "transactions" and understand his institutional economics intrinsically from there.

Commons' institutional economics aimed to move extreme individualism, collectivism, materialism, and static analysis to a dynamic analysis of human collective behavior. Commons summarized the content of this work in his later works, *The Legal Foundations of Capitalism* (Commons, 1924), *Institutional Economics* (Commons, 1934), and *The Economics of Collective Action* (Commons, 1950), published after his death. Commons himself emphasized that "transactions" are an essential concept that plays a central role in his theory; so taking up the concept of transactions itself is not particularly new. However, even though the Transaction Cost Economics has been attracting attention since the 1990s and Commons' transaction concept influenced Williamson, there have been few in-depth studies on the similarities and differences between the two. Among them, Ramstad (1996) states that "it is clear that Williamson's transaction cost economics cannot be grafted intact onto Commons's institutional economics" (Ramstad, 1996, p. 422), and it is particularly noteworthy that Williamson has no equivalent to Commons' "rationing transactions." Taka (1998) also points out that the only thing that the new institutional economics and Commons have in common is "bargaining transactions" among the three types of transactions (Taka, 1998, p. 68).[1] Based on these previous studies, this chapter aims to analyze the concept of transaction in more depth.[2]

Commons' theory is based on his practical activities and is difficult to grasp because of the many juristic concepts. On the other hand, the importance of law and institutions in economics is increasing. In this context, it is of great interest to know whether the institutional economics of Commons has only provided essential ideas to the new institutional economics or left behind an important message that the new institutional economists could only partially absorb. To do so, it is first necessary to systematically understand the institutional economics of Commons. What kind of overall picture can we obtain if we examine the concept of transaction as a core concept in which we can see

DOI: 10.4324/9781032701394-3

the methodological characteristics of Commons? These are the problems set for this chapter.

In order to address this issue, we will follow the following process. The first section summarizes why Commons chose the concept of "transaction" as the minimum unit of analysis. The following section presents the three characteristics of the transaction concept. Through these characteristics, we can understand that the legal and social elements, which are not emphasized in the "exchange" concept, are the axes of the transaction concept. The following section then explores the primary picture of transaction economics based on the transaction concept. The question is how to explain the relations among individuals and between individuals and groups in the micro dimension and how to explain collective behavior and its order in the macro dimension.

## Commons' transaction concept

Commons' consciousness of a problem was to construct a theory of the relations between individuals and groups and between groups, that is, the collective action in general, focusing on labor issues as capitalism moves toward monopolization. However, he pointed out that conventional economics did not solve these problems (Commons, 1950, p. 35). In *Institutional Economics*, he showed what position to take on economic phenomena. He criticized extreme individualistic economics and the resulting inaction at the time of the Great Depression, as well as extreme collectivistic economics and the resulting dictatorial communism and fascism. He stated that the error of such extreme economics is to transfer directly to economics the meanings derived from the physical sciences (Commons, 1934, p. 96). Specifically, he discussed the "mechanism," which treated individuals as material things such as electrons and atoms and explained the relations between individuals and the whole in terms of physics, and the "organism," which treated individuals as cells subject to the laws of nature and explained the relations between individuals and the whole in terms of biology.

Both theories have in common the view that the individual, a component of society, is a passive being to nature and society. However, while humans are passive beings, they are also proactive beings. Commons argued that economic theories based on "mechanism" and "organism" are mistaken in that they treat "ideas," which are intellectual tools, only as passive and objective. He believed that economics must deal not with relations between things but with relations between people and things, as well as between people and people, and therefore must not construct a theory based solely on passive ideas but must construct a theory based on active ideas with subjective "meaning." This method places the active elements that arise from the human will at the root of the theory. Commons called this active will of human beings "willingness," where he assumed an active economic agent instead of a passive economic agent.

Based on these assumptions, institutional economics of Commons will analyze the era of collective action in which modern political parties in mass society, joint-stock companies, and labor unions have developed. While "conflicts" between people with willingness arise, "dependence" on the group increases, and an "order" is needed to arbitrate the disputing parties. Commons aims to analyze collective action and needs to include these elements as the minimum unit of analysis. In academic terms, this is a law, economics, and ethics matter. In terms of law, it is a problem of analysis of the rights and duties of parties and the setting of rules, including the sanction of physical force to comply with them; in terms of economics, it is a problem of setting rules based on the exchange relations of goods and services and the profits and losses generated by the market; in terms of ethics, it is a problem of analysis of rights and duties within groups and organizations and the setting of moral rules.

> Thus, the ultimate unit of activity, which correlates law, economics, and ethics, must contain in itself the three principles of *conflict, dependence,* and *order*. This unit is a Transaction.
>
> (Commons, 1934, p. 58)

What is the difference between the "transaction" and "exchange" concepts? First, "exchange" is based on transferring material control of goods and money, resulting from the choice between pleasure and pain between goods. Conversely, "transaction" represents transfers of legal control, including transfers of ownership, and results from voluntary negotiations between human beings through persuasion or coercion. Commons noted that conventional economic theory defines materials and ownership as wealth, but ownership is an asset. In other words, "exchange" is basically for material goods, while "transaction" is for material and immaterial, including intangible things (assets and liabilities). In the "exchange" between commodities, people passively choose between pleasure and pain, and the starting point of discussion is individual desire. Furthermore, there is a difference in that the general concept of "exchange" is a momentary action based on accumulating past labor. In contrast, the concept of "transaction" is a present control with the expectation of future results, that is, we must be aware of "futurity." This is because:

> The *transfer of these rights* must therefore be negotiated between the parties concerned, according to the working rules of society, before labor can produce, or consumers can consume, or commodities can be physically delivered to other persons.
>
> (Commons, 1934, p. 58)

The "transaction" concept of Commons aims to elucidate human conflicts and interdependence through "transactions" and explain what is vital in providing order to these relations. In order to do so, we must consider what kinds of transactions are conducted by what kinds of actors and under what circumstances order formed. The contents of such transactions are the significant characteristics that constitute the "transaction" concept of Commons. In the next section, we will examine these three characteristics.

## Characteristics of Commons' transaction concept

### *Will of the actor*

The first characteristic is the assumption that the individual who executes the "transaction" is not a passive and static person who makes a momentary choice between two alternatives[3] but a proactive and dynamic person connected to actual actions.

As mentioned in the previous section, Commons held that "ideas" must not be treated only as passive and objective things but as active things, subjectively "meaning" by human beings. For example, Commons explains that if "red" is taken as 400 trillion vibrations per second, it can objectively explain the mechanism of the color world. However, "It may mean a murder or it may mean a rose" from red (Commons, 1934, p. 17). In other words,

> Our knowledge is not copies, but is, on the intellectual side, ideas actually created within; on the emotional side, meaning, which relate the ideas to the sensations.
>
> (Commons, 1934, pp. 17–18)

Thus, Commons criticized the idea that science is only the objective analysis of events, treating human beings like passive substances, and argued the need to shift the focus to familiar activities arising from human subjectivity. Based on the former passive view of man and science, economic analysis is basically the analysis of individuals' objective and material choices based on their physiological judgments. Supply and demand analysis appears when scarcity analysis is added to this. This value analysis is based on the objective meaning of "ideas," and general economics analyzes these objective, measurable objects. Commons emphasized, however, that social science requires an analysis of subjective meaning and objective analysis. To do this analysis, we require the assumption of a subjective and dynamic image of the human being.

Commons uses the term "willingness" to describe this image of man. Willingness is not a mere will but "a supposed similarity of cause, effect, or purpose, derived from experiences with human behavior" (Commons, 1934, p. 94). That is, it is a will linked to actions from the past to the future. The critical point is that willingness is connected to the future. Futurity would not be a problem if individuals had perfect knowledge and rationality since they would not be anxious about the future. However, since real people do not have perfect knowledge or rationality, "Not logic, but fear and hope are fundamental" factors at work (Commons, 1950, p. 105). In other words, humans consciously choose their current actions based on their concerns and expectations about the future and their accumulated past experiences. Commons' conception of economic agents is based on this willingness. In psychological terms, it represents the meaning of ideas; in economic terms, it represents the evaluation of value and the choice of action.

Among willingness, which is the totality of comprehensive will, Commons gives another name, "will-in-action,"[4] to the will mainly associated with an action. In actual transactions, an individual's choice to do a thing is "performance." His choice not to do it is "avoidance." However, in addition to these two choices, there is also the option of "forbearance"[5] in which the individual restrains his or her actions depending on the power relationship with the other party. It is a will that restricts one's actions. By assuming that a person has the will to refrain from his actions, he avoids a situation in which he accepts the demands of others in their entirety or refuses all of them.

### *Legal relations*

The second characteristic is the incorporation of legal relations in the transactions. Commons classified these transactions into three types: "bargaining transactions," "managerial transactions," and "rationing transactions." The purpose is to understand collective actions in terms of the legal and economic relations of transactions. The following is an explanation of each of the three types of transactions.

#### *Bargaining transactions*

Commons describes bargaining transactions that "*transfer ownership* of wealth by voluntary agreement between legal equals" (Commons, 1934, p. 68). Specifically, it is the transaction "on the markets which transfer ownerships of corporeal property and the new kinds of incorporeal and intangible property of bonds and stocks of corporations" (Commons, 1950, p. 43). Since it does not occur in a state of infinite existence of goods at all times and in all places, "the universal principle of bargaining transactions is scarcity," and its "unit of measurement" "is the dollar" (Commons, 1934, pp. 64, 66). The exchange of goods in the market, as generally assumed by economics, is included in this transaction. Commons, however, says that the "*individual* does not transfer ownership. Only the state, or, in medieval times, the 'market overt,' by operation of law as interpreted by the court, transfer ownership" (Commons, 1934, p. 60). Bargaining is the negotiation based on a unit consisting of "*four* parties, two buyers and two sellers" (Commons, 1934, p. 59), as explained in the next section. The price changes depending on how the negotiation is conducted. In other words, a reasonable price is constituted on the basis of the preceding conditions of equal opportunity to choose between the parties, fair competition, and equality of bargaining power (Commons, 1934, p. 63).[6]

*Managerial transactions*

Managerial transactions are for "the production of wealth" between "a legal superior who has legal right to issue commands" and "a legal inferior who, while the relation lasts, is bound by the legal duty of obedience." The relations between a manager and an employee in the workplace, or between a factory foreman and a worker, fall under this category. However, in this case, the legal superior does not refer to the entire management class but to individuals who belong to it and thus refers to "a relation between two parsons" (Commons, 1934, p. 64), whereas "bargaining transactions" consist of four persons. Moreover, while the universal principle of "bargaining transactions" is "scarcity," the universal principle of "managerial transactions" is the principle of "efficiency," which uses "man-hour" as the unit of measurement. It represents "the ratio of output per hour (physical use-values) to input per hour (average labor)" (Commons, 1934, pp. 64, 66).[7]

*Rationing transactions*

Rationing transactions "apportion the burdens and benefits of wealth creation by the *dictation* of legal superiors" (Commons, 1934, p. 68). A typical example is taxation because "the burden of taxation is apportioned by sovereignty without the consent or bargaining on the part of individual taxpayers" (Commons, 1950, p. 55). Rationing transaction is also a relation based on legal superiority but "differs from managerial transaction," which represents relations between two persons "in that the superior is a collective superior while the inferiors are individuals" (Commons, 1931, p. 653). Rationing transactions include "dictatorships," while they also include "the budget-making of corporate board of directors" and "the decisions of a court or arbitrator," which in the United States "are subject finally to the working rules (due process of law) of the Supreme Court" (Commons, 1931, p. 654). Commons then points out that, in addition to taxation, these economic outcomes include the distribution of wealth through "output-rationing" and "price rationing" (Commons, 1934, p. 68, 760). In this case, the former affects managerial transactions, and the latter affects bargaining transactions. Thus, the process by which a group or organization with legal power exercises legal means against an individual is rationing transactions.[8]

***Five members***

The third characteristic is the members who make up the transaction. It is not two individuals, but the transaction consists of four parties and a fifth person responsible for the legal settlement.

Taking a market transaction as an example, if the seller ($S_1$) offers only one bid price for the one offered by the buyer ($B_1$), there is no freedom of choice, and the transaction may take on a "hold-up" character. If there are two sellers ($S_1$) and ($S_2$) and two buyers ($B_1$) and ($B_2$), then choices are created on the part of both the seller and the buyer. In this way, a second set of "potential" transactions besides a set of "actual" transactions arises, the existence of which serves to eliminate or mitigate the "hold-up" character of the transaction (Commons, 1924, pp. 65–67). This force becomes stronger as the number of sellers and buyers increases, but what matters is the best "actual" transaction and the next best "potential" transaction.[9] Thus, four people, two on each side, are needed to reach a fair transaction. Commons states that "this typical transaction describes the minimum of all economic and social relations whatever, whether it be that of the family, of business, or politics" (Commons, 1924, p. 67) and is not limited to economic transactions.

However, there is still a possibility that disputes may arise between parties to a transaction, and such disputes occur constantly in the real world. In order to settle such disputes legally, "a fifth party to the transaction" exists. It is the role historically played by "a judge, priest, chieftain, paterfamilias, arbitrator, foreman, superintendent, general managers," and they "would be able to decide and settle the dispute, with the aid of the combined power of the group to which the five parties belonged" (Commons, 1924, p. 67). In some cases, however, this fifth party may be an autocratic and lawless person, but as long as he belongs to the same group as the other four parties, "arbitrary and lawless power has always been found to be itself limited by common rules, or working rules, the 'law' of the concern" (Commons, 1924, p. 67). Commons assumed as follows.

> A transaction, then, involving a minimum of five persons, and not an isolated individual, nor even only two individuals, is the ultimate unit of economics, ethics, and law.
>
> (Commons, 1924, p. 68)

Therefore, he analyzed collective action using this transaction concept. As described earlier, the transaction concept explains human "conflict" and mutual "dependence" and the "order" that arises from them through the three characteristics of the "will of the actor" linked to its actions, "legal relations," and a minimum of "five members."

## Institutional economics of Commons as transaction economics

### *Micro consideration: order formation through individual will and due process of law*

In this section, we will understand the institutional economics of Commons by analyzing markets and business organizations from a micro perspective as legal, economic, and ethical transactional relations.

As discussed previously, the methodology of Commons in the social sciences was to construct theories regarding active ideas that were subjectively "meaning." His fundamental idea of the economic agent is that an individual with the willingness select to perform, avoid, or forbear based on will-in-action. In *Legal Foundations of Capitalism* (Commons, 1924), Commons describes the legal relations of these individuals in transactions, using the diagram of legal relations by Wesley N. Hohfeld, a professor of law at Yale University (Hohfeld, 1913, p. 30, 1917, p. 710). In this section, we first consider the legal relations behind the transaction.

Hohfeld's basic legal conception of the transaction is the relations between "right" and "duty," plus "no-right," which expresses the absence of right, and "privilege," which does not extend to duty (Hohfeld, 1913, p. 30, 1917, p. 710).[10] Commons follows this relations between "rights" and "duties" but modifies it behavioristically for the remaining two concepts. In other words, he regarded "no right" as a state of "exposure" in which no protection of action is available and "privilege" as "liberty" to choose one's opportunities. In this way, he explained the legal relations among economic agents based on behaviorism.

In the two-party transaction (A to B) shown in Figure 1.1, the "right" possessed by party A represents the ability of A to execute A's will to A's counterparty B to the extent permitted. In contrast, B's "duty" means that it must "perform" or "forbear" its actions toward A and, in some cases, "avoid" them. We can say the same for A's "duty" and B's "right" from the opposite standpoint. Thus, "all rights and duties are relative," indicating that both parties have "a wish of one party to have a performance, avoidance, or forbearance of an opposite party whose wish is contrary" (Commons, 1924, p. 84). This correlation is also actual for "exposure" and "liberty." If B's "liberty" increases, A will not receive protection even if A appeals to a third party for A's protection. In other words, "exposure," the state without protection, increases. Thus, "the two are equal and opposite, that is, correlative" (Commons, 1924, p. 99). These legal relations are the "right-duty" and "exposure-liberty" correlation.

On the other hand, looking at Figure 1.1 vertically, the relations between "right" and "exposure" and "duty" and "liberty" represent opposite concepts: an increase in "right" in A means a decrease in the state of being in "exposure." In contrast, "duty" increases, and "liberty" decreases on the side of B. These legal relations are the "right-exposure" and "duty-liberty" opposition. Thus, legal relations in transactions include both correlation and opposition. Therefore, clarifying economic relations based on these correlations is essential for understanding transaction economics, which contains many legal elements.

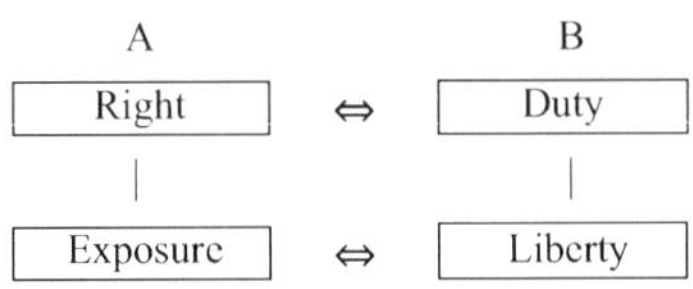


*Figure 1.1* Legal relations of transactions between two parties. Partially revised from Figure 9, changed from "no right" to "exposure" and "privilege" to "liberty," in Commons, 1924, p. 97.

Let us examine the economic relations by applying the transaction concept presented in the previous section to these relations. First, assuming transactions in a market, the relations between A and B are that of a bargaining transaction. If A's economic power is strong, B's "duty" will increase, and "liberty" will decrease. This relation narrows the opportunity for the choice of B. Since there is a risk that such a difference in power and inequality of opportunity may occur in bargaining transactions, the potential power of the second-best trading partners, A' and B,' is necessary to encourage "forbearance" in the actions of the stronger party. Thus, a competitive market consisting of A, A', B, and B' is created, and the price generated through "equal opportunity, fair competition, and equality of bargaining power" is what is called a "reasonable price" (Commons, 1934, p. 63). Thus, Commons did not emphasize on the natural adjustment mechanisms of the market but focused on the artificial relations that make the market work.

Next, A and B's relations correspond to bilateral "managerial transactions" relations when considering business organization transactions. Commons' concept of a corporation represents a "going concern," an organization that is continuously active. It is an organization composed of individuals with willingness, and, at the same time, it exists as an aggregate of transactions. To avoid complicating the discussion, let us treat a going concern as a company, and the legal power relations between manager A and employee B are like A > B from the beginning. The manager uses these relations to conduct production activities for "bargaining transactions" in the market. As indicated earlier, employees are evaluated on the basis of "efficiency." Management uses the amount of work per person per hour as the unit of measurement. It conducts scientific management to control the relations between input and output, but Commons considered it essential to manage the "limiting factor" and the "complimentary factor" (Commons, 1934, p. 90).

Complementary factors are those that work automatically without any particular action. When viewed from a volitional aspect, "routine transactions" (Commons, 1934, p. 634) occur. Since this is already a routine management method, creating this state will eliminate wasteful management in terms of production, thereby increasing production efficiency. On the other hand, limiting factors are required for the complementary factors to function well. When viewed from a volitional aspect, Commons called them "strategic transactions" (Commons, 1934, pp. 628–634). Managers of companies try to manipulate the limiting factor to make management as routine as possible. In other words, they aim to improve efficiency through customization. Thus, managers can organize companies and implement such management methods due to "managerial transactions" arising from differences in legal relations, and this point represents a significant difference from "bargaining transactions" in the market.

What does Commons have to say about establishing ethical relations between markets and business organizations? In the case of companies, there are a variety of internal rules. There are explicit articles of association and company rules, and there is also a customary company culture. Commons states that a going concern has "working rules," which exist in various forms and names, such as "common law, statute law, shop rules, business ethics, norms of conduct, and so on, which these governing or regulating groups of associated individuals have laid down for the guide of transactions" (Commons, 1924, p. 6).

These working rules are the four legal concepts presented at the beginning of this section: "right," "duty," "exposure," and "liberty." The question is, who imposes these rules? In terms of the transaction concept, it is the management class that conducts the "rationing transactions." They may impose direct rules on each member, or they may impose indirect rules. The foremost of the indirect rules is "custom," which Commons describes as "a kind of social compulsion imposed on individuals by the collective opinion" (Commons, 1934, p. 153). In this sense, working rules restrict individual activities and ensure individual freedom, as seen in the four legal concepts of "liberty" and "exposure." The managerial class sets the relations between these restrictions and freedoms, which forms the order within the company.

Thus, we can organize the micro aspects of the institutional economics of Commons by viewing markets and business organizations as legal, economic, and ethical transactional relations.

### *Macroscopic considerations: evolution of law and evolution of society*

Next, the macro aspect, adding the state and the courts, is viewed as a legal, economic, and ethical transactional relation.

Figure 1.2 adds an official C belonging to a group with legal power to the two-party transaction (A–B) shown in Figure 1.1 in the previous section. Commons uses this to explain how the group with legal power affects the transaction, which consists of four legal concepts. First, "power" represents a promise to protect A's "right." On the other hand, "liability" refers to enforcing the "duty" of party B if B fails to do so. Moreover, "disability" means that C cannot assist A when A is in "exposure." Finally, "immunity" refers to the state in which C does not need to use legal force when B is in "liberty" (Commons, 1924, pp. 117–119). In Figure 1.2, these horizontal connections are correlated so that as the "rights" of party A increase, the "powers" of official C also increase. Furthermore, the vertical connections are antagonistic; as the

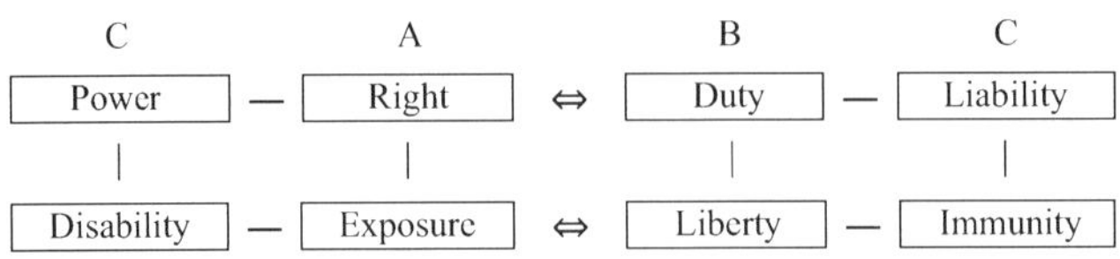


*Figure 1.2* Legal relations in transactions involving groups with legal power. Partially revised from Figure 16 in Commons (1924), p. 118.

"power" increases, the "disability" decreases. This relation is the legal relation of the transaction with the addition of the group with legal power.

The issue here is the type of collective power that official C exercises over parties A and B. The exercise of collective power from C to A is a positive guarantee of A's right to do something in the future. In contrast, the exercise of collective power from C to B is to force B to perform a duty created in the past. In other words, the collective power of official C is to guarantee the right of one and formulate new rules while at the same time protecting the existing rules by enforcing duty on the other (Commons, 1924, pp. 114–119).

If we apply these legal relations to economic issues, this problem concerns a liberal market economy and a state-controlled economy. If the transaction between A and B in Figure 1.2 is considered a "bargaining transaction" in the market, the official C intervenes in the market and sets and enforces the rules. C is unnecessary if the "bargaining transaction" between A and B goes well between the two parties. C is also unnecessary if it is possible to increase the number of buyer and seller participants and establish a fair transaction through competition. However, Commons, from the standpoint of his various investigations of the United States before and after the Great Depression, did not believe that the market order could function sufficiently on its own.

On the other hand, state control in fascism and autocratic communism represents the exercise of collective mighty power from C to A and B in Figure 1.2. This state is an economy where "managerial transactions" and "rationing transactions" are significant. Commons also rejected such extreme collectivist economies.

Thus, Commons' attitude was not exclusively toward "bargaining transactions," nor was it inclined toward "managerial transactions" or "rationing transactions." It is an economy in which these three "transactions" are not extreme and are in balance. There, the exercise of collective power from C to A and B in Figure 1.2 respects the "willingness" of the parties to the transaction. Therefore, it is necessary to have an entity that determines the balance among these three "transactions" and acts as a deterrent to exercising collective power. This entity is the fifth entity characteristic of the transaction concept, and Commons paid particular attention to the legal settlement function of the courts.

As already mentioned, order in the market is created by a minimum of five members, the ultimate goal of which is to achieve a "reasonable price." Commons cited the changing concept of property as one of the lessons learned from the U.S. Supreme Court's survey of precedents, providing an example of how court decisions affect the rules of society. Courts make judicial decisions on disputes of the moment through due process of law, influenced by past precedents and actual business practices. A court plays the role of the fifth person in the transaction, balancing the three kinds of transactions of "bargaining," "managerial," and "rationing." To prevent "market failures" and "state failures," a balancing agent is needed to control the sovereignty of these transactions. Commons sees this role in the courts and emphasizes the existence of the "visible hand" of the courts rather than God's "invisible hand" in the market. The visible hand of the courts performs the "artificial selection" of rules through "rationing transactions" that have gone through the due process of law.[11]

Based on the above, we can say that the transaction economics of Commons is a legal, economic, and ethical analysis of institutions, which are "collective action in restraint, liberation, and expansion of individual action" (Commons, 1934, p. 73) based on the concept of transactions.

## Conclusion

What this chapter has attempted to do can be summarized as follows. Transaction does not refer to "exchange," which implies a physical transfer; instead, it means a legal transfer of ownership. This concept has three features of Commons' institutional economics: (1) the volitional aspect based on human action; (2) three types of transactions—bargaining transactions, managerial transactions, and rationing transactions—determined by the legal relations; and (3) transactions comprising a minimum of five members—two buyers, two sellers, and one mediator. Then, this chapter reinterprets Commons' institutional economics as transaction economics. Using the theoretical construct of the transaction, we analyze the legal, economic, and ethical aspects of Commons' theory at micro and macro levels. From there, we captured the spontaneity of individuals, management by collective organizations, and customary order and artificial order as transaction economics consisting of bundles of transactions. This capture is an attempt to understand Commons, who has often been understood in comparison with other old institutionalists such as Thorstein B. Veblen and Wesley C. Mitchell, intrinsically from the conceptual device of transactions.

## Notes

1 Other studies focusing on Commons' transactions or Williamson's transaction costs include Dugger (1983, 1996), Pratten (1997), and Ito (1966). Pratten (1997) criticizes Williamson's deductive methodology from the standpoint of critical realism. Ito (1966) discusses the formulation of transactions from the standpoint of business administration.

2 A comparison of the transaction economics of Commons with the new institutional economics of Williamson et al. will be made in Chapter 8.

3 Such economic agents are what Veblen calls "a lightning calculator of pleasures and pains" (Veblen, 1898 (1919), p. 73) – passive, entirely rational "economic men."

4 The term "will-in-action" is used in the sense of the will connected with actual human action, in contrast to the term "will-in-vacuo," which refers to the physiological will to do things or not (Commons, 1924, p. 69). "Will-in-action" is distinguished from "willingness," which refers to active will in general.

5 Commons' explanation of "forbearance" in the major works is as follows:

> (W)e shall use the term "forbearance," not with its qualitative meaning of intentional omission, but with the quantitative, physical or economic meaning of a limit

placed on the degree of power put forth in overcoming resistance. Forbearance is a limit placed on performance.

(Commons, 1924, p. 76)

"(F)orbearance is the exercise, *not of the total* power except at a crisis, or under compulsion, but the exercise of a limited degree of one's *possible* moral, physical, or economic power. Thus, forbearance is the limit placed on performance" (Commons, 1934, p. 88). That is, "(f)orbearance is self-restraint in doing" (Commons, 1950, p. 39).

6 In the case of wage bargaining, workers are considered legally equal as negotiators in the market. However, they become legally inferior once they enter employment and must obey the management. There is an element that differs from commodity pricing (Commons, 1934, pp. 64–65).

7 However, the manager here is treated as one who plays the role of both the "employment department" as the legal aspect and the "technical department" as the productive aspect and is not treated as the "owner" of the enterprise (Commons, 1934, pp. 64–65). The following "rationing transactions" indicate the relations with shareholders as "owners."

8 We provide a detailed analysis and reclassification of rationing transactions in Chapter 7.

9 In addition to these two types of transactions, Commons also stated that a third type of "possible" transaction can occur if the conditions are different and an "impossible" transaction can occur in which the parties cannot approach the market due to time or location. The first "actual" transaction and the second "potential" transaction are the ones that have a decisive influence on the conclusion of a transaction (Commons, 1924, pp. 65–67).

10 Horwitz (1992) describes Hohfeld's analytical diagram of legal relations in the history of American law as follows. "Hohfeld sought to subvert the privileged position that rights had occupied as the starting point for orthodox legal analysis. He thus wished to relativize rights discourse by emphasizing that one might just as logically begin such an analysis with the concept of a duty created by law" (Horwitz, 1992, p.155).

11 Artificial selection of rules through rationing transactions is dealt with in detail in Chapter 9.

## References

### *English*


Commons, John R. (1924) 1995. *Legal Foundations of Capitalism*. New Brunswick and London: Transaction Publishers.

———. (1931). "Institutional Economics," *American Economic Review*, 21 (December), 648–657.

———. (1934). *Institutional Economics: Its Place in Political Economy*. New York: Macmillan.

———. (1950). *The Economics of Collective Action*. New York: Macmillan.

Dugger, William M. (1983). "The Transaction Cost Analysis of Oliver E. Williamson: A New Synthesis?" *Journal of Economic Issues*, 17 (1),, 95–114.

———. (1996). "Sovereignty in Transaction Cost Economics: John R. Commons and Oliver E. Williamson," *Journal of Economic Issues*, 30 (2), 427–432.

Hohfeld, Wesley N. (1913). "Some Fundamental Legal Conceptions as Applied in Judicial Reasoning," *Yale Law Journal*, 23 (November), 15–59.

———. (1917). "Fundamental Legal Conceptions as Applied in Judicial Reasoning," *Yale Law Journal*, 26 (June), 710–770.

Horwitz, Morton J. (1992). *The Transformation of American Law, 1870–1960: The Crisis of Legal Orthodoxy*. New York: Oxford University Press.

Pratten, Stephen. (1997). "The Nature of Transaction Cost Economics," *Journal of Economic Issues*, 31 (3), 781–803.

Ramstad, Yngve. (1996). "Is a Transaction a Transaction?" *Journal of Economic Issues*, 30 (2), 413–425.

Veblen, Thorstein B. (1898) 1919. "Why Is Economics Not an Evolutionary Science?" *Quarterly Journal of Economics*, 12 (July). Reprinted in Veblen (1919), 56–81.

———. (1919). *The Place of Science in Modern Civilization and Other Essays*. New York: B. W. Huebusch.

### *Japanese*

Ito, Fumio. (1966). "Shijō Torihiki no Hatten: J. R. Commons no Torihiki no Riron wo Chūsin ni" (The Development of Market Transactions: Focusing on J. R. Commons' Theory of Transactions), *Chiba-Shōdai-Ronsō*, 6, 91–114.

Taka, Tetsuo. (1998). "Commons ni okeru 'Hō to Keizaigaku' to Seido-shugi" ('Law and Economics' and Institutionalism on Commons), *Keizaigaku-Ronkyū* (The Journal of Economics of Kwansei Gakuin University), 52 (1), 65–84.

# 2 Theory of going concern

## Organization and institution

In this chapter, we will understand the institutional economics of Commons by examining his going concern theory.

A going concern is not merely an aggregation of individuals but rather an indication of the relations between individuals and groups or, in other words, the kind of institutions that need to be built for groups to continue. The transaction concept examined in the previous chapter is not intended to discuss the individual transactions of rational individuals but rather to analyze how individuals who have willingness but are influenced by their environment behave within the group. Therefore, the transaction concept of Commons makes more effective sense when combined with the going concern theory, which addresses the issue of the individual and the group or organization.

Although many previous studies treat the going concern theory as an essential concept in understanding the institutional economics of Commons, only a few studies focus on the going concern theory, such as Atkinson and Reed (1992) and Atkinson (2009).[1] While most applicable to corporate analysis, Commons' going concern theory is not limited to it. In Chapter 8, we will compare the going concern theory with other theories on whether the going concern theory can explain contemporary groups and organizations and explore the characteristics and contemporary significance of Commons' going concern theory.

To this end, in this chapter, we will first explain what a going concern is and then show that it consists of a going plant, a production sector, and a going business, a business sector, and consider how it relates to the going concern as a whole. The meaning of going concern as an aggregate will also be discussed. Based on the above considerations, we will view the overall institutional economics of Commons from the perspective of the going concern theory. We will discuss what kind of order institutions create between individuals and groups and how the freedom of individuals in institutions is secured.

### Institution as a going concern

The name "going concern" originated from the customs of business (Commons, 1924, p. 8), and Commons used this name after examining the reality

DOI: 10.4324/9781032701394-4

of such practices in the U.S. Supreme Court casebook. The representative example of a going concern is the corporation. However, the basis of a going concern in Commons' view is not labor, capital, or commodities but "transactions." Furthermore, the individual with "willingness" is assumed to be behind such transactions. These two terms have already been mentioned in the previous chapter, but let us review them again because they are essential for understanding going concerns. Willingness is not mere will but "a supposed similarity of cause, effect, or purpose, derived from experiences with human behavior" (Commons, 1934a, p. 94), representing a will that is associated with action from the past to the future.

Commons denies the individual with an unchangeable reason and sees the individual as a variable subject to change according to economic and political circumstances (Commons, 1934a, p. 46). The individual with willingness refers to someone who makes the following three choices: to do a thing (performance), not to do a thing (avoidance), and to limit the action and perform it (forbearance). It is not a person who simply chooses between doing or not doing a thing. Commons called this "will-in-action." By assuming a person has the will to limit his or her actions, it is possible to negotiate realistically, avoiding the situation in which one either fully accepts the demands of others or refuses all of them. This negotiation is a "transaction," as discussed in the previous chapter. As we have already seen, Commons classified the concept of transaction into the following three categories.

The first, bargaining transactions are transactions that "*transfer ownership* of wealth by voluntary agreement between legal equals" (Commons, 1934a, p. 68) and refer to general market transactions. The second managerial transactions are for "the production of wealth" between "a legal superior who has legal right to issue commands" and "a legal inferior who, while the relation lasts, is bound by the legal duty of obedience" (Commons, 1934a, p. 64). For example, the relations between a manager and an employee in the workplace fall under this category. The third type of rationing transactions "apportion the burdens and benefits of wealth creation by the *dictation* of legal superiors" (Commons, 1934a, p. 68). Typical examples are those related to the distribution of wealth, such as taxation or the distribution of shares by the board of directors.

These three transaction concepts are the "sub-concepts" that constitute a going concern. Thus, individuals with willingness as agents of action and transactions based on their will-in-action are the source of going concerns. Moreover, since the going concern is an accumulation and combination of willingness, it is an aggregate of wills.

On the other hand, the concept of a going concern differs from the following three. The first is "mechanism," which, according to Commons, explains the relations between the individual and the whole in physical terms, treating the individual as an electron or atom. Here, the individual is treated as a material thing and does not have willingness. The second is the "organism," a biological explanation that treats the individual like a living cell. Moreover,

*Table 2.1* Going concern with multiple meanings (compiled by the author).

| | | |
|---|---|---|
| Going Concern | Tangible meanings | Aggregate of **individuals** |
| | | Internal **governing body** |
| | Intangible meanings | Subjective: aggregate of **willingness** |
| | | Objective: aggregate of **transactions** |

the individual is subordinate to the whole, and the individual's rights are to be drawn from the whole (Commons, 1934a, pp. 25, 58–59). The third is the "corporation," which is the legal description of an enterprise that exists only by being granted juridical personality. A corporation was initially defined as an entity that engaged in the exchange of material goods. In contrast, the scope of a going concern has an economic meaning wherever transactions occur.[2]

In summary, as shown in Table 2.1, a going concern has both a tangible and an intangible meaning. In the tangible meaning, first, it represents a continuous body of activity as an aggregate of individuals. Second, as explained in the next section, it exists as an internal governing body, which functions as a coordinating and political entity that governs its internal economy. On the other hand, the intangible meaning has two aspects: subjective and objective. The subjective aspect is viewed as an aggregate of willingness, and the objective aspect is viewed as an aggregate of transactions. Thus, a going concern is not merely an aggregate of individuals, but it has multiple meanings: it is also an aggregate of subjective wills and an aggregate of objective transactions.

## Going plant and going business

The going concern economy creates an excellent value by effectively functioning its parts. The two subeconomies that comprise the going concern economy are the going plant and the going business.

### *Going plant*

A going plant is "a producing organization furnishing a service to the public" (Commons, 1924, p. 182). It is a technical economy where people work with nature to produce goods and services. It functions on the principle of "efficiency" to achieve maximum output with minimum input, and "managerial transactions" are carried out to produce wealth under the direction of a superior in legal relations. Wealth production here refers to the entire process of creating use value, so a going plant does not refer only to the physical plant (production facility). Commons says that the factors of production, "(t)he plant itself is the force of nature proportioned according to the qualities, supply and prices of each force" (Commons, 1924, p. 206) and that it is essential to add the production organization that manages these factors. If the plant is not integrated with the production organization, the plant becomes a "dead structure." Conversely, the production organization cannot produce anything if separated from the plant. Therefore,

> The production organization is fruitless without the going plant. They are inseparable relations of man to nature proportioned and economized according to the then state of arts, the sciences and engineering as understood by the members of the going concern.
>
> (Commons, 1924, p. 206)

However, the use value produced by a going plant is not limited to the social use value that integrates the physical parts. It includes intangible utility. Commons lists five components of use value: (1) the elementary utilities furnished by nature, (2) the form utilities furnished by labor, (3) the place utilities furnished by location, (4) the time utility furnished by investors, and (5) the confidence utility furnished by human character (Commons, 1924, p. 205). Commons describes the fifth "confidence utility furnished by human character" as follows:

> [E]ngineering economy, while it produces commodities, does not of itself produce confidence in the commodities. This springs from honesty and good service. So that the production of wealth is the inseparable union of arts, science, engineering *and ethics*. Ethics is the field of production of that invisible utility, confidence, without which the tangible utility are not even produced. The use-value of ethics is confidence in others, and the exchange-value of ethics is the market-value of their goodwill.
>
> (Commons, 1924, p. 206)

Therefore, a separate organization is needed to handle the intangible and ethical utility generated from the going plant in the marketplace. This organization is a going business as a business organization.

### *Going business*

A going business is "a bargaining organization obtaining prices from the public" (Commons, 1924, p. 182) and refers to the asset economy that handles all business transactions between people. It functions on the principle of "scarcity" because it transfers ownership of goods and services from where they are abundant to where they are scarce. Moreover, "bargaining transactions" occur here between legal equals. Commons recognizes the concept of a going business from a survey of court cases in the United States and notes that it is tied to changes in the concept of property.

> The going business was there but had not been recognized in the tax laws, owing to the primitive notion that property consisted only in physical things held for one's own use. When, however, the going business

> was recognized as property, then, not only physical things but also the "skill, diligence, fidelity, success and reputation" of the persons composing the concern were recognized as property, and property came to consist of the expected profitable transactions of the organized concern.
>
> (Commons, 1924, p. 182)

Commons divides the term "property" into three main categories. The first is tangible or corporeal property, which refers to material ownership. The second is incorporeal property, which is immaterial property and refers to ownership rights related to promises to pay such as debt, credit, or collateral. The third is intangible property, which refers to ownership rights that include the exchange value of all kinds of things such as goodwill and patent rights.[3]

While tangible property merely represents the accumulation of labor from the past to the present and existing material things, incorporeal and intangible properties have the added element of time in the future. Among them, intangible property refers to income in the future and thus includes tangible and intangible property. In concrete terms, tangible property, a material commodity, is handled in the commodity market, while incorporeal property, such as promissory notes and stocks, is handled in the financial market. On the other hand, intangible property such as goodwill, patents, trademarks, and credit represents the "intangible expectations" of the business, impacting the commodity market, the financial market, and even the labor market. Going business refers to the overall transactions of tangible, incorporeal, and intangible properties.

### *Going concern as a whole*

Going concern as a whole, on the other hand, functions as a coordinating and political entity that governs its internal economy. There, "rationing transactions" are conducted to share the burden of wealth and profits, and the economy of the going concern as a whole is managed. In other words, going plants and going businesses are managed so that they function well. Specifically, the going plant, which is the production organization, is to increase its output by improving efficiency, and the going business is to increase its income by smoothly conducting bargaining transactions. In doing so, the objective aspects of management called "limiting factors" and "complementary factors" are essential (Commons, 1934a, p. 90).

As explained in Chapter 1, complementary factors work automatically without any particular action. When viewed from the volitional aspect, Commons calls these "routine transactions." Since it indicates a management method that has already been routinized, once this state is established, in terms of production, it eliminates wasteful management and increases production efficiency. On the other hand, limiting factors are those required for how well the complementary factors function. When viewed from the volitional aspect, Commons calls these "strategic transactions." Going-plant and going-business

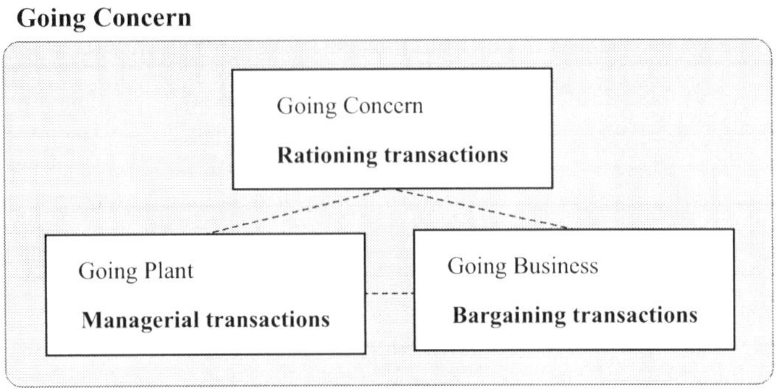


*Figure 2.1* The relation of going concern, going plant, and going business. Compiled by the author.

managers manipulate this limiting factor to make management routine. Moreover, the going concern's role as a governing body oversees this entire management (Commons, 1934a, pp. 628–634).

As described earlier, the economy of the going concern consists of two subeconomies. The going plant is a production organization tied to human management, creating value beyond mere production facilities. This, in turn, is combined with the going business, a mechanism that generates transactions in general and adds intangible values including ethical aspects such as goodwill. Thus, the economy of going concern, which combines both, is no longer a simple sum of parts but rather a multiplication of parts by parts.[4] Figure 2.1 summarizes the above relations.

## Active meaning of going concern

A going concern is a combination of partial elements that create overall value. However, it is only meaningful if such value is created continuously. Going concern, as the name suggests, is vital to be "going." It indicates that the going concern is active and behaviorist. Commons states at the beginning of *The Legal Foundations of Capitalism*, "The aim of this volume is to work out an evolutionary and behavioristic, or rather volitional, theory of value" (Commons, 1924, preface). In this section, we will examine the active elements of a going concern and analyze why going concern is to continue.

Commons distinguished between "concept" and "principle." The concept is similar to objective attributes or relations of things, while the principle is similar to actions. Thus, the principle would include time and represent similarities regarding things' cause, effect, and purpose. Then, the going concern concept would be a collection of transactional concepts, but what if we take it as a principle? Commons takes up the principle of mechanics and organisms as objects of comparison, stating as follows.

> (T)he principle of nature's mechanism is blind pressure; the principle of organisms is struggle for life; the principle of going concerns is concerted

> action for ends foreseen in the future. In other words, the principle of Nature's Mechanism is Energy, that of Organisms is Scarcity, that of Going Concern is Willingness.
>
> (Commons, 1934a, pp. 619–620)

In other words, the "principle" of the going concern is explained by viewing it as an aggregate of individuals with willingness. Furthermore, here, the dimension of time, especially the future, is essential, and at the same time, the purpose of things is essential. Futurity, purpose, and expectation are the driving forces of a going concern. Commons, influenced by Charles S. Peirce, states that "(t)he Past is Memory, the Present is Sensation, the Future is Expectation" (Commons, 1934a, p. 642). He then says, "(a) going concern exists only as long as there are expectations." Thus, "(i)f the expectations cease, they quit going" (Commons, 1934a, p. 620). It means that the going concern ceases to operate. Concerns that cease to be going are no longer going concern but merely a passive "group" that has no expectations and just got together.

On the other hand, the future is also essential when considering going plants and going businesses. That is because, as seen from the word "going" attached to each of them, they must be organizations that continuously create value. The going plant is a production organization that produces use value, and we have shown that the use value includes the utility of trust brought about by human nature. A going business is a business organization that deals with transactions in general, but it also deals with exchange value in general, including intangible value. They have in common the fact that both are deeply related to the intangible nature of value and future value. In other words, incorporeal property is a value based on the assumption that future debts and credits will be executed as contracted. In contrast, credit or trust, which is included in intangible property, is nothing but the present value of future potential, and the value of these properties is closely related to the future potential.

The same is true of transactions. A transaction is a contract with a counterparty, which promises the performance of a contract in the future, that is, rights and duties. Delivery of goods by a specific date, settlement of payments, repayment of debts, and production and sale of goods at favorable prices are all possible only if there is an expectation of the future. Commons states that the emphasis on the future significantly differs between institutional and preceding economics.

> Mathematically defined, "the present" is a moving *point* of time between the outgoing past and the incoming future. Psychologically, "the present" is an *instant* of time when feelings of pleasure and pain occur, modified by memory of the past and expectations of the future. Institutionally considered, however, the present is limited by the dates of concluding the negotiations of the several transactions which commit participants and subordinates to a line of behavior in the future. . . . The classical

> economists, followed by the communists, began with the exertions of labor in the production of *wealth* in the past time. . .. The hedonistic, or pleasure-pain economists, began with the pleasures of consumption of wealth in the present,. . . . The institutional economists begin with the legislative, administrative, and judicial decisions of both governmental and private collective action on which depend the *security* of present expectations of future profits, investments, jobs, and contracts.
>
> (Commons, 1950, p. 104)

When the concept of property referred only to tangible objects, viewing value as a visible thing produced by the accumulation of past labor was common. However, when liabilities and assets were added to the concept of property, and even goodwill, patent rights, and credit, the future became too important to ignore. Going businesses and bargaining transactions have an essential significance precisely because they deal with intangible property closely related to the future. Going business is not a one-time transaction but is based on the continuity of the transaction in general and on the parties' mutual expectations. Therefore, the significance of a going business lies is demonstrating business continuity based on intangible expectations.

On the other hand, going plants increase productivity by manipulating limiting factors through strategic transactions and making them routine transactions. It is because they are constantly aware of future profits, investment, and efficiency gains that the plant becomes a going plant that transcends mere production facilities and becomes a continuous production organization. The going concern as a governing body also manages various aspects of the concern on the premise that the concern as a whole will continue to exist into the future. In this way, "going" indicates collective action with an awareness of "futurity."

The going concern is, as explained before, a collective willingness. The individuals who make up the going concern are not passive but volitional. A going concern will continue going into the future only when closely connected to this volitional view of man. Commons describes the volitional man as follows.

> We find that people act in exactly opposite ways during periods of depression and prosperity. Not logic, but fear and hope are fundamental. People act to enlarge valuations in periods of hope and to depress valuations in periods of fear. Their reasons are expected consequences and immediate alternative opportunities. This, again, is negotiational psychology instead of rational or hedonistic psychology – it is "volitional psychology" or "will power."
>
> (Commons, 1950, p. 105)

The collective concern of people based on the volitional mind, according to their future goals and expectations, is the going concern, which refers to the collective will itself.

In this way, "willingness," "expectation," and "futurity" explain the "going" (continuity) of a going concern. Willingness is the basis of the economic subject by Commons, and at the same time, it is the root of a going concern as a collective will. When this willingness is combined with futurity, the meaning of "going," that is, the continuation of will into the future, becomes more explicit. Thus, the theory of going concern, driven by the principle of willingness, becomes "a volitional theory of economic activity directed towards purposes in the future" (Commons, 1934a, p. 643).

## Formation of order and individual freedom

In this section, we will capture the institutional economics of Commons from the perspective of a going concern's order formation and individual freedom. The institutional concept of Commons is defined as "collective action in control, liberation and expansion of individual action" (Commons, 1931, p. 648). Thus, the first role of institutions is to control individual actions within the concern. That means that working rules are enforced within the concern. Commons says the working rule:

> [T]aking many forms and names, such as the common law, statute law, shop rules, business ethics, business methods, norms of conduct, and so on, which these governing or regulating groups of associated individuals, which these governing or regulating groups of associated individuals have laid down for the guidance of transactions.
>
> (Commons, 1924, p. 6)

While the previous chapter explained working rules in terms of legal concepts, Commons explains them simply using English auxiliary verbs. The first is "can," which refers to what an individual "can" do with the aid of collective power and is a rule of entitlement expressing "right." The second is "must/must not," which refers to what an individual "must" or "must not" do for the concern and is a rule of compulsion indicating "duty." The third is "may," which refers to what an individual "may" do without interference from others and is a rule of permission indicating "liberty." The fourth is "cannot," a rule of non-assistance indicating "exposure" (Commons, 1924, pp. 6, 147–148, 1934a, p. 71).

Working rules include "right," "duty," "liberty," and "exposure." These rules are imposed by the governing bodies with legal superiority over each concern, which set the rules among their members through "rationing transactions." Working rules are not only explicit direct regulations, but they also include indirect regulations that are not explicitly stated. The foremost indirect regulation is "custom," which means "repetition by the continuing group of changing persons. It has a coercive effect on individuals" (Commons, 1934a, p. 155).

However, as we have already seen, working rules impose restrictions on individual action, but at the same time, they ensure individual liberty. Individuals gain liberty of action from the concern by belonging to the concern and abiding by the rules that have been established. It is because if everyone is obligated to do something, everyone has the right to do something at the same time. Also, liberty of action is expanded when the concern assists what the individual cannot do, and liberty of action is secured when the concern sets rules that others will not interfere with one's actions.

As we saw in the previous chapter, Commons distinguished between liberty and freedom. It is liberty that the individual obtains through working rules, which means liberty from obligation, whereas freedom has a more active and proactive meaning. Individuals belonging to the going concern have liberty through working rules. At the same time, they also have freedom because they have willingness that constitutes the going concern. Therefore, individuals with such freedom and the rules and conventions constraining them are not in an antagonistic structure but in relations of interdependence. Regarding customs and their evolution, Commons states as follows.

> (T)here is a continual selection of customs going on, and consequently there is a survival of customs fitted to the changing economic conditions and the changing political and economic dominance. Since this occurs by operation of human will, it is much like the artificial selection of Darwin's evolution, applicable, however, to practices and transactions suited to changing social conditions, instead of to Darwin's structures and functions of living organisms suited to changing geological condition.
> (Commons, 1934a, p. 45)

Thus, we need to consider the order within the going concern with together the individual with willingness. The going concern is directed by "artificial selection" of such customs and does not perish or survive by "natural selection." On the other hand, Veblen believes that the evolution of institutions, which are habits of thought, depends on what kinds of habits and tendencies are developed and preserved. He considers the evolution of institutions to be the "natural selection" of institutions – an evolution without a purpose. It differs from Commons, who emphasizes "artificial selection," and Veblen, who stresses "natural selection."

As described earlier, "working rule," which includes custom, is a keyword associated with "willingness" and "transactions," even when considering the going concern theory as a whole. These can be condensed into the following words of Commons.

> These three types of transactions are brought together in a larger unit of economic investigation, which, in British and American practice, is named a Going Concern. It is these going concerns, with the working rules that keep them agoing, all the way from the family, the corporation, the trade union, the trade association, up to the state itself, that

> we name Institutions. The passive concept is a "group"; the active is a "going concern."
>
> (Commons, 1934a, p. 69)

Commons takes a less pessimistic view of capitalism, assuming that the order within the going concern is an artificial order formed not to violate the willingness and freedom of the individual as much as possible. The representative of this is the "artificial selection" of customs by the Supreme Court. Commons' ideal was an economy in which the transactions generated a reasonable value. The Supreme Court, the highest judicial body, not the government or the market, was the final arbiter. The Supreme Court is influenced by working rules and stands in a position to mediate disputes occasionally. Commons learned the practical meaning of conciliation from his survey of Supreme Court cases and saw it as playing an essential role in the stability of capitalism.

Conversely, Veblen held that "enterprise" in capitalist society derives from a barbaric predatory instinct oriented toward acquisition, possession, domination, and pretense. On the other hand, "industry" is derived from a peaceful instinct that promotes production efficiency and helps increase social welfare. He also viewed "enterprise," which aims at monetary profit, and "industry," which aims at increased production, in opposition. He pessimistically observed that the enormous power of commercial enterprises was crushing the industry. Veblen thought that the way to overcome this situation would be realizing either a socialist system by industrial engineers or a regression to militarism through the unproductive consumption of corporations. This oppositional structure of "industry" versus "enterprise" is the composition of a "going plant" versus "going business" by Commons. However, Commons differs from Veblen in the fact that he advocates that it is possible to manage both by a "going concern" as a governing mechanism. Veblen also used the term "going concern," but only for corporations.[5]

In contrast, Commons, as noted earlier, applies to political and cultural organizations other than corporations. He believed that the capitalist society could be maintained and developed through the various categories of a going concern. As already mentioned, the working rules within a society are essential for this purpose, and, according to Commons, these rules have been historically phased in as follows.

> In this way we can see that the evolution of working rules in almost any concern or type of concern, passes through four stages. First the stage of ignorance and confidence, wherein faith, loyalty of submission accepts without protest the working rules as concealed and interpreted by those having authority. Second, the stage of skepticism and protest which is satisfied with the mere publicity of the rules. Third, the stage of resistance, revolt and insistence on a participating voice in amending and

recasting the rules. Fourth, a stage of an independent judiciary interpreting the rules as disputes arise.

(Commons, 1924, p. 142)

Thus, Commons' view of capitalism was neither an economic view based on the "invisible hand" or market universalism nor a planned economy based on state control. It is an economy in which the "visible hand of the court" (Commons, 1924, p. 204) balances the three kinds of transactions, and the institution evolves through "artificial selection" of working rules.

## Conclusion

In the last chapter of his *Institutional Economics* (1934), "Communism, Fascism, Capitalism," Commons lists the following problems with capitalism in the United States. First is the problem of banker capitalism on the economic side, which creates much unemployment because companies do not hire new workers when they have excess profits but instead distribute dividends to shareholders. The second is the political aspect: the power of the Supreme Court is growing stronger, while the power of the legislature and voluntary associations such as laborers, farmers, small business owners, and political parties is weakening (Commons, 1934a, p. 898).

In response to these problems, Commons stated that it was necessary that representatives of the interests of each of these associations were elected to Congress and they had the experience and ability to curb banker capitalism in the United States. He further points out that by establishing an administrative committee with representatives of the various interests in attendance, the administrative committee would effectively function as a quasi-legislature (Commons, 1934a, p. 155). The administrative commissions would also be discussed in his posthumous book, *The Economics of Collective Action* (1950), which will be discussed in a later chapter.

This chapter attempted to understand Commons' institutional economics through an analysis of the going concern theory. Commons developed his theory of going concerns not for analyzing corporations alone (joint-stock companies). He believed it was necessary to utilize the power of a wide range of groups and organizations to overcome capitalist society's crisis. The assertion of Commons against American capitalism mentioned earlier demonstrates the importance of the power of going concerns. Therefore, the going concern theory is essential in understanding the overall picture of the institutional economics of Commons.

## Notes

1 Atkinson and Reed (1992) focus on individuals within the going concern and see the interaction of active individuals as changing the environment, concluding that "(i)nstitutional economics requires a theory of the social individual." Moreover, Atkinson (2009) identifies "going concern," "futurity," and "reasonable value" as

the three features of the theoretical framework of Commons and argues that collective action as a going concern, conflict rather than cooperation, is the essence of economic inquiry and that rationing transactions based on due process of law are indispensable for the formation of order based on interrelation. On the other hand, in the Japanese-language literature, the main focus has been on analysis from a business administration perspective, such as corporate theory or business administration methodology, such as Ito (1969). In others, for example, Taka (2004) in Chapter 4 deals with something other than the going concern theory. It is interesting to note the differences between Veblen's going concern concept (Taka, 2004, p. 202) and the similarities with Keynes' "semi-autonomous bodies" (Keynes, 1926, p. 41). We will discuss Commons and Keynes in Chapter 5.

2 Supreme Court decisions, such as the Pittsburgh Plus case (1920), Commons says, transformed the corporate organization in the United States from a legal entity to an economic going concern (Commons, 1934a, p. 53). He noted in his autobiography (Commons, 1934b) that "seeing the intense political conflict in Wisconsin over this same economic issue, I got my first idea of a 'going concern' existing wherever it does business, distinguished from a 'corporation' existing only in the state of its incorporation" (Commons, 1934b, pp. 97–98).

3 Veblen recognized intangible property and its introduction into economics before Commons. Commons stated the following in this regard.

> Thorstein Veblen, to his great credit, was introducing the same idea of intangible property into economics during the period following 1900, and is was mainly on that ground that he became known as an 'institutional' economist. But the difference was that Veblen obtained his case material from the testimony of the fiscal magnates before the United States Industrial Commission of 1900, so that his notion of intangible property ended in the Marxian extortion and exploitation. But my sources were my participation in collective action, in drafting bills, and my necessary study, during these participations, of the decisions of the Supreme Court covering the period; so that my notion of intangible property ends in the common-law notion of reasonable value.
>
> (Commons, 1934a, p 4)

4 To touch on the relation with organization theory, Commons' concept of going concerns has something in common with Chester I. Barnard's view of organization, who is regarded as the founder of modern organization theory. Barnard said,

> An organization comes into being when (1) there are persons able to communicate with each other (2) who are willing to contribute action (3) to accomplish a common purpose. The elements of an organization are therefore (1) communication; (2) willingness to serve; (3) common purpose.
>
> (Barnard, 1938, p. 82)

The idea that individuals are motivated to contribute to achieving a common purpose and realize what cannot be accomplished by individuals alone is familiar to Commons' going concern theory. However, the significant difference is that Commons' theory places the concept of transactions at its foundation, which is also different from other organizational theories (such as the divisional system of a company).

5 Veblen, in his *The Theory of Business Enterprise*, states,

> But in so far as business procedure and business conceptions have been shaped in the image of the modern corporation (or limited liability company), the basis of capitalization has gradually shifted, until the basis is now no longer given by the cost

of material equipment owned, but by the earning-capacity of the corporation as a going concern.

(Veblen, 1904, p. 137)

For a detailed discussion of Veblen, see Taka (1991).

## References

### *English*

Atkinson, Glen. (2009). "Going Concern, Futurity and Reasonable Value," *Journal of Economic Issues*, 43 (2), 433–440.

Atkinson, Glen, & Mike Reed. (1992). "The Individual in a Going Concern," *Journal of Economic Issues*, 26 (2), 469–476.

Barnard, Chester I. (1938). *The Functions of the Executive*. Cambridge, MA: Harvard University Press.

Commons, John R. (1924) 1995. *Legal Foundations of Capitalism*. New Brunswick and London: Transaction Publishers.

———. (1931). "Institutional Economics," *American Economic Review*, 21 (December), 648–657.

———. (1934a). *Institutional Economics: Its Place in Political Economy*. New York: Macmillan.

———. (1934b). *Myself*. New York: Macmillan.

———. (1950). *The Economics of Collective Action*. New York: Macmillan.

Keynes, John M. (1926) 1931. "The End of Laissez-Faire," in Keynes (1931).

———. (1931). *Essays in Persuasion*. London: Macmillan.

Veblen, Thorstein B. (1904). *The Theory of Business Enterprise*. New York: C. Scribner.

### *Japanese*

Ito, Fumio. (1969). "J. R. Commons no 'Going Concern' Ron ni tsuite no Oboe-gaki" (Memorandum on J. R. Commons' 'Going Concern' Theory), *Aoyama-Keiei-Ronshū*, 3 (4), 82–94.

Taka, Tetsuo. (1991). *Veblen Kenkyū: Shinka Ron teki Keizaigaku no Sekai* (Studies on Thorstein Veblen: The World of Evolutionary Economics). Kyoto: Minerva Shobō.

———. (2004). *Gendai America Keizai Shisō no Kigen: Pragmatism to Seido Keizaigaku* (Origins of Modern American Economic Thought: Pragmatism and Institutional Economics). Nagoya: Nagoya Daigaku Shuppan-kai.

# Part II

# Basis of cumulative causation

## Markets and business organizations

# 3 Pricing theory

## Pricing by scarcity, abundance, and stabilization

In this chapter, we aim to understand the pricing theory of Commons. His theories explained the collective actions to overcome challenges of capitalism, such as monopoly and depressions. Therefore, Commons' theories are profound yet complex because they include the concepts of law, ethics, and psychology.

Glen Atkinson and Charles Whalen placed the basis of post-Keynesian institutionalism on the concept of "futurity" by Commons (Atkinson & Whalen, 2011). Hiroyuki Uni analyzed the newly discovered manuscript (Commons, 1927–29) and highlighted two issues between 1927 and 1934. First, Commons expanded the concept of "proprietary scarcity" arising from control by the supply and demand sides. Second, the "judicial transaction" became the "rationing transaction" (Uni, 2014). This chapter focuses on Commons' theory of price and its significance based on these previous studies.

### Pricing factors in the historical development of capitalism

Commons analyzed prices in Chapter 10 "Reasonable Value," section 7 "Collective Action" in *Institutional Economics* (Commons, 1934) and stated "scarcity," "efficiency," and "profit" as factors impacting prices. Commons studied these factors with the historical development of capitalism. He said, "Capitalism is not a single or static concept. It is an evolutionary concept of three historic stages – 'Merchant Capitalism,' 'Employer Capitalism,' 'Banker Capitalism' " (Commons, 1934, p. 766). Table 3.1 shows the historical development period of capitalism, pricing, and transactions by Commons.

#### *The era of merchant capitalism*

At first, merchant capitalism, before the Industrial Revolution, arose from the extension of markets. At this stage, "relative scarcity" in the market, that is, the "law of supply and demand," affects the price. If demand exceeds supply, relative scarcity will arise, and the price will increase. On the other hand, if supply exceeds demand, relative scarcity will fall, and the price will decrease. Commons called this stage a period of "scarcity" (Commons, 1934, p. 773).

DOI: 10.4324/9781032701394-6

*Table 3.1* Historical development of capitalism, pricing, and transactions by Commons. Compiled by the author.

| | *Capitalism* | *Historical period* | *Factors of pricing* | *Transactions* | *Money* |
|---|---|---|---|---|---|
| 1 | Merchant Capitalism | Scarcity | Relative scarcity (law of supply and demand) | Bargaining transactions | Metallic money |
| 2 | Employer Capitalism | Abundance | Efficiency and proprietary scarcity | Managerial transactions | Paper money |
| 3 | Banker Capitalism | Stabilization | Margins for profit (futurity) in addition to scarcity and efficiency | Rationing transactions | Credit money |

He thought that the main transactions in this stage were "bargaining transactions," which transfer the ownership of wealth by a voluntary agreement between legal equals (Commons, 1934, p. 68), and metallic money was the intermediation of trade. The principle of bargaining transactions relies on scarcity because these transactions do not occur during an excess supply. The unit of measurement in the bargaining transaction is the dollars (Commons, 1934, p. 66), that is, the price.

### *The era of employer capitalism*

The next stage is employer capitalism after the Industrial Revolution. Commons called this a period of "abundance" (Commons, 1934, p. 773) in which commodities are produced efficiently using new technology. In this stage, "managerial transactions" were prominent, which created wealth by commands of legal superiors. The principle of managerial transactions is "efficiency" based on maximum output from minimum inputs. Efficiency is measured in man-hours (Commons, 1934, pp. 64–68). At this stage, the relative scarcity (law of supply and demand) affects prices directly, but Commons drew attention to the concept of "proprietary scarcity," which occurs when sellers "withhold" supply to maintain the price in the wholesale market. Commons differentiated proprietary scarcity from relative scarcity.[1]

### *The era of banker capitalism*

The last stage is banker capitalism in which the credit system is extended. Commons called this stage a period of "stabilization" (Commons, 1934, p. 773). At this stage, "profit" (the margin for profit) in addition to scarcity and efficiency is strongly correlated with price. The main transactions in this stage were "rationing transactions," which "apportion the burdens and benefits of wealth creation by the dictation of legal superiors" (Commons, 1934, p. 68). At a micro level, rationing transactions correspond to "the activity of a board of directors of a company in making up its budget for the ensuing year" and the like. The macro-level corresponds to "the activity of members of a legislative body in apportioning taxes" and "distribution of wealth" by "quantity rationing" or "price rationing"[2] (Commons, 1934, pp. 68, 760). This connects to the decision of a profit level, which is the expected profit, through the decision of drawing its budget by the board of directors of a company. Then, by rationing transaction, capitalism is controlled, and market economy stabilized. So Commons claimed that the most important factor of stabilization was "the principles of futurity and narrow margins of profit" (Commons, 1934, p. 788). He pointed out the importance of "expected events" termed "futurity" (Commons, 1934, p. 738). As stated earlier, Commons considered factors of pricing by analyzing the historical stage.

## Relations of price and Commons' concepts of transactions

### *Relations of price and bargaining transactions*

This section considers how the three kinds of transactions and factors affect prices. Commons said,

> In a money economy, as in Menger's commodity economy, Demand and Supply cannot be measured directly, but the effects of their variations are measured. This measurement of effects is Price, so that price is the measure of the variable relations of Scarcity, and is the pecuniary equivalent of his marginal utility.
>
> (Commons, 1934, p. 381)

This does not refute the law of supply and demand but considers that relative scarcity appears as price. However, this outcome depends on the bargaining transactions of sellers and buyers in a market.

As we saw in Chapter 1, bargaining transactions in a market constitute two sellers and two buyers. When there are only two people in the market, a seller ($S_1$) and a buyer ($B_1$), the transaction tends to be like a robbery. If the seller has the strong bargaining power, the price will rise. On the other hand, if the buyer has the strong bargaining power, the price will fall. Then if there are four persons, that is, two sellers ($S_1$)·($S_2$) and two buyers ($B_1$)·($B_2$), there emerge a set of "actual" transaction and another set of "potential" transaction as alternatives (Commons, 1924, pp. 65–67). Therefore, bargaining transactions need to have a minimum of four persons. Furthermore, he believed that a fifth person, such as, historically, a judge, priest, chieftain, or an arbitrator, who has legal powers, was needed. Thus, "A transaction, then, involving a minimum of five persons, and not an isolated individual, nor even only two individuals, is the ultimate unit of economics, ethics, and law" (Commons, 1924, p. 68). As shown in Figure 3.1, these bargaining transactions decide the prices based on relative scarcity.

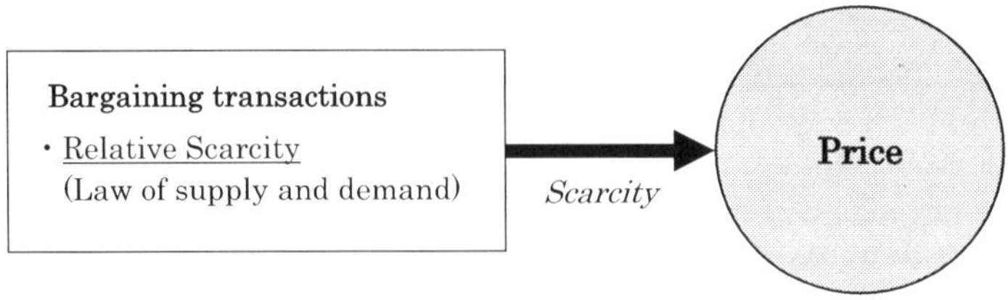


*Figure 3.1* Relations of price and bargaining transaction. Compiled by the author.

### *Relations of price and managerial transactions*

How does the efficiency of managerial transactions affect scarcity? Commons said, "This is what we mean by Capitalism, double process of creating use-value for others and restricting its supply so as to create scarcity-value. Hence capitalism, unlike the Marxian Communism, requires two units of measurement, the man-hour and the dollar" (Commons, 1934, p. 284). He insisted that we could perceive scarcity as price and abundance producing use value, which is, in fact, efficiency measured in man-hours. These affect the relative scarcity, which is the law of supply and demand by the managerial transactions.

Abundance is achieved by managerial transactions based on the principle of efficiency. We can perceive it as quantity. If abundance increases, relative scarcity will decrease. If abundance decreases, relative scarcity will increase. These changes will affect the prices; however, this is not all. Proprietary scarcity will increase if a supplier "withholds" the supply to the market. Commons explained about proprietary scarcity as a historical shift from producing power to bargaining power.

In all of these cases, in varying degree, a historical shift from concerted action may be seen in order to increase the production of wealth, highly favored in the past by the economists and courts, to concerted action in order to restrict the production of wealth, highly disfavored by them in the past. For, it is the shift from producing power to bargaining power, which, when authorized by law, becomes a reasonable restraint of trade (Commons, 1934, p. 346).

Figure 3.2 confirms the past trend, that is, price is decided by relative scarcity (the law of supply and demand) by way of the bargaining transactions. However, an abundance resulting from the efficiency by way of the managerial transactions affects relative and proprietary scarcity.

### *Relations of price and rationing transactions*

Finally, we study what affects price during a period of stabilization. As seen in the previous section, rationing transactions are important to apportion the burdens and benefits about creation of wealth in this stage. Rationing transactions work by connecting the concept of "futurity," which is "expected events."[3]

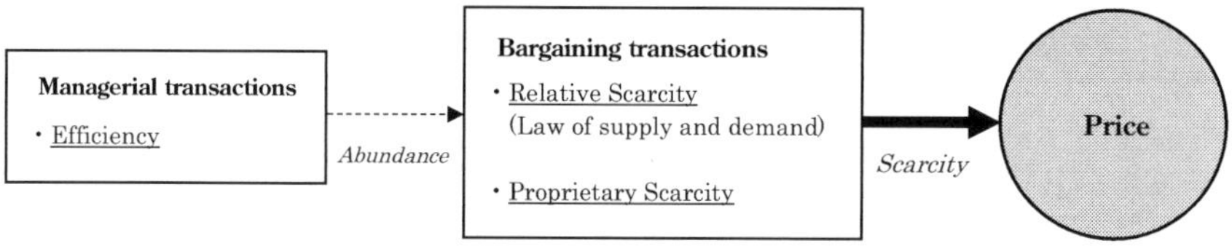


*Figure 3.2* Relations of price and managerial and bargaining transactions. Compiled by the author.

The board of directors in a company estimates the level of "the margin for profit" (current net profit), which is the expected profit. These estimates affect production planning and pricing, namely, the managerial transactions and the bargaining transactions. Commons elucidated profit maximization by producers as follows.

> Thus, producers can enlarge their profits in three directions: first, as sellers by raising the prices of their products; second, as buyers by reducing the prices paid to others for materials and labor; or, third, as producers by increasing their efficiency.
>
> (Commons, 1934, p. 797)

The first and second methods affect prices by bargaining transactions. The first method can increase proprietary scarcity by withholding supply or increase the price by using bargaining power if one is in a stronger position than the opponent. The second method can decrease the relative scarcity by restricting demand or decrease the price by using bargaining power if one is in a stronger position than the opponent. The third method can produce many things from few inputs by managerial transactions, that is, the method can increase the abundance by improving efficiency (man-hour). If the price and cost do not change, you can maximize the profit by increasing the quantity. If the board of directors aims at profit maximization, rationing transactions affect the bargaining and managerial transactions. As shown in Figure 3.3, the connection between the rationing transactions at the micro-level and the bargaining and managerial transactions can affect the price. Mentioned in the figure are the three kinds of transactions as described by Commons and the factors impacting prices.

## Relations of price and Commons' concepts of going concerns

Next, we look at the relationship between price and going concerns. Figure 3.4 reflects the going concern in the relations between price and the three types of transactions shown in Figure 3.3. In this figure, within the going concern as a whole (e.g., a company), there is a going plant as the production department, a going business as the sales and marketing department, and a going concern as the governing department. The roles of each are described next.

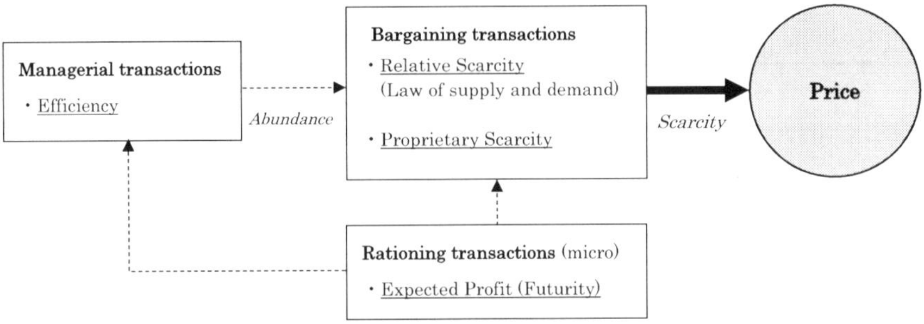


*Figure 3.3* Relations of price and rationing and managerial and bargaining transactions. Compiled by the author.

### *Relations of price and going plants*

The going plant is the production department within the going concern, which conducts managerial transactions to create wealth based on efficiency. Commons describes the role of this department as "control of nature" (Commons, 1934, p. 628). That is, it follows the orders of its superiors within the department to use fixed capital to generate use value and to track its production activities in the form of "man-hours" in pursuit of efficiency. The result is expressed as more output with less resource input.

Commons summarizes the going plant as "the whole of the fixed capital and inventory, measurable by the man-hours required for its production" (Commons, 1934, p. 296). Stated differently, it is an organization that controls limiting factors through its labor force – factors whose control in the proper form, at the right time and place, cause complementary factors to work to bring about the intended result. For example, he describes it in *Institutional Economics* as follows.

> A very little potash, if that is the limiting factor, will multiply the grain yield from perhaps five bushels to twenty bushels per acre. The sagacious mechanic is the one who busies himself with control of the limiting factor, knowing that the complementary factors will work out the results intended.
>
> (Commons, 1934, p. 629)

If the "abundance" created in this way is supplied to the market as is, it will lead to a collapse in commodity prices, which will be regulated by the going business.

### *Relations of price and going business*

A going business is the sales and marketing department within a going concern that conducts bargaining transactions for transferring wealth based on scarcity. Commons describes the role of this department as "control of other

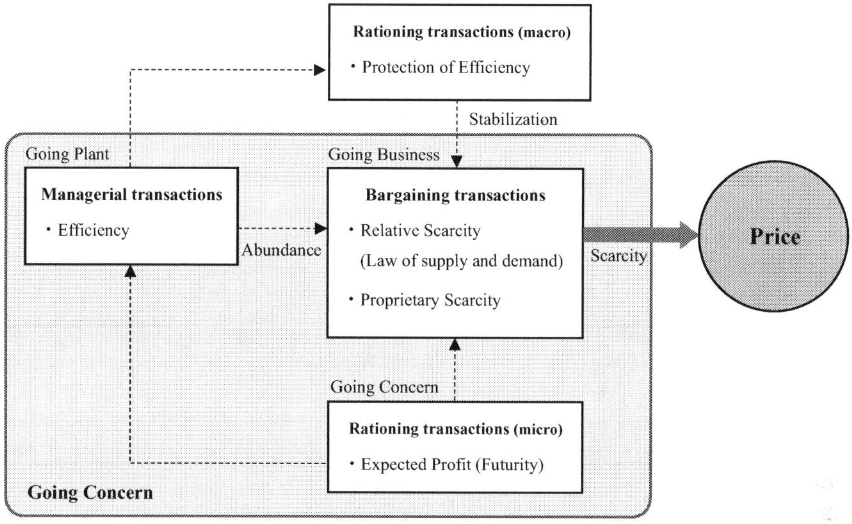


*Figure 3.4* Relations between price and three kinds of transactions and a going concern. Compiled by the author.

person" (Commons, 1934, p. 628). That is, it supplies its products through bargaining in the market, but in doing so, it creates exchange value through relative scarcity and proprietary scarcity and captures those sales in the form of "money," that is, "dollars."

Relative scarcity is the law of supply and demand, which determines a commodity's price. On the other hand, proprietary scarcity is created by withholding supply to prevent the price collapse caused by the "abundance." Commons is unique in that he distinguishes between two types of scarcity and argues that both affect price formation. He summarizes the going business as "the whole of the capital assets, measurable by money" (Commons, 1934, p. 297). He specifically describes the following in *Institutional Economics*.

> The terms "internal economy" and "external economy" are sometimes used to distinguish these two aspects of a going concern. But the "internal" economy turns out to be the engineering economy of managerial transactions producing use-values; the external economy becomes the proprietary economy of bargaining transactions which maintain or enlarge, if possible, the total value of assets.
>
> (Commons, 1934, p. 297)

Going businesses are organizations that sell goods, but what are their relations to going plants, which are production organizations? It is because, in *The Theory of Business Enterprise* (Veblen, 1904), Veblen regards contemporary capitalism as the dominance of the industrial system by business enterprises.

Veblen's view of capitalism is expressed in his view of the two as opposites. Commons, however, does not view the two oppositely as Veblen does because it emphasizes the role of the going concern as a mechanism that coordinates and governs the two.

### *Relations of price and micro's going concern*

As we saw in Chapter 2, there are two types of going concerns: going concern as a whole and going concern as an internal (micro-level) governing body. It is the latter role that is described here. Rationing transactions are used to distribute wealth, which can be easily understood by imagining a board of directors in a corporation. Companies decide on operating budgets and stock dividends to increase their profit margin, which is total sales minus total expenses. In Commons' terms, this is the decision of an "expected profit" regarding futurity. Specifically, this means directing production volume, targets, or technological development for a going plant. For a going business, it would direct sales volume and sales targets.

On the other hand, the going concern, in its coordinating role, also shapes corporate ethics. As explained in Chapters 6 and 7,[4] if goodwill as a good relationship between labor and management is fostered within the going concern, the going concern as a company can move in the same direction without conflict. Therefore, it is essential to form order within the going concern.

A going concern as an internal governing body is also affected by economic prices. What is important here is the relations between price fluctuation and profit margin. Commons explained the relations between the two in *Institutional Economics* as follows: For example, at 10 cents per copy, 600,000 copies were sold, yielding $590,400 per week. At this time, he assumed that the margin for profit of this corporation was 3% of the selling price. This amounted to 600,000, leaving $58,200 as the total cost of production per week. Here, he assumed a decline of 1% per month, close to the rate of decline of commodity prices from 1929. He supposed that the debt of $58,200 was incurred at the beginning of the month and paid at the end of the month. If the prices fall by 1%, the gross sales fall from $600,000 to $590,400. However, this $600 is one-third, or 33%, of the margin for profit ($1,800). Thus, a general fall in prices reduced the margin for profit by 33% through a fall of 1% in the selling prices (Commons, 1934, pp. 577–579).

In this example, if the profit margin is 10%, a 1% reduction in selling price is suppressed with a 10% reduction in profit margin. However, in Commons' estimate, a medium average margin for profit of 3% on sales for manufacturing corporations was the base line (Commons, 1934, p. 570). Thus, the above example applies, and slight changes in price have a major impact on the profit margin of the company. That is, as prices fall, debt payments such as interest do not change, so the profit margin falls sharply. On the other hand, as prices rise, debt payments such as interest do not change, so the profit margin rises significantly.

As described earlier, since price fluctuations significantly impact company profits, the role of the going concern in making macro policies is required in addition to the part of the micro going concern.

## Relations of price and macro's rationing transactions

Commons states, in *Institutional Economics*, "Yet while prices are institutional and exchange-values are 'real,' prices are very real in the capitalistic sense—they determine who shall get the results of efficiency" (Commons, 1934, p. 792). He stated as follows:

> The answer to the political and ethical question would then seem to be, Every person seeking his purely selfish increase of profits or wages should get his largest gain as a producer through increasing his efficiency, not as a seller gambling on the rise of prices, and not as a buyer gambling on the fall of prices.
>
> (Commons, 1934, p. 800)

Increasing prices as a seller leads to the increase of gross sales by means of the rise of a commodity price in case of a company and the increase of the income by the rise of wage level in case of a laborer. On the other hand, lowering prices as a buyer leads to the reduction of costs by the fall in price of investment goods in case of a company and the improvement of living standards by the fall in price of consumer goods in case of a laborer. However, a company is not only a seller of a commodity but also a buyer of raw materials. A laborer is not only a seller of a labor power commodity but also a consumer. Then, the results would be offset when they pay higher prices as buyers, even if they can earn money at high prices as sellers. Therefore, Commons insisted that they should not increase their gain by these methods but increase their gain by improving their efficiency.

He judged that reducing prices was not appropriate because it deprived producers of their gains and vice versa – that is, raising prices was not appropriate because it deprived consumers of their gains. In other words, he recommended stable prices. In particular, he believed that increasing efficiency through use of the new technology and brands guaranteeing high quality should be protected by law. That is, he insisted that the government should control a law of supply and demand to secure the profit of a producer, who adopts new technology to improve efficiency, by the patent law and the protection of brand. Commons said, "At first they give all the gains in efficiency to the producer. Then eventually they give all the gains to the buyers. The patent law do this by controlling the 'law' of supply and demand" (Commons, 1934, p. 802). He thought of both securing the gain of inventors as producers and securing the gain of consumers.

Efficiency of the new technology and the brand are "intangible properties," and so the patent law and protection of the brand mean to protect the "intangible properties" by a nation. Figure 3.4 shows that efficiency backed by new technology at a micro level and the protection of efficiency by rationing transactions at a macro level lead to the "stabilization" of bargaining transactions, hence maintaining the price and protecting the interest of inventors. Concerning "stabilization" at the macro level, Commons believes that the worldwide stabilization of the average purchasing power of money, that is, of the movement of prices (Commons, 1934, p. 804), is needed. This leads to a proper control of general prices to protect intangible property such as patents and brands. Commons had focused on the role of money from his early times and thought of proper control.[5]

According to Commons, central banks frame monetary policy for public interests prior to private interests. However, Governor Benjamin Strong of the New York Reserve Bank discovered the powerful regulative influence of open market operations. This led to a substitution of private purpose for public purpose (Commons, 1950, p. 260). As Véronique Dutraive and Bruno Théret argued, this situation is that the political factors, which have more of a public purpose, are subordinate to the economic factors, which have a more of a private purpose. It is consistent with the model of banker capitalism and inconsistent with the reasonable capitalism of Commons (Dutraive & Théret, 2013, p. 108). Therefore, according to Commons, we should safeguard the public interest by stabilizing the prices through macro monetary policy[6] and protection-efficient producers' profits.

As stated earlier, Commons thought price should be stable, because economic-efficient agents at the micro level can benefit. To attain that, the government should intervene in pricing through policy and law. Furthermore, he insisted on a worldwide stabilization of the average purchasing power of money, that is, the movement of prices.

## Conclusion

Commons' pricing theory includes not only economic factors but also historical, political, and legal elements. The theory is closely related to the concepts of transactions and going concern in addition to historical analysis. Commons focused on the concept of "efficiency" and the original "scarcity" at the micro level before the Great Depression (Commons, 1927–29). However, after the Great Depression, he insisted on price stabilization by analyzing price movement at a macro-level, in addition to the profit margins (Commons, 1931). In *Institutional Economics* (1934), he emphasized on the importance of the economic stabilization policy that includes distribution of the gains resulting from efficiency.[7] Commons' pricing theory is an institutional economics theory that includes the protection of intangible property such as patent and brand, particularly in modern economy, which has several new technologies at the micro level and stabilization or problems of distributions at the macro level.

As in previous research,[8] we can see cumulative causation. That is, economic actions on a micro-level affect the economy on macro level, and economic stabilization policy on macro level impact pricing by micro economic agents. This point is theoretically crucial. It is because one of the theoretical links between Veblen, Commons, and Mitchell, who founded the institutional school, is the idea of cumulative causation. Although the three men do not share the same view of institutions, cumulative causation is a common feature of their theories. It is a theoretical characteristic of the old institutional school.

Another finding of this chapter is that in Commons' pricing theory, going plants and going businesses are not antagonistic but are coordinated by both micro and macro going concerns. It is a clear distinction from Veblen.

## Notes

1 Uni explained that the concept of "proprietary scarcity" extended from 1927 to 1934. In the manuscript (Commons, 1927–29), this concept meant only the control of supply by sellers. In 1934, this concept expanded to include the control of supply and demand for the sake of public welfare and public necessity (Uni, 2014, p. 82).
2 Quantity rationing and price rationing are explained in Chapter 7.
3 More on Futurity is covered in Chapter 5.
4 Chapter 6, Labor Theory and Labor Policy: Labor Problems and Social Security, deals with goodwill within going concerns. Chapter 7 deals with the relations between policy formation and reasonable value, where we attempt to reconsider rationing transactions.
5 Commons (1893a) and (1893b) insist that money should have elasticity.
6 Commons' views of money and monetary policy theory are discussed in Chapter 5.
7 Commons' stabilization policies are discussed in Chapters 5 and 6 of Part III.
8 See Uni (2014).

## References

### *English*

Atkinson, Glen, & Charles J. Whalen. (2011). "Futurity: Cornerstone of Post-Keynesian Institutionalism," in *Global Financial Crisis, 2008-2009, Financial crises, Neokeynesianismus, Rezession, Wirtschaftstheorie*, ed. by Whalen, Charles J., 39–61. Cheltenham: Edward Elgar.

Commons, John R. (1893a) 1986. "Economic Reform," *The Voice*. Reproduced in *John R. Commons Papers* (microfilm edition: reel 15, 58–63). State Historical Society of Wisconsin.

———. (1893b) 1986. "Sound Currency," *The Voice*. Reproduced in *John R. Commons Papers* (microfilm edition: reel 15, 64–66). State Historical Society of Wisconsin.

———. (1924) 1995. *Legal Foundations of Capitalism*. New Brunswick and London: Transaction Publishers.

———. (1927–29). *Reasonable Value: A Theory of Volitional Economics*. Manuscript. (Collection of the National Agricultural Library. NAL call number: HB501 C66 1927, Identifier: CAT10844889001 and CAT10844889002).

———. (1931). "Institutional Economics," *American Economic Review*, 21 (December), 648–657.

———. (1934). *Institutional Economics: Its Place in Political Economy*. New York: Macmillan.

———. (1950). *The Economics of Collective Action*. New York: Macmillan.

———. (1986). *The John R. Commons Papers* (microfilm edition), ed. by Miller, Harold L. Madison: State Historical Society of Wisconsin.

Veblen, Thorstein B. (1904). *The Theory of Business Enterprise*. New York: C. Scribner.

### *Japanese*

Dutraive, Véronique, & Bruno Théret. (2013). "Political Sovereignty and Monetary Sovereignty: An Interpretation from J. R. Commons" (Takayuki Nakahara, Trans.), *Keizai-Ronso* (The Economic Review), 187 (1), 83–110.

Uni, Hiroyuki. (2014). "J. R. Commons no Ruisekiteki Inga Renkan Ron: *Seido Keizaigaku* to 1927 nen Sōko no Hikaku Bunseki" (J. R. Commons' Theory of Cumulative Causation: A Comparative Analysis of *Institutional Economics* and Its Manuscript in 1927), *Kikan-Keizai-Riron* (Political Economy Quarterly), 51 (2), 77–88.

# 4 Business cycle theory

## Expectations and cumulative causation

The main objective of this chapter is to examine the characteristics of Commons' business cycle theory. He is regarded as the founder of institutional economics that follows Thorstein B. Veblen and Wesley C. Mitchell, who grasped changes in economic society as cumulative causation. The business cycle theory is a concrete description of the cumulative causation in which institutions influence the economy. To understand Commons' institutional economics, after dividing the business cycle theory into the profit-share and profit-margin theory, we will confirm how the business cycle theory is more consistent with the latter. Next, we consider the economy analysis by the business cycle theory of Commons. After that, we discuss his cumulative causation in light of price and business cycle theories.

### Factors of business cycle: profit-share and profit-margin

#### *Profit-share theory*

In Chapter 9, "futurity," section 7, "The Margin For Profit" in *Institutional Economics* (Commons, 1934), Commons analyzed two theories – the "profit-share" and "profit-margin" theories – to explain the cause of prosperity and depression.[1] Both theories focus on profit, which is most important for businessmen in capitalism, but the profit-share theory considers the share of profit in total production. Regarding the profit-share theory, Commons stated the following:

> [T]he Profit-share theorists have argued that too much of national income goes to the proprietary incomes, such as rent, interest, and profit, and too little to consumer's income, especially wages and salaries. Therefore consumers are not able to purchase back all of the products which they as laborers have produced. Hence overproduction, followed by business depression and unemployment.
>
> (Commons, 1934, p. 527)

DOI: 10.4324/9781032701394-7

He explained this theory by illustrating different stages, namely "the Consumption stage," "the Savings stage," "the Dividends-Lag stage," and "the Sales-Lag stage." The "Consumption stage" takes the view of communists – by eliminating property income including rent, interest, and profits through common ownership, workers should receive the total value of products as wage, which they can then use for consumption. Commons used Alfred B. Lewis' argument that people who earned property income also consumed goods, and expenditure by company owners was enough to repurchase part of the whole product.

Next, the "Savings stage" adopts the perspective of socialists – company owners will contribute to overproduction because they save or invest a larger portion of their income than they spend. Commons also introduced Lewis' objection that savings are, in other words, expenditure on capital equipment to produce goods.

The other two theories are part of profit-lag theory focusing on the gap between the time when profit occurs and the time when distribution occurs. Commons divided this into "the Dividends-Lag" theory and "Sales-Lag" theory. In "the Dividends-Lag" theory, there will be unsold products in the case of expanded production even if the profit generated in the previous year is used for repurchasing the product not purchased by workers in the next year. Therefore, we should reduce the share of profits and dividends and raise the share of wages. So, Lewis insisted on strengthening labor unions, etc. Commons, on the contrary, argued that undistributed profits could also lead to an expansion of investment through bank deposits.

In the final "Sales-Lag" theory, even if goods are increased in the previous year, the increasing purchase power is not available until the goods are sold. Therefore, the idea is that a shortage of purchasing power will result from an increase in production, and unsold goods will accumulate. Commons criticized this thought as well as other theories, because paying wages was possible through the use of the banking system to disburse loans before selling and also through a means of checks and discounting checks. At the end of Chapter 9 in *Institutional Economics*, he stated the following.

> We may then conclude that the fundamental reason why *share* theories of national monetary income do not account for the alternating booms and depressions is because increasing the share of one class reduces the shares of other classes and does not change the total purchasing power of all classes. The purchasing power of all classes, whether expended as savings or expended for consumption, furnishes the same employment for labor, barring temporary difficulties of adjustment.
>
> (Commons, 1934, p. 589)

Therefore, for the above reasons, Commons did not adopt the profit-share theory but adopted the profit-margin theory, which is examined in the next section.

### *Profit-margin theory*

Profit-margin is the difference between the total of all liabilities incurred for all purposes and the gross income obtained from all product sales. Simply, this margin is equivalent to net profit (Commons, 1934, p. 527). Commons stated the following:

> The profit-margin theorists have argued that the cause of business depression and unemployment was the inability of businessmen to obtain a sufficient revenue over and above all expenses to enable them to make a profit and to continue in business without suffering loss and bankruptcy.
>
> (Commons, 1934, p. 527)

"To continue in business" means to continue a company as a going concern. In *Institutional Economics*, Commons divided this profit-margin theory further into two theories. One is the Ricardian theory, wherein profit margins can be secured only through wage cuts when price declines. Commons criticized this by saying that the debt's nominal amount does not actually change and thus increases the real burden on businesses. This ultimately suppresses debt-financed investment, even when profit margins are secured by wage cuts during a price decline.

The other theory is one inferred from Knut Wicksell's idea that if the market interest rate falls below the natural interest rate, economic activity will be stimulated, but if the market interest rate exceeds the natural interest rate, economic activity will be suppressed. Commons incorporated this idea and presented the relations between the market interest rate (the central bank rate) and the natural interest rate (marginal productivity of capital) as the following.

> If the central bank rate is reduced, by world-wide action, below the marginal productivity of capital, that is, "natural" interest, then the bank customers are induced to increase their demand for bank credit by which they increase their demand for commodities and labor, and thereby raise the general level of prices. In the opposite direction, if the central bank rate, by world-wide concerted action, is raised above the marginal productivity of physical capital, the business customers owing to narrow margins for profit, reduce their borrowings, reduce their demand for commodities and labor, and a fall in prices and employment is the result.
>
> (Commons, 1934, p. 596)

However, Commons thought that the natural interest rate used by Wicksell to represent "marginal productivity" pertained to physical aspects, so it was necessary for him to translate this into an institutional concept. That is, "capital-yield" or profit divided by capital or ratio of profit to capital was replaced with natural interest rate or marginal productivity.[2] After that,

*Table 4.1* Comparison of Commons and Wicksell. Compiled by the author.

| | |
|---|---|
| Wicksell | Market interest rate (%) < natural interest rate (%) → economic activity ↑ |
| | Market interest rate (%) > natural interest rate (%) → economic activity ↓ |
| Commons | Market interest rate (%) < expected profit rate (%) → economic activity ↑ |
| | Market interest rate (%) > expected profit rate (%) → economic activity ↓ |

Commons discussed the relations between the central bank rate, which is the market interest rate, and the capital-yield in the following manner.

> [I]t is not the *absolute* rise or fall of the bank rate that affects the average movement of output and prices, it is the *relative* rise or fall of the bank rate compared with capital-yield. If the capital-yield is 6 per cent, then a bank rate of 41/2 per cent, as in 1919, is low rate, and will initiate a tendency towards a rise of average of commodity prices. If the capital-yield falls to 4 per cent, as in 1929, then the same bank rate of 5 per cent is a *high* rate and will initiate a tendency towards a fall in commodity prices.
> (Commons, 1934, p. 605)

However, as pointed out by Kitagawa (2017), Commons noted "expected capital-yield," that is, "expected profit margin" or "expected profit rate."[3] Commons said, "The business owner is looking forward, and what he might call his wage or salary, if he gets it, is merged into the expected margin of profit remaining after he pays all his debts" (Commons, 1934, p. 605). Using this concept, as Shibata (2021) states, if the market interest rate falls below the expected profit rate, the debt-dependent investment will expand, and if the market interest rate exceeds the expected profit rate), debt-dependent investment is suppressed. Table 4.1 summarizes the differences between Wicksell and Commons.

What is important is the business owner's expectation on how much profit margin can be obtained. Commons made the following statement at the time in 1931 after the Great Depression: "In capitalistic countries it is the expectation of profit that makes possible the employment of labor and the payment of interest and rent" (Commons, 1931, p. 8). With this, we turn to Commons' explanation of the business cycle through profit-margin theory using "World Depressions" written in 1931.

## Explanation of business cycle by profit-margin theory (1924–1931)

### *Upturn in the economy (1924–1927)*

Commons summarized the rising phases of the economy from 1924 to 1927 in "World Depressions" in the following manner.[4] First of all, during this period in the United States, as a policy of the Federal Reserve system, credit provision was extended to support England's gold standard restoration. The rate of interest in the United States was induced to a lower level than the interest rate in England through this policy, which means that the companies' expected profit was expanded because of the compression of interest payment costs. Then, the investment was expanded in the United States, which resulted in overproduction and soaring stock prices. This led to an increase in demand for production goods and an accompanying increase in production price, resulting in rising product prices. In the profit-margin theory, the rise in prices led to an increase in the profit-margin because the nominal amount of debt did not change. This resulted in the upward spiral that led to a further increase in expected profit. Eventually, if marginal business that could not be realized developed and the expected profit was not achieved, the expectation was finally revised. This was the movement until the fall of 1929.

#### *Downturn in the economy (1929)*

On the other hand, in the downturn from the fall of 1929, some companies went into bankruptcy due to excessive debt through failure to achieve expected profit. Then, expected profits decreased, which led to a reduction in production and a decline in stock prices. This led to a decline in demand for production goods and the accompanying decline in production price, eventually resulting in a decline in product prices. In the profit-margin theory, the decline in prices led to a decline in the profit-margin because the nominal amount of the debt did not change. This resulted in the downward spiral that led to a further decline in expected profit. When further price declines emerged due to the sale of assets for interest payment, debt deflation eventually occurred. This is the Great Depression analysis using Commons' profit-margin theory.

Table 4.2 summarizes the above. What is important here is the relations between price fluctuation and profit margin. That is, slight changes in price have a major impact on the profit margin of the company. As prices fall, debt payments such as interest do not change, so the profit margin falls sharply. On the other hand, as prices rise, debt payments such as interest do not change, so the profit margin rises significantly.

### Basis of cumulative causation of Commons' transaction economics

In this section, we will look at the basis of cumulative causation in the transaction economics of Commons, taking into account the price theory of the previous chapter. Cumulative causation refers to the cyclical and cumulative progression of changes in these various factors through mutually reinforcing actions that operate among multiple factors. Put another way, it can be described as a "micro-macro loop" in which micro phenomena affect the macro and macro phenomena affect the micro.

*Table 4.2* Explanation of business fluctuations by Commons. Compiled by the author based on Commons (1931).

| *Upturn in the economy (1924–1927)* | *Downturn in the economy (1929)* |
|---|---|
| To support Britain's return to the gold standard U.S. interest rate < U.K. interest rate | Companies fail to achieve expected profits and become insolvent |
| ↓ | ↓ |
| Interest expense in the U.S. ↓ | **Expected profit** of the company ↓ |
| ↓ | ↓ |
| **Expected profit** of company ↑ | Production ↓ ⇒ Stock price ↓ |
| ↓ | ↓ |
| Investment ↑ ⇒ Production ↑ ⇒ Stock price ↑ | Demand for production goods ↓ |
| ↓ | ↓ |
| Demand for production goods ↑ | Production and **Product price** ↓ |
| ↓ | ↓ |
| Production and **Product price** ↑ | Nominal price of debt unchanged |
| ↓ | ↓ |
| Nominal price of debt unchanged | Profit ↓ ⇒ **Expected profit** ↓ |
| ↓ | ↓ |
| Profit ↑ ⇒ **Expected profit** ↑ | Sale of assets |
| ↓ | ↓ |
| Investment relying on debt ↑ | Asset deflation |
| ↓ | |
| Extending credit ↑ | |

### *Cumulative causation in micro dimensions*

Figure 4.1 adds profit-margin theory to the "transaction," "going concern," and "price" theories of the previous chapters.

In turn, the starting point is the "expected profit" in the company as the going concern. Based on the profit-margin theory, if the expected profit rate (%) is higher than the market interest rate (%), then the going concern as the governing body (rationing transactions in micro) will give instructions to the going plant to increase capital investment or production in the next year. In addition, the going business is instructed to set sales prices and profit targets in the market. As a result, the going plant increases production, and the going business conducts sales to ensure the target profit. Higher demand for production goods will eventually lead to higher production and product prices. If this happens, the expected profit in the next period will be even higher since the nominal amount of debt will remain unchanged. If expectations are high, investment and production plans that depend on debt can be made by the going concern as the governing body (rationing transactions in micro). The above is the case in a booming economy, but in a recession, the opposite occurs, as discussed in the previous section.

Thus, investment and production plans based on the expected profits of companies in the micro dimension affect capital investment and production volume, which in turn affect market prices. Then, changes in market prices affect the expected profits of the companies in the next period, and the cause and effect are cumulative.

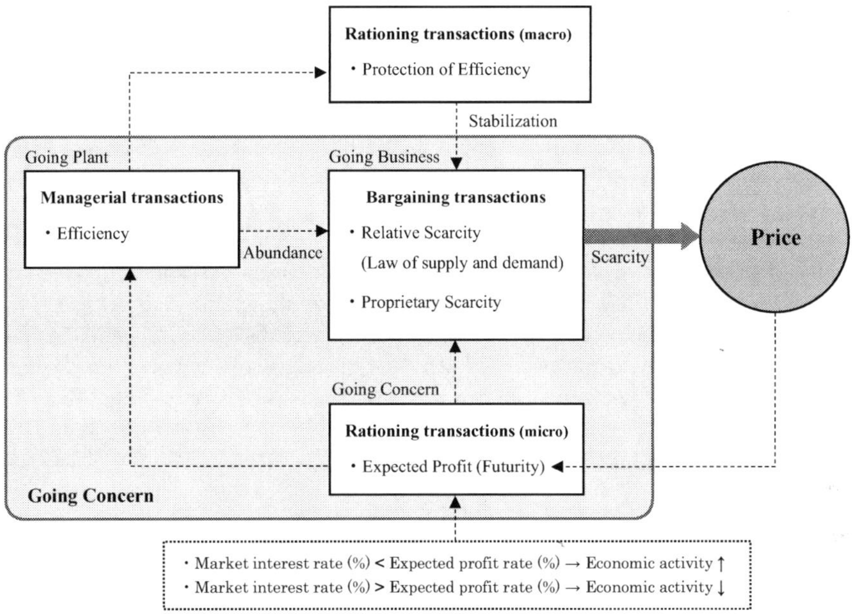


*Figure 4.1* Basics of cumulative causation and business cycle. Compiled by the author.

***Cumulative causation between micro and macro***

As explained earlier, the starting point in the micro dimension is "expected profit," but what influences that expected profit is the market interest rate, which is determined at the macro-level. In other words, as will be explained in detail in the next chapter, a country's interest rate policy determines the official discount rate, impacting the market interest rate. It is not micro-level but macro-level rationing transactions. Based on the profit-margin theory, if the market interest rate can be induced to be low, it will stimulate the economy, leading to economic stabilization. Conversely, asset deflation may occur in a recession due to asset sales, making such stimulus measure necessary. Economic restraint measures are necessary when the economy is overheated, and there is a risk of an economic bubble due to an increase in debt-dependent investment and a rapid increase in credit availability. In other words, monetary policy in the macro dimension will affect business activity in the micro dimension, as explained precisely in the next chapter. As we have seen in the previous chapter, small price changes significantly impact company profits, so an important goal is stabilizing prices.

On the other hand, protecting intangible properties is also an important macroeconomic policy. As shown in Figure 4.1, if the government protects a new technology invented by a going plant as a patent, the value added by the technology will bring the product to market at a higher price. Without such a system, there would be no expectation of securing profits and no plans to develop new technologies. In other words, this stabilization policy leads to reasonable prices, and an incentive policy encourages companies to pursue new technologies and efficiency.

These macroeconomic policies or institutions, such as monetary policy and the protection of intangible properties, are the basis of cumulative causation that affects microeconomic corporate activities, or in other words, a micro–macro loop. This methodology is different from "methodological individualism," which takes the individual as the starting point, or "methodological totalitarianism," which takes society as a whole as the starting point and is a methodology common to the old American institutional school, which Veblen and Mitchell also share. Furthermore, from this analysis, especially about price stabilization by economic policy (rationing transactions), we can say that Commons was one of the few economists of his era (pre-Keynes) to appreciate the role and impact of a flexible monetary system on real economic cycles. In the next section, we compare Veblen and Mitchell to clarify the characteristics of Commons' business cycle theory.

## Comparison with T. Veblen and W.C. Mitchell

### *Veblen's business cycle theory*

Veblen (1904) regards contemporary capitalism as the dominance of industrial system by business enterprises. Veblen identified monopoly by business enterprise, location, natural resource control, and goodwill as impacting prices. This goodwill includes established customary business relations, honest trade reputation, privileges, trademarks, brands, patents, copyrights, and exclusive control of special raw material resources. He understood that business enterprises use advertisements to raise the value of goodwill and make these costs part of production costs. He thought that the rise in the value of goodwill through these advertisements raised the expected rate of return of business enterprises, thereby ensuring credit loans.

Veblen understood that the gap between industrial equipment, which is a tangible property, and corporate capital, which is an intangible property, caused the business cycle. That is, if the demand in an industry increases and price rises, the expected rate of return of the companies will rise. Accordingly, the value of goodwill and collateral of the companies rise, and credit loans based on this increase will be issued. Thus, it is a characteristic of boom that the corporate capital of intangible property is larger than the industrial equipment of tangible property.

However, as the production cost rises, the difference between the selling price and the production cost shrinks, and the firm's expected rate of return declines. As a result, the value of goodwill and collateral of the relevant enterprise are reduced, and credit loans based on this decrease. Thus, a characteristic of recession period is that the difference between tangible property and intangible property shrinks. Furthermore, at this time, if bankruptcy occurs in chain due to the default of debt, it becomes a depression as a liquidation process ensues.

As a way to escape from such a depression, Veblen gave the following two means: one is nonproductive consumption of goods – that is, government waste such as armaments and construction of public facilities. The other is the elimination of excessive competition by allowing monopolies and trusts. Monopolies can restore profit by setting production limits and managing price. As such, it was goodwill, that is, an intangible property that was attracted as a result of corporate mergers carried out in the process toward monopolization.

As described earlier, in the case of Veblen, there is a salient characteristic of the existence of business enterprises closely linked with goodwill, advertisement, expected rate of return, and credit loans. In addition, the understanding of goodwill, which is an intangible property, also affected Commons. The intangible value generally refers to the balance obtained by subtracting the amount of tangible property valued at reproductive cost from the total value. However, according to Commons, Veblen's understanding of intangible value is regarded as "exploitation" theory, meaning a financial assessment based on the strategic power of a company for "getting something for nothing" (Commons, 1934, pp. 650–651).

### *Mitchell's business cycle theory*

Next, we will look at the overview of the business cycle theory of Mitchell, who worked on business cycle research for many years. As Mitchell was influenced by Veblen, he regarded the fundamental character of capitalism as a monetary economy centered on money-making. First of all, Mitchell (1941) thinks that the business cycle depends on the "prospect for profit." Companies expand their business if the prospect for profit in the future exceeds the profit of the past, and in the opposite case, they will shrink the business. This reflects the understanding that companies give priority to making money rather than producing goods. Here, we will concretely look at his business cycle theory divided into four phases of recovery, prosperity, promotion of crisis, and depression.

In the recovery period, wages and profits generally rise as a whole. Along with this, consumption demand and investment demand increase, causing an increase in inventory (assets) due to an increased production. At this time, Mitchell thought that companies' "optimism" attitudes arose. Following this, the selling price rises, and the purchase of goods (for production) increases. Wages and general expenses, which are a part of the costs, rise, but companies' profit increases because the rise of wages and general expenses is delayed until the selling price rises. That is, there is a time lag. In the next prosperous period, new capital such as new factories increase, and the wage increase is caused by general expenses rising and increased working hours due to increased demand, etc. In other words, although business cost rises, companies cannot easily increase selling prices due to an improvement of production capacity, which is an effect of price reduction and regulation of antitrust laws.

Then, in the next crisis promotion period, all costs rise, so profits decrease and production and sales capacity decline. If oversupply occurs in this phase, prices fall. Mitchell thought that "financial difficulties" caused this situation to become a depression because it was difficult to obtain financing due to the rising interest rate during prosperous periods. When the recession occurs in this way, the company makes efforts to reduce costs through dismissal and reducing wages. Since prices fall during the recession period, borrowing and investment increase due to cheap capital goods and falling interest rates, which lead to a recovery phase. This is the summary of Mitchell's business cycle theory.

Mitchell proposed the following three ideas as a plan to control such a business cycle. The first is to reorganize the American banking system to make it easier for interbank financing, and to prevent the panic from the recession. The second is the adjustment of government projects. To alleviate the seriousness of the depression, it is necessary to take measures to suspend government projects until they goes into recession. The third is the stabilization of the dollar. This narrows the fluctuation range of prices and makes the business cycle flatter. This makes it possible to eliminate the factors that cause fluctuation in the company's expected profit.

## Conclusion

From the above, how can we summarize Commons' business cycle theory? We would like to present three points.

The first is the existence of the commonality of the old American institutionalists, Veblen, Commons, and Mitchell, in their business cycle theories. First of all, the three business cycle theories are neither accidentally caused by external disturbing factors nor are ways of thinking that it converges toward equilibrium. The three business cycle theories are cumulative causation theories in which there is an accumulation of the endogenous causal relations. In addition, a common idea between the three institutionalists is that the business cycle is a phenomenon originating not from the industrial production side, that is to say, not from the physical natural economy, but from the business enterprise side, such as price, revenue, and capital, that is, from the money economy. Furthermore, common between them is the pointing out of the importance of expected profit in the business cycle.

The second point is the uniqueness of Commons' business cycle theory. He learned the importance of intangible properties in modern capitalism from Veblen and the courts. As for Veblen, Commons stated in *Institutional Economics* the following.

> The problem set by Veblen of a dualism in economics between materials and intangible property has only recently been attacked by economists whose work we epitomize under the terms transactions, going concerns,

> stabilization of prices, and reasonable value. Each transaction is a valuation, not of materials, but of Veblen's ownership of materials; each concern is both Veblen's going plant and the business man's going business; each fluctuation of general prices is Veblen's exploitation; each approach towards a better understanding of reasonable value reduces this exploitation. And these are scientific, not in the sense of Veblen's physical sciences, but in the sense of the human will in action (Commons, 1934, p. 677).

In this way, although Commons was influenced by Veblen, he explained the business cycle using his own terms of transaction, going concern, and reasonable value. We can understand deeply his business cycle theory by considering his pricing theory. In another place, Commons said that Veblen's theory of intangible property was exploitation theory and that his scientific concept was a traditional concept of physical science and one with no purpose. On the other hand, Commons said that the court's intangible property theory which he adopted was the theory of reasonable value that defined a proper level with public purpose. The concept of science was an institutional concept, which was social science with public purpose (Commons, 1934, p. 654). This is an important issue separating Veblen and Commons, while paying attention to the keywords such as intangible property.

The third point is the contemporary meaning of Commons' business cycle theory. Shibata (2021) analyzes his business cycle theory by focusing on the concept of incorporeal property and intangible property. In particular, he analyzes the subprime financial crisis from the view of converting incorporeal property into intangible property by expanding negotiability. This point shows the effectiveness of Commons' business cycle theory as a modern analytical tool. Furthermore, his business cycle theory, in which price stability and realization of reasonable value are achieved through the protection of goodwill, is suggestive for the modern economy, where intellectual property and labor–management relations are important in the global economy.[5]

## Notes

1 See Shibata (2021) and Kitagawa (2017) for a detailed explanation of profit-share theory and profit-margin theory of Commons.

2 Uni (2019) analyzes Commons' criticism of Wicksell's theory of interest. Uni focused on the influence of Ralph G. Hawtrey by comparing Commons (1927–29), which was the manuscript of *Institutional Economics*, with *Institutional Economics* (1934).

3 Kitagawa (2017) analyzes the difference between financial statement analysis and Commons' *Institutional Economics* (1934) regarding this point. According to him, *Institutional Economics* shows the present decision for the future, while financial statement analysis is a posteriori analysis.

4 See Terakawa (2017) for details.

5 Reasonable value is discussed in detail in Chapter 7 and labor policy in Chapter 6.

## References

### *English*

Commons, John R. (1927–29). *Reasonable Value: A Theory of Volitional Economics.* Manuscript. (Collection of the National Agricultural Library. NAL call number: HB501 C66 1927, Identifier: CAT10844889001 and CAT10844889002).

———. (1931) 1986. "World Depressions," reproduced in *John R. Commons Papers* (microfilm edition: reel 18, 613–624). State Historical Society of Wisconsin.

———. (1934). *Institutional Economics: Its Place in Political Economy.* New York: Macmillan.

———. (1986). *The John R. Commons Papers* (microfilm edition), ed. by Miller, Harold L. Madison: State Historical Society of Wisconsin.

Mitchell, Wesley C. (1941). *Business Cycles and Their Causes.* Berkley: University of California Press, 1941.

Veblen, Thorstein B. (1904). *The Theory of Business Enterprise.* New York: C. Scribner.

### *Japanese*

Kitagawa, Kota. (2017). "J. R. Commons Seido Keizaigaku ni okeru Shinyō Seido to Tōchi: Shinyō Kahei no Naisei-Setsu no Kanten kara" (Credit System and Its Governance of J. R. Commons' Institutional Economics: From the Perspective of Endogenous Credit Money), *Keizai-Ronshu* (Economic review of Kansai University), 67 (3), 83–121.

Shibata, Tokutaro. (2021). *J. R. Commons no Seido-teki Keizaigaku* (Institutional Economics of J. R. Commons). Tokyo: Nihon-Keizai-Hyōronsha.

Terakawa, Ryuichiro. (2017). "Commons wa Daikyōkō wo Dou Toraetanoka" (How did Commons perceive the Great Depression?), Japan Society for Evolutionary Economics, Institution and Governance meeting. Handout, January 15.

Uni, Hiroyuki. (2019). "J. R. Commons no Wicksell Rishi Riron Hihan: R. G. Hawtrey no Eikyō wo Chūshin ni" (John. R. Commons' Criticism of Wicksell's Theory of Interest: Focusing on an Influence of R. G. Hawtrey), *Keizai-Ronso* (The Economic Review), 193 (1), 85–105.

# Part III

# Stabilization policy

## Role of the state

# 5 Futurity and monetary policy

## Money and credit management

Commons was primarily a contributor to the trade union movement and to the creation of various reform legislation centered on conciliation in labor–management relations. However, he was also president of the National Monetary Association (1922), a collaborator on the Federal Reserve Bank's price stabilization legislation, and the first to report on open market operations to the American Economic Association (1924). Commons understood the close relations between monetary and labor issues, as he stated, "The credit problem is our biggest labor problem" (Commons, 1921, p. 288). The content of Commons' views on money has been taken up since the 1990s, and there have been previous studies that have found the inseparability of money and labor, and comparisons with Keynes, especially the similarities between the two.[1]

However, most of these previous studies discuss Commons' view of money, and only some deal in detail with specific policy theories such as monetary reform theory under the gold-silver double standard or open market operations theory under the central banking system. Only a few, such as Ramstad (2001) and Whalen (1993), point out that these monetary policy theories can be understood as institutional economics, and little literature even touches on Commons' view of class.

In this chapter, we take the monetary issues discussed by Commons as a monetary policy theory.[2] Then, we will examine what Commons, who said that "[s]ince purpose or policy looks to the future, it is the realm of ethics as well as economics" (Commons, 1937, p. 694), based his judgment of the goodness or badness of policy on.

In what follows, we begin our discussion by reviewing Commons' view of money. Then, we examine the characteristics of monetary policy under the Federal Reserve System and discuss the relations between open market operations and price stabilization. Next, focusing on the criteria for judging whether the monetary policy to be implemented is appropriate or not, we will discuss specific measures of what Commons considers an appropriate monetary policy. We will deal with the relations between monetary policy and workers/consumers. In addition, we will compare Commons' monetary policy with that of Keynes, pointed out in previous studies, and discuss the similarities and differences between the two. From this, we will discuss the characteristics of

DOI: 10.4324/9781032701394-9

Commons' monetary policy theory as institutional economics. Finally, we will grasp it in the context of the whole picture of transaction economics.

## Commons' view of money

As we have seen in the previous chapters, Commons had read from a survey of U.S. Supreme Court cases that a significant change in the concept of property occurred in the second half of the 19th century. The change was from corporeal property, representing material ownership, to incorporeal property, representing immaterial ownership, such as debt instruments and credit, and to intangible property, representing goodwill and patent rights.[3] Commons' emphasis in thinking about money was on the money as incorporeal property or money as debt.

> Economists speak of the "quantity of money," or the "quantity theory of money," whereas it is not a quantity of money but a quantity of debts, and this quantity of debts has somewhere an equal quantity of credits. The quantity of money is the quantity of debts, and the quantity of debts is the quantity of credits.
>
> (Commons, 1934a, p. 472)

The understanding is that money arises from the creditor–debtor relations and is equal to the amount of credit extended. Commons also defines the money market as "not where money is exchanged, but where ownership of debts is exchanged," and the commodity market is also "not where commodities are exchanged, but where ownership of commodities is exchanged" (Commons, 1934a, p. 427). It is due to the recognition that real business is conducted on credit and debt and that World War I was also financed by credit.[4]

The core of money as debt is bank debt (deposits). Bank deposits are defined as "money" because they are not "time-discounted," meaning they are past due and unpaid liabilities. On the other hand, securities are classified as "capital" rather than "money" because they are unpaid liabilities. Therefore, the money market is a "market for debts past due," and the capital market is a "market for debts not yet due" (Commons, 1934a, p. 449), and both markets constitute a "debt market." With credit, the "commodity market," consisting of retail, wholesale, and so on, is associated with the "debt market," consisting of the money and capital markets. Commons states the following.

> Thus, we begin our economic theory, not with Adam Smith's assumption of individual liberty to produce and acquire wealth, but with Hawtrey's assumption of a duty to produce and deliver wealth.
>
> (Commons, 1934a, pp. 473–474)

Commons supports Hawtrey's view of money as "the means for the legal discharge of a debt" (Hawtrey, 1919, p. 15).[5] Commons appreciated that

Hawtrey linked the commodity market to the debt market by the two aspects of prices: "prices in the commodity market" and "prices in the money market (which determine the extent of debt)" (Commons, 1934a, p. 483).[6]

Bank deposits, which belong to the debt market and are central to the money market, mean that banks supply purchasing power to consumers and companies through debt. Since it is the supply of purchasing power through the transfer of credit and debt relations, bank debts represent the supply of purchasing power through credit. Since credit transactions in the market take place in a world with futurity and uncertainty, money becomes credit money strongly linked to futurity and uncertainty rather than metal money as past labor accumulation. The idea of "credit money as debt" linking the commodity and debt markets is Commons' basic view of money.

In 1893, Commons wrote a paper on money (Commons, 1893a, 1893b) in which he argued that money should be elastic. Money on the gold standard or the gold-silver double standard would be convertible to gold or silver, and it would also be resilient to allow for credit creation.[7] Commons emphasized the role of elastic issuable money by emphasizing the purchasing power supply function through bank credit creation. According to him, in late 19th-century business in the United States, more than 90% of payments were made on credit, and the money supply was four times greater when credit existed than when it did not. Thus, if there were no credit, the money supply would be one-fourth, and the value of money would rise by that amount. As a result, commodity prices were reduced by a quarter. Thus, he states that credit is both a substitute for and a representative of money (Commons, 1893a, p. 59). Furthermore, of course, credit also depends on the industry's confidence level. If the industry is stable, a lot of credit lending will occur; if it is sluggish, lending will be reluctant, and reserves will be increased (Commons, 1893a, p. 59). From the statistical data, Commons states that the long-run price fluctuations result from changes in the money supply, with a cumulative rise in credit.

> When the supply of money is increasing and the secular movement is upward, as in the years 1850 to 1873, then an upward movement of credit acts cumulatively, and prices leap forward with bounds, as in 1850 to 1857 and 1869 to 1873.
>
> (Commons, 1893a, p. 60)

He analyzed that this led to excessive speculation, trade, production, and the subsequent depression (Commons, 1893a, p. 60). Therefore, his paper "Economic Reform" (Commons, 1893a) argued that monetary reform was needed to achieve a stable price level to prevent wild fluctuations. His proposal in this paper was to replace the fixed exchange ratio of gold to silver (1:16) with a flexible exchange ratio under the gold–silver double standard adopted in the U.S. at the time and to authorize the Secretary of the Treasury to redeem government bills (Treasury bills) for gold or silver bullion at market prices.

The issuance of Treasury bills convertible to gold or silver had already been authorized by the Brand-Allison Act of 1878 and the Sherman Silver Purchase Act of 1890. However, the amount of the issue was defined by the amount of silver purchased.[8] This was unsatisfactory to the farmers of the time, who were engaged in the free silver movement in hopes of alleviating currency shortages. Therefore, Commons proposed that when prices tended to fall, the government issued legal tender (silver certificates) to purchase silver bullion and increase the amount of currency to prevent prices from falling. On the other hand, when prices were rising, he proposed an elastic money system in which the quantity of money would be reduced by selling silver bullion at market prices to absorb legal tender (silver securities), thereby preventing prices from rising.

Commons came to this view because of legal changes in the concept of property from American business practices and changes in the corporate form and its accompanying legal provisions, as seen in the joint-stock companies, that is, the legal foundation of capitalism was changing. In this context, he found a limit to the materialistic view of money and its separation from the actual market. It is reflected in how he views the role of banks (issuing banks) as money suppliers. Commons praises H.G. Moulton, who emphasized the shiftability theory that banks' liquidity is maintained through the sale of stocks and bonds, for correcting the materialist doctrine of the classical school by linking the credit structure to capital formation. However, Commons criticizes Moulton for making little reference to debt in Moulton and giving credit only a passive role (Commons, 1937, pp. 682–683). The reason for this is that Commons emphasized the active role of credit by banks, that is, the impact of credit currency on the actual market through the supply of purchasing power.

Thus, considering money as debt and that the function of banks is to supply credit currency in the form of bank debt, Commons considered that credit management must take into account the positive role of credit. Therefore, it is necessary to consider the role of the central bank, which plays a central role in credit management under financial capitalism.

## Price stabilization by the Federal Reserve System

The Federal Reserve System was created by the Federal Reserve Act of 1913. The Central Bank of the United States was established twice (1791–1811 and 1816–1832) in the form of the Bank of the United States, but both failed. The cause of its failure is mainly deep-seated opposition to the centralized banking system and its inability to serve a neutral role because it was developed in a way that was tied to the interests of specific regions.[9] In addition, credit management prior to the establishment of the Federal Reserve System consisted only of manipulating the rate of interest. However, changes caused by a rise in the rate of interest were too slow to stop the expansion of credit, and, conversely, changes caused by a fall in the rate of interest also occurred after a depression (Commons, 1925a, pp. 49–50).

Against this background, the Federal Reserve System was established during the Wilson presidency. The Federal Reserve System was a decentralized organization consisting of 12 district Federal Reserve Banks (Feds) under the Federal Reserve Board in Washington, D.C. These Feds have jurisdiction over national and state banks that meet membership requirements. Each had the initiative to negotiate with their counterparties but were obliged to maintain a reserve of deposits with the Fed. Initially, each bank endeavored to hold reserves above the legal minimum to prepare for emergencies. However, after the Federal Reserve System was established, it began to extend the legal minimum reserve, or demand deposit, to the legal maximum to provide an elastic money supply.

As the inflow of gold from exports to European countries increased between World War I (1914) and the U.S. entry into the war (1917), the question arose about how to control inflation and regular credit management. While interest rate policy and open market operations are taken for granted today, the Federal Reserve System at that time had a complex system of official interest rates that differed from district to district, making it difficult for the Federal Reserve to carry out uniform and rapid operations. Open market operations, a more direct monetary policy tool, were not yet fully recognized for effectiveness.

Open market operations originated when the Fed took the initiative and purchased securities from brokers. In the sequence of events, the brokers who sold the securities deposited them with the Federal Reserve System member banks, which deposited them as legal reserves with the Feds. The member banks then increased their demand deposits as their credit reserves increased. When the Feds purchase securities, bond prices rise, and interest rates on commercial bills fall, reducing the rediscount rate on the bills. On the other hand, when the Fed sells securities, bond prices fall, and the interest rate on commercial notes rises, increasing the rediscount rate on the bills.

However, only some understood what their security purchases were causing since the Federal Reserve Banks then purchased securities merely to increase their assets and earnings by using their gold reserves. Nevertheless, Benjamin Strong, president of the Federal Reserve Bank of New York, was among the first to recognize the effects of open market operations in the early 1920s. He led the creation of the Open Market Investment Committee (OMIC) in 1923. Under Strong's supervision, Commons learned about the American banking system and open market operations. It was to have a significant impact on his future. In his autobiography, Commons wrote as follows.

> Curiously enough, though I was a late comer in the field of banking, I was, in December, 1924, the first to expound to economists at the American Economic Association the principles of control of the money market by a central bank through buying and selling securities on the open market at current prices.
>
> (Commons, 1934b, pp. 192–193)

One advantage of open market operations is that it allows the Reserve System to take the initiative in providing funds to the market without having to wait for member banks to act. According to Commons, 1923 was more inflationary than 1919, but the Reserve Banks' open market operations and warnings of higher interest rates were effective. However, he states that 1919 failed to implement these things promptly and that if the 1923 decisions had been adopted, the extreme inflation and credit collapse of 1919–1920 would have been mitigated (Commons, 1925a, pp. 46–47).

Commons learned about the effects of securities purchases through open market operations, including rising prices of profitable assets, declining interest rates on commercial bills, expanding the quantity of money on credit, and rising wholesale prices. He later addressed the relations among these monetary problems, business cycles, and labor problems. In 1920, Commons established the National Bureau of Economic Research (NBER) with Mitchell and others to study business cycles. From that study, he stated that "[t]he most important labor problem was the stabilization of the average of employer's wholesale prices" (Commons, 1934b, p. 190). It is a question concerning the criterion of economic stabilization. After establishing the Federal Reserve System, price level stabilization was expected, but Commons says that the role of price level stability has been eliminated (Commons, 1927a, pp. 386–387). Meanwhile, concerning the discount rate (rate of interest), Section 14 of the Federal Reserve Act was vague: rates of discount to be charged by the Federal Reserve Bank for each class of paper, which shall be fixed with a view of accommodating commerce and business.

Commons recognized that "credit inflation demoralized labor and then deflation pauperized it" (Commons, 1927a, p. 386). After World War I, as the increase in credit creation and the inflow of gold became problematic, inflationary concerns grew, and the need for price stabilization increased. Against this backdrop, Commons argued that "the Reserve System should hold itself responsible primarily only for the stability of the general average of wholesale prices" (Commons, 1927a, p. 394). One reason for choosing the wholesale price was its quick response to manipulation. It is based on the understanding that stock prices are profit forecasts that depend heavily on wholesale prices and that wholesale prices also determine wages and retail prices. The other reason is that wholesale prices are related to managers, and their amplitude leads to determining employment and unemployment, so he focused on the wholesale price index (Commons, 1927a, pp. 394–395). Thus, the stability of wholesale prices through open market operations by the central bank is at the core of Commons' theory of monetary policy.

In 1924, a year after the creation of the Open Market Investment Committee, the American Bankers Association issued a statement criticizing the Federal Reserve's open market operations. They suggested that open market operations by the Federal Reserve System could accelerate financial market turbulence rather than stabilize it and that the Federal Reserve Banks should be limited to ticketing and rediscounting operations. Commons countered that open market operations by the Federal Reserve System are not solely in order to make a profit but mainly in order to safeguard "the general credit situation" (Commons, 1925a, p. 49). It was based on the idea that open market operations took less time to affect the real economy than interest rate operations and that by impacting the supply of credit, open market operations could stabilize financial markets.

However, the above arguments of Commons were misunderstood and condemned by those who did not favor an aggressive monetary policy by the central bank. Wissler and Comer criticized Commons' argument to be based on the "fiat" of the Federal Reserve System. Commons responded by explaining why it should be called "fiat" when the inflation is brought about by a concerted action of 10,000 member banks united in the Federal Reserve System (Commons, 1927b, p. 402). It indicates that the policies that emerge from the decentralized structure of the Federal Reserve System do not constitute "fiat." The coordinated actions of many member banks, supervised by the Federal Reserve and guided by the 12 Reserve Banks, are analogous to "collective bargaining" in a labor union. Therefore, he thought the Federal Reserve's policy decisions were not "fiat."

In addition, Commons acknowledged the existence of the solid legal and economic power of the Federal Reserve System concerning general price levels and, at the same time, pointed out that within that system, there are rules of conduct in legal documents, rules by custom, and "working rules" in the language of Commons (Commons, 1927b, p. 398). About open market operations, it is assumed that the Federal Reserve Banks buy and sell securities independently of business demand and their interests, while member banks invest in securities in response to business demand. In addition, the Federal Reserve Board, which administers the system, has established rules such that the Chairman does not make decisions on purchasing and selling securities at his discretion but only after consulting with the other Board members. Furthermore, he thought that the practice of member banks to lend up to their maximum limits and the practice of avoiding obligations to the Federal Reserve Banks as much as possible are primarily responsible for the open market purchases and sales of securities and the Federal Reserve's quick reaction to changes in the rediscount rate. In other words, he emphasized that the Federal Reserve System has a collective practice (working rule) and that member banks' presence with the initiative prevents "fiat."

## Monetary policy to create a reasonable price and value

Commons explained the importance of credit management by the central bank as "the passive role of credit is likewise the *laissez-faire* role of the state" (Commons, 1937, p. 692). For credit management, it is essential to make appropriate policy decisions for price stabilization through a decentralized structure that takes advantage of the individual initiative (willingness in Commons' terminology) and intragroup customs that make up the institution. In other words, it is an appropriate intervention in the market, but what are the criteria for judging whether it is appropriate or not? Commons' discussion of the failure of the initial New Deal provides a clue.

The Agricultural Adjustment Act (AAA) in 1933 and the National Industrial Recovery Act (NIRA) in 1933, which represented the early New Deal, were ambitious attempts. Still, both experiments were ruled unconstitutional.[10] On the other hand, the Securities Exchange Act (1934) was a similar attempt but not unconstitutional. According to Commons, regulation by the Securities and Exchange Commission is a general regulation imposed on all industries, while the first two (AAA and NIRA) were problematic because of the specificity of the regulations.[11]

Fair competition is preserved when the policy of increasing or stabilizing average prices through credit management is applied generally to all businesses. However, suppose one tries to implement a specific price reduction policy through the free competition to produce low-cost, low-priced goods for export, which compete with the low-priced goods of European countries. In that case, the viable companies will be limited to large companies capable of mass production. It would put small independent producers in a situation where they would be converted into wage laborers or unemployed. In addition, reducing labor costs through efficient production will also cause a decline in the status of employees of large companies due to a fall in wages. In contrast, "the general price stabilization policy" protects the employment of small-scale producers and ensures that they have opportunities to participate in the market as producers. Commons, therefore, argued that "[t]he preservation of small independent producers is also a democratic ideal" (Commons, 1937, pp. 695–697).

On the other hand, in *Institutional Economics* (1934), Commons wrote: "Savings occurred in the past, but capital is the discounted expectations of future income. There is no identity whatever between them" (Commons, 1934a, pp. 556–557). Moreover, "[s]aving is saving money. But investment is spending the money. The one accumulates *capital*, the other 'forms' *capitals*" (Commons, 1934a, p. 490). Therefore, he does not believe that excess savings equal excess investment, resulting in excess capital and production. He is concerned with the mismatch between the behavior of consumers and companies in response to rising prices.

> [W]hen the consumer buys *less* instead of more, on a rising market, because prices *have* risen, the business man buys *more* instead of less, on a similar rising market, because prices are *expected* to rise.
>
> (Commons, 1934a, pp. 556–557)

Consumers curb their consumption in order to make the most of their limited purchasing power to satisfy their desires, while companies increase their production in order to "expect" to sell more to earn profits. It is where the discrepancy between the two arises, resulting in the problem of consumers' lack of purchasing power and companies' declining profits.[12] Since profits disappear in many companies during a recession, companies cannot be expected to expand employment or contribute to an increase in workers' purchasing power through higher wages. In addition, new businesses decline during a recession, so new borrowing from banks also declines. Thus, even if the credit supply capacity of commercial banks increases, there may be a shortage of borrowers. In such a case, the supply of purchasing power from banks will not be sufficient to reach wage earners, who are the employees of companies, and will lack the immediate effect of boosting the consumer demand. Therefore, Commons states that the most effective monetary policy in a recession directly increases the purchasing power of workers and consumers as follows.

> In order to increase the purchasing power of labor, the unemployed must be put to work by *creation of new money*, and not by *transferring* the existing purchasing power of taxpayers to laborers, as Malthus proposed, nor by borrowing money by government which *transfers* investments but does not augment them. This new money cannot be created and issued by banks, either in commercial, investment, or central banks, because, in a period of depression, the margins for profit have disappeared, and there are no business borrowers willing to cooperate with bankers in creating the new money. In order to create the *consumer demand*, on which business depends for sales, the government itself must create the new money and go completely over the head of the entire banking system by paying it out directly to the unemployed, either as relief or for construction of public works, as it does in time of war.
>
> (Commons, 1934a, pp. 589–590)

Commons emphasized the issuance of "government money" that directly increases the purchasing power of consumers, rather than income redistribution policies that merely "transfer" purchasing power or public investment that merely "transfers" investment. He argues that it is necessary to increase aggregate consumer demand by distributing these government bills not only to wage earners but also to farmers, business establishments, and virtually all companies (Commons, 1934a, p. 590). In other words, he argued that while the central bank needed to stabilize prices through open market operations, the government needed to take emergency measures, such as issuing government money during recessions, especially depressions, when aggregate demand was declining.

These policies must be implemented promptly and effectively, considering timeliness. Commons states that "[t]he essence of administrative ability is to do the right thing at the right time, the right place and in the right amount" (Commons, 1927b, p. 400). He also criticizes the fact that in decision-making, managers must decide on purchase contracts for the future before past statistical data are available, something that is ignored by economists who focus on past statistical data. Therefore, policymaking requires not only the analysis of past data but also the consideration of the impact on the bargaining power of market participants. The policy allows each participant in market transactions to make decisions on an equal footing. Otherwise, capitalism would be mired in unfair competition favoring a few large companies. Commons called the price resulting from "Equal Opportunity," "Fair Competition," and "Equality of Bargaining Power" a "reasonable price" (Commons, 1934a, p. 63). Finally, the value that is "objective, measurable in money" as determined by the "Court's decision" is called "reasonable value" (Commons, 1936, p. 244).[13]

Therefore, a monetary policy that creates reasonable price and value is legally and ethically significant. Credit management that favors certain companies or monetary policy that does not improve workers' opportunities to participate in the market and their weak bargaining power cannot be said to be a monetary policy that creates reasonable price and value. Conversely, credit management policy through open market operations stabilizes the price level. It is a legally and ethically equal intervention, that is, a policy that creates reasonable price and value, because the scope of the policy is broad and includes workers. The issuance of "government money" is also a policy that realizes reasonable price and value because, if spread to all economic agents, it will increase trading opportunities and the bargaining power of each economic agent due to the increased purchasing power.

## Keynes and Commons on monetary policy

### *Similarities with Keynes*

To summarize what has been said so far, the characteristics of Commons' monetary policy theory are, first, to implement price stability through open market operations by the working rules of the Federal Reserve System. Second, by issuing government money in times of severe recession, the government increases the purchasing power of consumers and creates reasonable prices and value through equal opportunity, fair competition, and bargaining power. Commons held that the institutional concepts of equal opportunity, fair competition, equality of bargaining power, or due process of law "are involved in the transactional system of money, the monetary meaning of value, and the collective action of society" (Commons, 1934a, pp. 219–220). His argument indicates that money and labor issues are closely related through price changes and purchasing power.

Commons' contemporary Keynes shares this problematic view, which has been addressed in several previous studies. Atkinson and Oleson (1998) find commonalities between Commons and Keynes in that both addressed uncertainty or futurity while addressing the economic theory of money and monetary institutions. Furthermore, they both spoke of the need for economic stabilization through institutions that reduce uncertainty and guarantee people's expectations. Tymoigne (2003) also noted that "Keynes and

Commons were developing the same theoretical foundations. Both were looking for an analytical system in which money and expectation concerning the future play an essential role in the explanation of the business cycles" (Tymoigne, 2003, p. 541). Tymoigne also cites the theory of investment determination as a similarity between the two. In other words, while Keynes asserted in his General Theory that the rate of interest and the marginal efficiency of capital determine the amount of investment, Commons also recognized that the rate of interest is not a reward for saving and that the "capital-yield," which is the marginal efficiency of capital, determines the amount of investment and that future expectations affect the present (Tymoigne, 2003, pp. 540–541). On the other hand, Taka (2004) points out that Keynes' concepts of economic binding through joint action and "semi-autonomous body" are identical to the going concern of Commons (Taka, 2004, pp. 219–220).

In "Am I a Libertarian?" (1925), Keynes quotes Commons' theory of "stages of economic development" (period of scarcity → period of Abundance → period of Stabilization) as follows.

> An eminent American economist, Professor Commons, who has been one of the first to recognise the nature of the economic transition amidst the early stages of which we are now living, distinguishes three epochs, three economic orders, upon the third of which we are entering. The first is the Era of Scarcity, "whether due to inefficiency or to violence, war, custom, or superstition." In such a period "there is the minimum of individual liberty and the maximum of communistic, feudalistic or governmental control through physical coercion." This was, with brief intervals in exceptional cases, the normal economic state of the world up to (say) the fifteenth or sixteenth century. Next comes the Era of Abundance. "In a period of extreme abundance there is the maximum of individual liberty, the minimum of coercive control through government, and individual bargaining takes the place of rationing." During the seventeenth and eighteenth centuries we fought our way out of the bondage of Scarcity into the free air of Abundance, and in the nineteenth century this epoch culminated gloriously in the victories of laissez-faire and historic Liberalism. It is not surprising or discreditable that the veterans of the party cast backward glances on that easier age. But we are now entering on a third era, which Professor Commons calls the period of Stabilisation, and truly characterises as "the actual alternative to Marx's communism." In this period, he says, "there is a diminution of individual liberty, enforced in part by governmental sanctions, but mainly by economic sanctions through concerted action, whether secret, semi-open, open, or arbitrational, of associations, corporations, unions, and other collective movements of manufacturers, merchants, labourers, farmers, and bankers."
>
> (Keynes, 1925, pp. 334–336)

On these grounds, Skidelsky states that Commons has had an important, if unacknowledged, influence on Keynes (Skidelsky, 1992, p. 229).

In "The End of Laissez-faire" (1926), Keynes wrote,

> Many of the greatest economic evils of our time are the fruits of risk, uncertainty, and ignorance. . .. I believe that the cure for these things is partly to be sought in the deliberate control of currency and of credit by a central institution.
>
> (Keynes, 1926, p. 29)

In April 1927, Keynes sent the following letter to Commons as follows:

> Many thanks for sending me your article in the "Analyst." I am entirely in sympathy with it. Indeed, a good deal of your analysis runs on very closely similar lines to some material which I already have in manuscript for a forthcoming book on the Theory of Credit. I quite agree with your practical proposals. Particularly with the point that the reserve system "should hold itself responsible primarily only for the stability of the general average of wholesale prices; and secondarily responsible for the other factors only in so far as they may be expected to swerve the average wholesale prices away from stability." I am sure that the reserve authorities will never succeed in attaining stability of the price level if they keep their eyes on Wall Street as much as they have been doing lately. I should very much like to have some conversations with you on this and other matters. Judging from limited evidence and at great distance, there seems to me to be no other economist with whose general way of thinking I feel myself in such genuine accord.
>
> (Keynes, 1927)

From the discussion so far in this chapter, it is clear that this view of Keynes' policy is consistent in its fundamental ideas with those of Commons – that is, similarity in terms of the impact of money markets on goods and labor markets, expectations about the future, and economic stabilization through institutions (improvement of capitalism).

### *Differences from Keynes*

However, they differ in the following two points: "the importance of custom and reasonable value" and "the class perspective and emergency policy measures." First, Keynes noted in *The General Theory of Employment, Interest, and Money* (1936) that with respect to investment incentives, "[i]n practice we have tacitly agreed, as a rule, to fall back on what is, in truth, a *convention*" (Keynes, 1936, p. 152) and that the unreliability of the practice creates a problem when considering investments. Although Keynes addresses the "convention," there is little explicit reference to the role of custom or the common law.

In the case of Commons, on the other hand, there is a strong awareness of the legal and ethical validity of policies, which manifests itself as the importance of custom and practice in influencing reasonable price and value. Commons has been researching U.S. Supreme Court cases for many years and has been influenced in no small measure by the American legal community. The idea of the importance of custom and the common law has been interpreted by Horwitz, an expert on American legal history, as follows:

> [C]ustom was employed for the purpose of overthrowing post-revolutionary natural rights individualism, which represented an anarchic threat to order. On the other hand, custom was used to deny the legitimacy or necessity of most legislative and social coercion.
>
> (Horwitz, 1992, pp. 122–123)

In the case of Commons, he was not using the term in a conservative sense. However, instead, he took custom and the common law to prevent extreme individualism and extreme collectivism, and he sees these as having an essential influence on creating "reasonable value." He argues as follows:

> Reasonable value, as formed in the practices of courts, juries, commissions, arbitration arrangements, and so on, is a concept of collective action in terms of money, arrived at by consensus of opinion of reasonable men – "reasonable" in that they are men who conform to the dominant practices of the time.
>
> (Commons, 1934a, pp. 206–207)

For example, notes and checks became the means of payment not because they were first legislated by statute but because they arose from business customs. From these customs of credit transactions, the banking system of discounting developed, which eventually led to the sovereign's approval of these customs. Thus, "[c]ustom is a kind of social compulsion imposed on individuals by the collective opinion of those who feel and act alike" (Commons, 1934a, p. 153), and "even a dictator cannot overrule them." "[T]he common-law *method* is universal in all collective actions, . . . is itself custom" (Commons, 1934a, p. 72). He defined "institution" as "collective action in restraint, liberation, and expansion of individual action" (Commons, 1934a, p. 73) through working rules within the collective organization, including customs.

The Federal Reserve System, as the executor of monetary policy, also has working rules within its "system" and is influenced by customs other than statute law. As noted earlier, Commons emphasizes that the decentralized structure of the Federal Reserve System avoids "fiat" while making monetary policy more effective through member banks lending up to their maximum limits. If rules are established that deprive market participants of "equal opportunity," "fair competition," and "equality of bargaining power," the Supreme Court has the power to strike down the rules because the rules deprive market participants of their property and liberty without due process of law, in violation of the Fourteenth Amendment to the U.S. Constitution. However, the Supreme Court has its own working rules, which change with "due process of law" and under the influence of custom (Commons, 1934a, pp. 62–63). On the other hand, when equal opportunity, fair competition, and equality of bargaining power are ensured, "reasonable value" or, more specifically, "reasonable price" in the market is realized. Thus, in this context, as Ramstad states, Commons' theory of reasonable value is an inquiry into the economics of "just price" (Ramstad, 2001, p. 274). It is not automatically derived from the market mechanism but is heavily influenced by custom.

Second, while Keynes, in his "A Tract on Monetary Reform" (1923), presents a triple classification of "the investing class," "the business class," and "the earning class," or a double classification of "inactive" class (investors) and "active" class (businessmen and workers), Commons is unique in that he does not establish clear class divisions.

In "A Tract on Monetary Reform," Keynes argued that post-World War I, Britain should realize "devaluation" rather than "deflation," "stability of price" rather than "stability of exchange," and the "restoration of a gold standard" rather than a "gold standard." As a premise for this, he thought,

> For the purpose of this inquiry a triple classification of Society is convenient – into the Investing Class, the Business Class, and the Earning Class. These classes overlap, and the same individual may earn, deal, and invest; but in the present organisation of society such a division corresponds to a social cleavage and an actual divergence of interest.
>
> (Keynes, 1923, p. 5)

Then, a reason why deflation is worse than inflation is as follows:

> Deflation, as we have already seen, involves a transference of wealth from the rest of the community to the *rentier* class and to all holders of titles to money; just as inflation involves the opposite. In particular it involves a transference from all borrowers, that is to say from traders, manufacturers, and farmers, to lenders, from the active to the inactive.
>
> (Keynes, 1923, p. 143)

Thus, Keynes was distinctive in his view of British society at that time in class terms and in his judgment that "it is worse, in an impoverished world, to provoke unemployment than to disappoint the rentier" (Keynes, 1923, p. 40).

On the other hand, the basic idea of Commons is that there is not a "class" but a "classification" of people (Commons, 1925b, p. 384). He then focuses on the existence of "spectators," who know they do not belong to the working or capitalist classes. He then calls these bystanders "the public" (Commons, 1913, p. 72) and recognizes that the masses are discretely located as a consumer class (Commons, 1913, p. 83). Therefore, policies conscious of their impact on "the public" and "consumers" are central.

Hence, in addition to price stabilization by the central bank, he insisted that the government develop policies to directly increase the purchasing power of consumers through the issuance of government bills in recession emergencies. The active participation of "the public," who are thus guaranteed purchasing power in the market with equal opportunity and equal bargaining power, is a policy that generates reasonable price and value. As for public investment, Commons is also unique in that, in contrast to Keynes, who insists on its effectiveness, Commons believes that public investment through the issuance of public bonds is merely a transfer of investment (Commons, 1934a, p. 589). Thus, fiscal policy is not emphasized as an effect that increases the consumer's purchasing power.

In summary, Keynes and Commons have something in common in their basic policy views: price stability is based on the idea that monetary policy affects the real economy and that capitalism can be sustained through government and central bank market intervention. However, in the case of Commons, the common law and customs other than statutes are emphasized to stop the runaway movement toward dictatorial capitalism. They are reflected in the fact that in open market operations to stabilize prices, the Federal Reserve emphasizes nondiscretionary policies based on "custom," which emphasizes autonomy through decentralized organizations or, in the language of Commons, willingness, in order to suppress deep-seated criticism of the Federal Reserve's leadership. It is unique in that it emphasizes the creation of reasonable prices and value through the issuance of government bills rather than public investment from the perspective of increasing the consumer purchasing power.

## Conclusion

The discussion in this chapter can be summarized as follows. Commons' theory is based on a fundamental view of money that emphasizes an elastic money supply based on credit money as a debt. The Federal Reserve System, as the central bank, coordinates with its member banks to stabilize prices, and the central focus of monetary policy is to adjust the economy by aiming to stabilize prices. The specific adjustment method is credit management through open market operations, emphasizing creating reasonable prices and value from equal opportunity, fair competition, and equality of bargaining power.

Commons understood collective action as a network of transactions based on willingness, so he discussed the decentralized structure of the Federal Reserve System, which he believed would play a role in preventing dogmatic policies. However, as was the case with the Federal Reserve System in the 1920s and 1930s, while the effects of open market operations were recognized, there was an aspect in which policies were not implemented with agility according to the times. Galbraith said, "In fact, the Federal Reserve was helpless only because it wanted to be" (Galbraith, 1979, p. 32), and he was scathing in his criticism of the Fed's passive attitude.

Whether monetary factors caused the Great Depression has long been debated in the United States. Friedman and Schwartz, from the monetarist standpoint, held that the contraction of the money supply due to inappropriate monetary policy caused prices to fall and output to decline (Friedman & Schwartz, 1963). However, since they did not systematically analyze the relationship with countries other than the United States, we don't have a definitive conclusion. On the other hand, a comparison of data on national economies during the interwar period by former Fed Chairman Bernanke and others has revealed the importance of monetary factors. They asserted the importance of elastic money supply as follows:

> Countries that left gold were able to reflate their money supplies and price levels, and did so after some delay; countries remaining on gold were forced into further deflation. To an overwhelming degree, the evidence shows that countries that left the gold standard recovered from the Depression more quickly than countries that remained on gold.
>
> (Bernanke, 2000, p. 8)

Therefore, although Commons' monetary policy theory was correct in pointing out the importance of elastic money supply and credit management, it needed help regarding policy feasibility and decision-making methods. Central banks need help with similar problems in their decision-making today. The Bank of Japan (BOJ) Policy Board and the Federal Reserve Board (FRB) have adopted a multimember committee system. According to the former BOJ Governor, the advantage of the committee system is that the collective wisdom of many people is more likely to arrive at the correct decision than a decision by the Governor alone, and the legitimacy of the decision is expected to be higher. On the other hand, the disadvantage is that a more significant number of committee members reduce the incentive to think about policies on one's own and make it easier to agree with the majority opinion (Shirakawa, 2008, pp. 112–113).

On the other hand, Commons' theory of monetary policy seeks the role of the central bank to stabilize prices. The idea that the objective of central banking is price stability is consistent with the objectives of today's national central banks. The emphasis on open market operations as a monetary adjustment is common in today's monetary policy. However, the argument that the government, rather than the central bank, should issue government bills in times of emergency, such as depression, is one argument that considers the roles of the central bank and the government. In the case of Commons, its contemporary significance lies in its intention to consider policy from the standpoint of consumers, who constitute the majority of society, and to realize fair competition through policy.

These are Commons' monetary policy theories. This policy is illustrated in Figure 5.1, which shows that rationing transactions in the macro dimension contribute to the "stabilization" of prices.

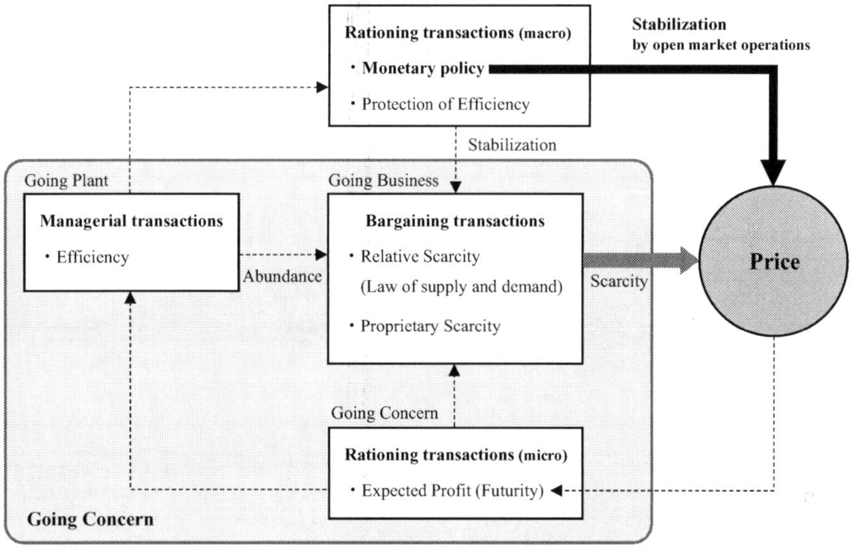


*Figure 5.1* The impact of monetary policy. Compiled by the author.

## Notes

1 Earlier studies dealing with Commons' view of money and monetary theory include Whalen (1993), (2008), Atkinson and Oleson (1998), Tymoigne (2003), and Ramstad (2001). Whalen (1993) emphasizes that money and labor of Commons are inseparable, especially credit being at their root. Atkinson and Oleson (1998), Tymoigne (2003), and Whalen (2008) point out the similarities between Keynes and Commons.

2 In Whalen (1993), "the monetary issues addressed by John R. Commons have generally received little attention, even from his closest followers" (Whalen, 1993, p. 1167).

3 In the "Slaughter House Cases" decision (1873), the majority opinion of the U.S. Supreme Court interpreted property as material use value. However, a minority of justices argued that "[p]roperty is everything which has exchange value." This minority opinion has since permeated the constitutional definition. Finally, in the decision in the "Minnesota Rate Case" (1890), the definition of property was changed to include not only material things but also exchange value (Commons, 1924, pp. 11–14).

4 Government bonds issued by Britain and France to finance war expenditures were underwritten by a syndicate of bond underwriters led by the U.S. Morgan Companies, and from then on, private financing to the Allied side became more active. After the United States entered the war, the Federal Reserve System set the interest rate on loans lower than the interest rate on wartime government bonds issued by the U.S. government and extended credit to sell wartime government bonds. For details, see Nishikawa and Matsui (1989), Chapter 6.

5 For Hawtrey's view of money, see Kojima (1997), Chapters 3 and 6, Ito (2006), Chapter 4; and Furukawa (2012), Chapter 2.

6 Commons held that price is not attached to and paid for a thing but is attached to and paid for ownership. He takes the position that in a transaction of goods, there is a contractual transfer of ownership first, followed by a transfer of goods. Thus, in Fisher's exchange equation, MV = PT, "we should always expect PT to precede MV" (Commons, 1934a, p. 513). As can be seen from this, Commons does not support the quantity theory of money.

7 However, he points out that a currency under a gold–silver double standard would be less elastic than a currency under a gold standard because it is difficult for only one country, the United States, to maintain the free minting of silver coins under a constant gold/silver price ratio (Commons, 1893a, pp. 61–62).

8 According to Nishikawa and Matsui (1989), the government-issued Treasury bill, the greenback, created as legal tender in 1862, had been circulating as a complete fiat currency since 1863. However, the Specie Payment Resumption Act was enacted in 1875, and the fiat greenbacks were intended to be promptly withdrawn and replaced with banknotes issued by the national banks. It also sought to resume the conversion of the greenback to gold, which was virtually the only legal tender at the time. The shortage of currency caused by the recovery of greenbacks and the restriction on gold led to the formation of the Greenback Party, the Free Silver Movement, and a series of other movements calling for an increase in the currency issue. The Brand-Allison Act of 1878 authorized the Secretary of the Treasury to purchase a certain amount of silver at market prices and issue silver certificates. It restored silver as a currency. The Sherman Silver Purchase Act of 1890 authorized the government to purchase a fixed amount of silver at market prices and to use Treasury bills to pay for the purchases. However, because the amount of silver purchased was limited, those seeking increased currency remained dissatisfied. For details, see Nishikawa and Matsui (1989), Chapters 3–4.

9 For the U.S. central bank (Bank of the United States and Federal Reserve System), see Meulendyke (1998), Chapter 2, and Nishikawa and Matsui (1989), Chapter 1.

10 The AAA was a law intended to maintain agricultural prices and restore the purchasing power of farmers by restricting agricultural production and purchasing surplus agricultural products from the government. The government paid benefits to farmers who cooperated with the production restrictions, financed by a processing tax imposed on the primary processing of agricultural products. Lawsuits were filed by companies opposed to this processing tax, and in 1936, the law was ruled unconstitutional. NIRA was a law intended to restore production and purchasing power by regulating production through covenants between the government and individual industries, guaranteeing fair profits to industries, fair prices to consumers, and fair wages and working conditions to workers. In addition to the price and production controls favoring large corporations, industries that agreed to the terms were exempted from the "antitrust" laws, thus allowing monopolies to flourish. It led to protests from small- and medium-sized enterprises, which resulted in an unconstitutional ruling in 1935. See Akimoto (1995), Chapter 11.

11 However, the Agricultural Adjustment Act made sense as a quick administrative adjustment in times of credit depression (Commons, 1942, p. 384).

12 Commons lists "a rate of profit" (profit divided by total stock price), "a profit yield" (profit divided by total stock market value), and "a margin for profit" (profit divided by total sales). As we saw in the previous chapter, he states that the last of these, the "margin for profit," is particularly important (Commons, 1934a, p. 562).

13 The difference between reasonable price and reasonable value is dealt with in Chapter 7.

## References

### *English*

Atkinson, Glen, & Theodore Oleson, Jr. (1998). "Commons and Keynes: Their Assault on Laissez Faire," *Journal of Economic Issues*, 32 (4), 1019–1030.

Bernanke, Ben S. (2000). *Essays on the Great Depression*. Princeton: Princeton University Press.

Commons, John R. (1893a) 1986. "Economic Reform," *The Voice*. Reproduced in *John R. Commons Papers* (microfilm edition: reel 15, 58–63). State Historical Society of Wisconsin.

———. (1893b) 1986. "Sound Currency," *The Voice*. Reproduced in *John R. Commons Papers* (microfilm edition: reel 15, 64–66). State Historical Society of Wisconsin.

———. (1913). *Labor and Administration*. New York: Macmillan.

———. (1921) 1996. "Unemployment: Compensation and Prevention," *The Survey*, 42 (October). Reprinted in Commons (1996), 288–298.

———. (1924) 1995. *Legal Foundations of Capitalism*. New Brunswick and London: Transaction Publishers.

———. (1925a). "The Stabilization of Prices and Business," *American Economic Review*, 15 (March), 43–52.

———. (1925b) 1996. "Marx Today: Capitalism and Socialism," *Atlantic Monthly*, 136 (November). Reprinted in Commons (1996), 371–385.

———. (1927a) 1996. "Price Stabilization and the Federal Reserve System," *The Annalist*, 29 (April). Reprinted in Commons (1996), 386–396.

———. (1927b) 1996. "Reserve Bank Control of the General Price Level: A Rejoinder," *The Annalist*, 30 (July). Reprinted in Commons (1996), 397–403.

———. (1934a). *Institutional Economics: Its Place in Political Economy*. New York: Macmillan.

———. (1934b). *Myself*. New York: Macmillan.

———. (1936). "Institutional Economics," *American Economic Review*, 26 (March), 237–249.

———. (1937). "Capacity to Produce, Capacity to Consume, Capacity to Pay Debts," *American Economic Review*, 27 (December), 680–697.

———. (1942). "Legislative and Administrative Reasoning in Economics," *Journal of Farm Economics*, 24 (May), 369–391.

———. (1986). *The John R. Commons Papers* (microfilm edition), ed. by Miller, Harold L. Madison: State Historical Society of Wisconsin.

———. (1996). *John R. Commons: Selected Essays*, eds. by Rutherford, Malcom, & Warren J. Samuels. London and New York: Routledge.

Friedman, Milton, & Anna J. Schwartz. (1963). *A Monetary History of the United States 1867–1960*. Princeton: Princeton University Press.

Galbraith, John K. (1979). *The Great Crash 1929*. Boston: Houghton Mifflin (1st ed. 1954).

Hawtrey, Ralph G. (1919). *Currency and Credit*. London: Longmans, Green & Co.

Horwitz, Morton J. (1992). *The Transformation of American Law, 1870–1960: The Crisis of Legal Orthodoxy*. New York: Oxford University Press.

Keynes, John M. (1923) 1924. *A Tract on Monetary Reform*. London: Macmillan.

———. (1925) 1931. "Am I a Liberal?" in Keynes (1931).

———. (1926) 1931. "The End of Laissez-Faire," in Keynes (1931).

———. (1927) 1986. Letter to Professor Commons (April 26), in Commons (1986), reel 4, 448.

———. (1931). *Essays in Persuasion*. London: Macmillan.

———. (1936) *The General Theory of Employment, Interest and Money*. London: Macmillan.

Meulendyke, Ann M. (1998). *U.S. Monetary Policy and Financial Markets*. New York: Federal Reserve Bank of New York.

Ramstad, Yngve. (2001). "John R. Commons's Reasonable Value and the Problem of Just Price," *Journal of Economic Issues*, 35 (2), 253–277.

Skidelsky, Robert (1992). *John Maynard Keynes: The Economist as Saviour 1920–1937*. London: Macmillan.

Tymoigne, Éric. (2003). "Keynes and Commons on Money," *Journal of Economic Issues*, 37 (3), 527–545.

Whalen, Charles J. (1993). "Saving Capitalism By Making It Good: The Monetary Economics of John R. Commons," *Journal of Economic Issues*, 27 (4), 1155–1179.
———. (2008). "John R. Commons and John Maynard Keynes on Economic History and Policy: the 1920s and Today," *Journal of Economic Issues*, 42 (1), 225–242.

### *Japanese*

Akimoto, Eiichi. (1995). *America Keizai no Rekishi: 1492–1993* (A History of the American Economy, 1492–1993). Tokyo: Tokyo Daigaku Shuppan-kai.
Furukawa, Akira. (2012). *R. G. Hawtrey no Keizaigaku* (The Economics of R. G. Hawtrey). Kyoto: Nakanishiya Shuppan.
Ito, Nobuhiro. (2006). *Gendai Keizaigaku no Tanjō: Cambridge Gakuha no Keifu* (The Birth of Modern Economics: A Genealogy of the Cambridge School). Tokyo: Chuō Kōron Shin-sha.
Kojima, Hirotaka. (1997). *Keynes Riron no Gensen: Sraffa, Hawtrey, Abbati* (Sources of Keynesian Theory: Sraffa, Hawtrey, Abbati). Tokyo: Yūhikaku.
Nishikawa, Junko, & Kazauo Matsui. (1989). *America Kinyū-shi: Kenkoku kara 1980 nendai made* (American Financial History: From the Founding to the 1980's). Tokyo: Yūhikaku.
Shirakawa, Masaaki. (2008). *Gendai no Kinyū Seisaku: Riron to Jissai* (Modern Monetary Policy in Theory and Practice: Central Banking and Financial Markets). Tokyo: Nihon-Keizai-Shinbun-Shuppan-sha.
Taka, Tetsuo. (2004). *Gendai America Keizai Shisō no Kigen: Pragmatism to Seido Keizaigaku* (Origins of Modern American Economic Thought: Pragmatism and Institutional Economics). Nagoya: Nagoya Daigaku Shuppan-kai.

# 6 Labor theory and labor policy

## Labor problems and social security

Commons attended a joint labor and management meeting in 1900, after which he published several works on labor–management relations. First, we will research labor history and the labor theory of Commons. This section will examine the characteristics of Commons' labor history research through his article "American Shoemakers, 1648–1895" (Commons, 1909), him being the founder of the Wisconsin School in labor history research. Then, the content of the labor theory derived from historical research and practical activities of labor–management mediation will be examined in *Industrial Goodwill* (Commons, 1919) and *Principles of Labor Legislation* (Commons & Andrews, 1916). Next, we will research labor–management negotiations and the administrative commission system as the fourth branch of governance, in which Commons ultimately found hope. We will focus on "agricultural administration" as presented in his posthumously published *The Economics of Collective Action* (Commons, 1950). There, we will show that he would use the dispute resolution methods he had acquired in his earlier labor–management mediation. After that, we will research the labor policy of Commons through workers' compensation and unemployment compensation. Concerning labor policy, the formation of goodwill will be necessary. Finally, we will summarize labor policy and institutional economics of Commons, especially the relations between labor issues and pricing, business cycles, and reasonable value.

### Labor history and labor theory of Commons

#### *Research on American labor history*

Commons is considered one of the founders of institutional economics and the founder of the Wisconsin School in the study of labor history. According to Kobayashi (1988), the strength of the Wisconsin School lies in its fact-based research attitude. However, in Commons' time, when existing literature and materials were scarce, there was no other way to research than to construct necessary concepts from facts and experience, and this was also a way to become an authority in the field (Kobayashi, 1988, p. 16). Commons worked in a unionized printing plant from his undergraduate days, which was the

DOI: 10.4324/9781032701394-10

basis for his later thinking on labor issues. Here, we will outline Commons' seminal work on labor history, "American Shoemakers, 1648–1895" (Commons, 1909), a paper that provided the framework for subsequent labor history research in the Wisconsin School, and we will capture the characteristics of Commons' study of labor history.[1]

### *Formation of guilds*

A hallmark of Commons' analysis in labor history studies is the change in labor–management relations based on the "expansion of the market." He historically illustrates this change by examining the protective organizations of American shoemakers. He begins by examining the Company of Shoemakers in Boston, formed in 1648 and considered the first guild in America. Early shoemakers were itinerant shoemakers who went to their customer's homes to make shoes from materials provided by the customers. In contrast, the settled shoemaker, who had his workshop and made shoes from materials he had prepared, formed guilds among shoemakers. The Boston Shoemakers' Guild was the latter, and its purpose was to eliminate itinerant shoemakers who made inferior products (Commons, 1909, p. 222).

The resident craftsman of this period had the three functions of "merchant," "master," and "journeyman." The merchant function was based on the ability to control the type and quality of work and to negotiate with customers for compensation based on the quality of the work. The master function controlled the workshop and tools and passed on orders received from the merchant to the journeyman, who was compensated for his labor and capital. The journeyman's function depends on the skill and quality of labor, the work speed, the employment amount, and its regularity and stability (Commons, 1909, pp. 223–224). In this phase, individuals mainly made "bespoke work" to the order of customers. Thus, quality was more of an issue than the price of the goods since eliminating inferior goods meant having only good-quality goods.

### *Differentiation of masters and craftsmen*

However, to respond immediately to the orders of temporary visitors and visitors, some began to make shoes in standard sizes. It becomes difficult for one person to make more shoes than before, so the master and the journeyman were differentiated. In order to cater to a broader market, the master would give the raw materials to the craftsman, who would make and deliver the finished product. In addition to "bespoke work," journeymen make "shop work" (High-end ready-made products for retail), and the master becomes a retail merchant and employer (Commons, 1909, p. 230). Thus, the union at the stage where individuals were responsible for the three functions became differentiated by function. The Society of Master Cordwainers (1789) and the Federal Society of Journeyman (1794) were founded in Philadelphia. Journeymen formed self-defense organizations out of fear that their masters would cut their wages. However, the interests of the masters and journeymen were not in conflict since the early masters formed a price control organization to eliminate cheap traders. This is because the early masters' associations were centered on the merchant function, especially the retail merchant function.

Some of the masters then began to develop outside markets. They sent samples to outside markets, took product orders, and manufactured and shipped them. In other words, they became "wholesale merchants and employers." Commons referred to this stage as the "wholesale-order stage" of the industry (Commons, 1909, p. 230). From this stage, the masters held a large stock of goods, and, at the same time, they expanded their fierce competition with other competitors. Therefore, "the wage-bargain assumes importance, and the employer-function comes to the front." As a result, "[t]he conflict of capital and labor begins" (Commons, 1909, p. 240).

*Response to Market Expansion*

After these relations had been in place for some time, a situation arose that further aggravated the relations between labor and management. It is the emergence of merchant capitalists who "subdues both the master and the journeyman through his control of the new widespread market of the South and West" (Commons, 1909, p. 241). This was partly due to the development of transportation networks and the establishment of the banking system. The provision of bank credit made it possible to have a large stock of goods before actual orders, making the market speculative (Commons, 1909, p. 243).

Merchant capitalists, who controlled the commodity sales network, would control the masters and journeymen, that is, the production mechanism, in various ways. They could have the journeymen work in their warehouses or give raw materials to the journeymen and have them deliver the finished product. They could also outsource production to contractors who would perform menial labor, or they could use prison labor to lower the price of their products (Commons, 1909, pp. 244–245). Journeymen's opposition to these trends was also expressed in the statement by the United Beneficial Society of Journeyman Cordwainers, which was formed in 1835, that mentioned declining wages and long working hours. The Trades' Union, under the leadership of the United Beneficial Society of Journeyman Cordwainers, would lead the first ten-hour strike in the United States (Commons, 1909, p. 241).

In shoemaking, shoemakers used various tools, which were essentially tools, not full-fledged factory machines. The early shoe-soled sewing machines also did not threaten shoemakers because they played a complementary rather than a labor-substituting role. However, the pegging and sole-sewing machines that appeared around 1860 were extremely labor-substituting, and factory systems that introduced these machines appeared and expanded rapidly due to increased demand caused by the Civil War.

During this period, the "Knights of St. Crispin" were formed in 1868, but they were not opposed to introducing machinery per se. They opposed the substitution of "green hands," which is unskilled labor for journeymen. However, shoes made with unskilled labor and steam engines were more competitively priced than those made with prison labor or Chinese labor, which were considered less expensive, and the quality was equal to or better than journeymen's shoes (Commons, 1909, pp. 256–257).

The factory system of shoemaking was primarily established in the early 1880s, and labor changed from cooperative and manual labor to work divided into detailed, piece-rate work. The Boot and Shoe Workers' Union, formed in 1895, was also intended to be a union of all employees in an industry rather than a job classification. They advocated protectionist trade and opposed immigration, prison labor, child labor, and long working hours (Commons, 1909, p. 258).

Given above is a history of the development of the shoe industry in the United States and the accompanying labor history of shoemakers. The sequence of shoemaker papers can be summarized in Table 6.1.

Through this examination of shoemakers, Commons showed that market expansion and changes in labor–management relations are linked. In the last section of this paper, he states as follows.

> Karl Marx was the first to challenge the world with a keen analysis of economic evolution, but his standpoint is that of the mode of production and not the extension of the market. His two assumptions of a given "use value" and a given "average social labor" serve to obliterate,

*Table 6.1* Market expansion and union development in the "American shoemakers." Compiled by the author based on Commons (1909), p. 220.

| *Extent of market* | *Kind of bargain* | *Competitive menace* | *Protective organization* |
|---|---|---|---|
| 1. Itinerant | Wages | Family workers | None |
| 2. Personal | Custom order | **Bad ware (by itinerant)** | Craft guild |
| 3. Local | Retail | **Market work (cheap goods)** | Retail merchants' association |
| 4. Waterways | Wholesale order | **Scabs**<br>**Interstate producers** | Journeymen's society<br>Masters' society |
| 5. Highways | Wholesale speculative | **Prison sweatshop**<br>**Foreigner**<br>**Speeding up** | Journeymen's society<br>Employers' association<br>Manufacturers' association* |
| 6. Rail | Wholesale speculative | **Green hands**<br>**Chinese, foreigner**<br>**Women, children** | Trade union<br>Employers' association<br>Manufacturers' association* |
| 7. World | Factory order | **Long hours**<br>**Immigrants**<br>**Foreign products** | Industrial union<br>Employers' association<br>Manufacturers' association* |

*Manufacturer's association is based on the merchant or price-fixing function.

> the one the part played by the price-bargain, the other the played by the wage-bargain.
>
> (Commons, 1909, p. 259)

This shoemaker's study is purely a labor history study in the United States. Commons states the following at the end of his paper.

> Thus have American shoemakers epitomized American industrial history. Common to all industries is the historical extension of markets. . .. The shoemakers have pioneered and left legible record. Their career is 'interpretative,' if not typical.
>
> (Commons, 1909, p. 264)[2]

The assertion that the conflict between laborers and employers, here master and artisan, arose "not as a result of changes in tools or methods of production, but directly as a result of changes in markets" (Commons, 1909, p. 231) became a common approach of the Wisconsin School in subsequent years and had a significant influence on the study of labor history.

### *Labor theory consisting of four stages*

Ten years after his shoemaker paper, Commons developed his labor theory in *Industrial Goodwill* (Commons, 1919). Here, we will follow Commons' labor theory through this work.

#### *Commodity theory of labor*

As a starting point for his discussion, he cites the example of a visit to an employment office in a factory. In that factory, he saw immigrant workers from abroad being treated like commodities at low wages. He said as follows.

> This is the workings of what I call the commodity theory of labor. Demand and supply determine wages. You cannot overcome the law of demand and supply. If labor is scarce, wages will go up. If labor is abundant, wages will go down. The ebb and flow of the labor market is like the ebb and flow of the commodity market.
>
> (Commons, 1919, p. 5)

As mentioned in the previous section, employers treated them as commodities since most immigrants could only perform simple physical labor due to language barriers.

#### *Machine theory of labor*

Next, Commons discusses introducing F. Taylor's scientific management method into factory production. Here, a piece-rate system was implemented on the basis of sectional control, and workers were paid bonuses or premiums as an incentive to increase efficiency, in addition to the basic wage rate. Commons describes this method as follows.

> This I call the machinery theory of labor. Labor is not a commodity – its value determined by demand and supply – but each laborer is a machine – its value determined by the quantity of its product. The theory is not new. Its application is a new discovery in science and engineering. The commodity theory is the merchant's theory of buying and selling. The machinery theory is the engineer's theory of economy and output.
>
> (Commons, 1919, p. 14)

But Commons says, "The machinery theory, like the commodity theory of labor, is not false, it is incomplete" (Commons, 1919, p. 17). The reason is that it does not consider the costs of labor mobility.

### *Goodwill of labor*

Workers moving between companies quickly cost companies extra time and money to provide job training. Commons gives the example of the automobile company Ford, which doubled wages but increased profits by reducing the cost of labor mobility, stating that "the intangible goodwill of labor may be as profitable as the scientific management of labor" (Commons, 1919, p. 18). This "goodwill of labor" is the third theory of labor to replace "commodities" and "machines."[3]

What Commons calls "goodwill" indicates "mutual concession" and a "beneficial reciprocity of wills" between labor and management (Commons, 1919, p. 19). The reason why he presented this idea is because "[t]he laborer is not only a productive machine, he is a customer" (Commons, 1919, p. 18). It is because there is a recognition that the workers are not a "working class" but "the public" or "consumers" as we have already seen. Individuals as such pluralistic economic agents belong to various going concerns. The "goodwill" is essential in considering the continuity of the going concern as a company. Commons explained it as follows.

> [G]oodwill is coming to be an intangible asset of business more valuable than the tangible properties. It is the life of a going concern. Business goodwill, commercial goodwill, trade names, trade reputation, trade marks, often exceed in value the physical plant and the inventory of stock on hand.
>
> (Commons, 1919, p. 25)

The importance of goodwill is valid for today's companies, but companies are exposed to severe price competition under free competition. Only a few blue-chip companies can maintain high wages for their workers by emphasizing goodwill. Most companies strive to keep labor costs low and offer low-priced products. Therefore, if only one company focuses on goodwill, it will be shut out of the market. Commons knows this and says, "[g]oodwill is an individual matter" (Commons, 1919, p. 29). In other words, he recognizes that without government intervention, it is difficult to achieve because it is achieved through the efforts of individual companies.

### *The public utility theory of labor*

If all companies pursue profit under free competition, product prices will fall during a recession due to price-cutting competition. If this occurs in other industries, it will also lead to deflation. This situation will ultimately lead to lower wages for workers, worsening labor–management relations or goodwill. Commons then explains the need for government intervention in the marketplace as follows.

> Goodwill does not reach the entire field. For those whom it does not reach, who do not care for the goodwill of labor, or who are unable, incompetent or unprogressive, the state comes in and tries to force them to do something nearly as good or to eliminate them entirely. This may be called the public-utility theory of labor.
>
> (Commons, 1919, p. 30)

This "public utility theory of labor" becomes the fourth theory of labor. Legislation supplements goodwill so that "legislation raises the class as a whole" (Commons, 1919, pp. 29–30). In other words, the idea is that the enactment of labor legislation should nurture the consumer class of a country as a whole. Goodwill is an individual company's issue, but protecting workers as a consumer class will increase their purchasing power and stimulate demand in the domestic market. Therefore, the idea is that labor legislation should not favor only a particular class of workers.

Commons came to this view because of the Supreme Court's decision. In *Industrial Goodwill*, Commons discusses the 1898 case of Holden v. Hardy. In this case, the Utah and Colorado legislatures passed bills reducing the working hours of mine and refinery workers to eight hours a day. However, the Supreme Court of Colorado ruled unconstitutional, and the Supreme Court of Utah ruled constitutional, but the Supreme Court of the United States upheld the Utah decision and declared it constitutional (Commons, 1919, pp. 31–32). Commons interpreted the decision in this case as follows:

> Prior to that time the health of consumers was, of course, recognized as a public purpose. By that decision it came to be recognized that workers also were a part of the public, and legislation on behalf of their health

> while at work would not be class legislation but reasonable classification for a public purpose.
>
> (Commons, 1919, p. 32)

Workers in mines and refineries do not have the same bargaining power as company managers, and they also physically exert themselves under harsher working conditions than other workers. State intervention in this regard is not to give them preferential treatment but to improve their working conditions and ensure that they can lead economic lives as "the public." Therefore, such labor legislation is "reasonable." It is the same as the policy of creating reasonable prices and values described in the previous chapter. In other words, policies that ensure "equal opportunity," "fair competition," and "equal bargaining power" are necessary legally, economically, and ethically. These are the four levels of Commons' labor theory.

## Discussions on policy formation

### *Labor–management negotiations*

What Commons learned from attending what he called "my discovery of 1900" (Commons, 1934b, p. 73), a joint labor–management conference, was that it was not for third-party arbitrators to hand down rules and regulations but collective agreement through conciliation (Commons, 1934b, pp. 72–73). However, there was a significant difference in bargaining power between workers and employers in labor–management negotiations.

While employers were allowed to rally as corporations in the mid-19th century with the passage of the General Corporation Law, unity on the workers' side was not readily recognized in practice. In *Principles of Labor Legislation* (Commons & Andrews, 1916 (1936)),[4] which Commons wrote with his student Andrews, they divided social attitudes in collective bargaining into four categories: repression, toleration, encouragement, and intervention.

"Repression" refers to the restriction or prohibition of workers' unity with the goal of higher wages or better work, which is regarded as an illegal conspiracy. "Toleration" means that workers may organize and bargain collectively, but at the same time, employers may prevent or deny workers' unity. It was in keeping with the laissez-faire philosophy, which believed that while workers' rights should be protected, employers' rights should also be protected. "Encouragement" implies that collective bargaining is seen as a sound public policy that should be encouraged by the government so that the government protects the workers. The final "intervention" is that collective bargaining is encouraged by the government, but if negotiations are not concluded, the government intervenes to adjust the dispute and prevent a strike (Commons & Andrews, 1916 (1936), pp. 374–376).

According to Commons, "toleration" took place in the United States before 1933 (Commons & Andrews, 1916 (1936), p. 376). In such a situation, even if workers united, they would be disadvantaged if the employer prevented or refused to do so. He defines *bargaining power* as the "power, protected by law, to hold back and wait until an agreement can be reached upon the exchange value of the property before permitting others to take it or use it" (Commons & Andrews, 1916 (1936), p. 507). Thus, if a worker personally withholds his labor, what awaits him is unemployment due to a decrease in income or dismissal. However, finding a replacement is easy even if the employer withholds employment and fires one worker. In other words, in a "toleration," there is an overwhelming difference in bargaining power between labor and management. However, this does not mean that Commons endorsed violent revolution by united workers. He said as follows:

> It is not revolutions and strikes that we want, but collective bargaining on something like an organized equilibrium of equality. This I take it, was the social philosophy of Samuel Gompers. It seems to me the only way to save us from Communism, Fascism, or Nazism.
>
> (Commons, 1934b, p. 73)

It is for workers to unite and organize in trade unions. In his 1925 article "Marx Today" (Commons, 1925), he describes the "self-recovery" and "forced recovery" of capitalism. As an example of "self-recovery," the passage of the general incorporation law promoted the concentration of capital. In contrast, the "ownership" of capital by the joint-stock company system was dispersed. It adopted the new device to exploit investors like corporations exploited laborers, attracting many Americans who wanted to preserve capitalism, he says (Commons, 1925, p. 372). The foreseeing capitalists also opposed unions but copied the shop rules they established (Commons, 1925, p. 374). Commons criticized Marx for failing to foresee capitalism's ability to "self-recovery," but he also described the need for "forced recovery." He also pointed to two types of legislation: legislation to protect corporations, such as blue-sky laws, and labor legislation to protect workers (Commons, 1925, p. 373). Having grasped these two aspects of capitalism, Commons shows how to resolve labor–management conflicts in a scarcity-based economy.

> These conflicts over scarcity ultimately press upon the judiciary and the legislatures for decision. Yet these two branches of government have shown themselves often incompetent to decide class conflicts. The legislature does not accurately represent the parties to the dispute. It is the lobbies that are more truly representative of classes than the legislatures. The judiciary, on the other hand, while it is suited to decide individual conflicts where the rules of the game have previously been laid down, yet is unsuited to decide the conflicts of classes themselves where the rules themselves are developed. This incompetency of legislature and judiciary has led the people of various states and the nation to install a

> set of commissions designed to deal with the more urgent of these class conflicts.
>
> (Commons, 1925, pp. 383–384)

This committee would be the administrative approach to economic problems that Commons would emphasize in his later years. It is because collective agreements agreed to by joint labor–management meetings lacked binding force, with no investigative capacity to monitor individual situations closely and no judicial branch. The "administrative committee," discussed in the next section, is the solution to these problems.

## *Administrative commission as fourth governance sector*

### *Role of administrative commission*

In this section, we will look at the role of administrative commissions as indicated by Commons. First, an administrative committee deals explicitly with the following conflicts of interest.

- Industrial commission: conflict of interest between employers and employees.
- Market commission: conflict of interest between buyers and sellers.
- Tax commission: conflict of interest between taxpayers.
- Railroad commission: conflict of interests between public utilities and shippers of goods

(Commons, 1925, p. 384).

These commissions differ in that they deal with conflicts of interest between "classes" (Commons, 1925, p. 384), whereas the courts deal with conflicts of interest between individuals. Of course, Commons does not believe that individuals belong to one "class," so each individual can be a party in various cases and capacities. These committees are needed as "commissions" because they can conduct investigations based on objective statistical data and interviews of the parties involved when considering individual cases. This administrative section for investigative purposes is what Commons calls the fourth branch of governance.

He says that under the American system of separation of powers, only the president as commander in chief of the military and subordinate branches of government, the governor of a state, and the judicial branch, which gives orders to prosecutors, have executive power with coercion. The legislature and the executive branch, to which the legislature delegates power, have no executive power in the sense of having physical coercive power (Commons, 1950, p. 224). The legislative branch and the executive branch, delegated power by the legislative branch, have no executive power in the sense of physical coercion (Commons, 1950, p. 224). While it may be usual to think that only government intervention with coercive and executive power makes sense, Commons says the opposite is true regarding administrative commissions.

> This command is effective because the administrative department, as just now suggested, is not itself an executive department in command of physical force needed to carry its own decisions into effect. It may not arrest or imprison anybody. It may not resist the marshal or sheriff. It must make application to the Court to issue its own order to use force, and must submit its arguments. Its power is only investigational and advisory in so far as the legislature authorizes and the Court approves. As a so-called "fourth branch" of government, it is more nearly like a standing committee for economic investigations and recommendations to the three recognized branches and to the people generally.
>
> (Commons, 1950, p. 225)

According to him, since the court does not have a staff specializing in statistics, it relies on the opinions of administrative agencies, prosecutors, and lawyers. It is not a problem in normal times, but in times of emergency, such as depression, it is impossible to make timely decisions using statistical data. He also says that since the legislature does not have statistical examiners, it is impossible to reach a consensus without starting from the extreme and using the means of suppression of the minority by the majority (Commons, 1950, pp. 233–234). Therefore, it is necessary to have an administrative department or administrative committee that conducts economic research to obtain detailed information.

As a specific organization, in the first edition of his *Principles of Labor Legislation* (1916), he included an organizational chart of the New York Industrial Commission (1915) (Commons & Andrews, 1916, p. 434). Under five members, there was an "Advisory Council" of employers and employees, a "Legislative Bureau" for criminal prosecution and legal advice, and seven bureaus directly under the commission. One of these bureaus is the "Bureau of Statistics and Information," and it introduces the "Industrial Investigation," the "General Labor Statistics," and other subordinate divisions. Commons noted that the administrative commission has such a specialized organization for statistical research, which enables it to make policy recommendations in line with the latest economic situation.

### *Administrative commission in the New Deal*

He would show that these commissions were significant in the economic emergency of the depression. After the Great Depression and the New Deal, the administrative commission is discussed in Chapter 14, "Agricultural Administration," of his posthumously published work, *The Economics of Collective Action* (1950).[5] What is discussed is the pros and cons of government intervention regarding the Agricultural Adjustment Act (1933).

The Agricultural Adjustment Act, a law intended to maintain agricultural commodity prices and restore farmers' purchasing power by limiting agricultural production and purchasing surplus crops from the government, was ruled unconstitutional in 1936. At the time, the U.S. Supreme Court had a majority of negative justices and a minority of positive justices for the law. The law was intended to use the government's economic power to balance the economic power (such as property rights and purchasing power) between unorganized farmers and other organized economic entities. The majority, however, rejects the use of government economic power. Like most economists, they believed that the government's economic power could only be exercised against those who would impede free competition among equal individuals or companies. Since they basically believed that a law was constitutional or unconstitutional in light of the Constitution, Commons characterized this as a legislative method of theory or deductive reasoning (Commons, 1950, p. 214).

The minority, on the other hand, does not think in terms of constitutional or unconstitutional or extreme claims against the Constitution but rather in terms of the statistical likelihood of falling between the two extremes. Commons described this as an administrative method of reasoning or experimental reasoning that deals with quantity, degrees of economic power, and timeliness of action (Commons, 1950, p. 214).

They agreed that the exercise of economic power by the government, like taxation, was coercive and potentially abusive. Moreover, they agreed that the Agricultural Adjustment Act was also coercive and not voluntary. The issue that divided interpretations was the question of administration. In the industrial sector, prices are maintained during recessions by closing factories and laying off workers. However, when the same thing is done in the agricultural sector, the tragedy is that six million pigs were slaughtered in an administrative process in order to maintain prices. The majority was wary of going from these extreme cases to the other extreme (communism or fascism) (Commons, 1950, pp. 218–220).

However, Justice Stone, a minority member, held that giving money to the unemployed, for example, does not require work in return and that it is all right if such expenditures serve the purposes of all the people (Commons, 1950, p. 221). He also stated that the judiciary has the power to declare laws unconstitutional but that the power is only concerning the power to enact laws, not the wisdom of those laws. He further stated that self-restraint is the only check on the judiciary's power (Commons, 1950, p. 223).

Commons supports Justice Stone's idea and says that a possible guide for the courts in exercising restraint is a statistical survey submitted by an administrative agency (the Department of Agriculture) (Commons, 1950, pp. 223–224). At the same time, he says, it will bring about the following economic changes.

> [T]he reliance on statistics is characteristic not only for the modern science of economics, it is also, more emphatically, characteristic of modern administrative economics in carrying out the legislative policy.
>
> (Commons, 1950, p. 226)

Here, Commons' ideas are condensed from his study of historical and inductive research methods with Richard T. Ely, his investigation of business cycles with Mitchell and others, and his involvement in various labor legislations. He was concerned about the danger of going to extremes if power was misused but that this could be prevented by the objectivity of "statistical research" and "due process of law." He said this was not new at all but following the history of Anglo-American law.

> On the legal side the statistical method of reasoning from actual cases had always been, in fact, the historical method in Anglo-American jurisprudence in cases of "fair competition" located somewhere between the extremes of "destructive competition," or "chiseling," and monopolistic competition. As such, it was the point, to be discovered by proper judicial investigation and "due process" of notice and hearing, where each of the conflicting interests at the time and place was given its "due weight" in reaching a judicial decision.
>
> (Commons, 1950, p. 227)

Commons emphasizes the role of the administrative commissions because of the "due process of law" of conducting such statistical studies, holding public hearings with interested parties, and then making executive decisions. But that is not the only role of the administrative commissions. One of the things that Commons emphasized is the timeliness of the policy proposals that this committee has.

The Agricultural Adjustment Act paid benefits to farmers who cooperated with production restrictions. The funding for this came from a processing tax imposed on the primary processing of agricultural products. As a result, lawsuits were filed by those opposed to the processing tax, and the law was ruled unconstitutional in 1936. Rexford G. Tugwell, who was a key player in drafting the bill, resigned that same year.[6] Commons, however, has some appreciation of this law as a law for emergencies and when urgent measures are required.

> An administrative department alone can meet promptly the "adjustments" needed to ward off inflation and deflation of prices, or bring relief promptly in time of deflation. The Adjustment Act of 1933 is almost the first act of American legislation designed specifically to counteract this credit cycle.
>
> (Commons, 1950, p. 231)

In times of emergency, such as a depression, judicial decisions by the courts take too long. Legislatures enacting laws also often delay their decisions because of political wrangling. There is also the problem that those representing the interests are lobbies outside the House. Therefore, policies that have undergone study and deliberation by the administrative commission are superior in their immediate effect. However, since this is only an emergency measure, in the case of the Agricultural Adjustment Law, it is necessary to increase the protection of agriculture during the depression but to reduce that protection once agriculture recovers.

Such an idea was always a problem because it involved discretionary decisions, as the majority justices feared in the Agricultural Adjustment Act. Besides, such an administrative approach could lead to bureaucratic politics. Commons says that administrative commissions have "the power of custom" (Commons, 1950, p. 227) and that "the administrative 'orders' are analogous to the force of custom" (Commons, 1950, p. 225). If this is good practice, it is good, but it will be ineffective if the bureaucracy has absolute power and conducts arbitrary investigations and formal hearings. Commons, in *Principles of Labor Legislation*, states as follows.

> It is not rotation in office that cures bureaucracy. The most democratic of Americans often become bureaucrats as soon as installed in office. Bureaucracy is just the ordinary human instinct for exclusive possession of power. Its essence consists in imposing its will upon others without really consulting them.
>
> (Commons & Andrews, 1916 (1936), p. 476)

*Process and objectivity in policy formation*

Thus, public hearings that are bureaucracy-centered and merely "ask" for expert opinions are meaningless. The administrative committee referred to here adopts an "interest representation system" in which interested parties are directly included. In this way, formal bureaucracy is prevented, and, at the same time, the direct opinions of interested parties are reflected more than in the legislature via the lobby.

Thus, as the fourth branch of governance, the administrative commission system becomes an administrative economics based on actual cases and occupies an essential place in the institutional economics of Commons.

> [B]etween these contradictory extremes of the north and the south poles of reasoning are the actual transactions of individuals governed by the actual collective action of corporations, unions, and governments, at the time and place. This is the field of institutional economics based on good judgment and full investigation of issues between conflicting interests. It is the problem of administrative economics in actual cases rather than unconstitutionality in all cases.
>
> (Commons, 1950, pp. 237–238)

For the institutional economics of Commons, the significance of a statistical survey by an administrative commission is that it serves as a criterion for determining "reasonableness." As has been repeatedly stated, "reasonable value" is an "objective, measurable in money" (Commons, 1936, p. 244) that emerges from a balance of transactions that achieves a reasonable price arising from equal opportunity, fair competition, and equal bargaining power, and a court decision ultimately determines that.

Commons states that in cases of conflicting economic interests, this should be ascertained by "comparing relatively the gains and losses" (Commons, 1950, p. 237). In the case of the Agricultural Adjustment Act, the economic liberties gained (the amount received) and lost (the amount paid) by the farmers during the emergency are calculated. Similarly, we calculate the economic liberties gained (amount received) and lost (amount paid) by the rest of society during the emergency. Then, if we compare the gains and losses of the farmer and the rest of society relative to each other, we will have "a fair measure of the balanced equilibrium of public welfare" (Commons, 1950, p. 237).

Although he did not conduct an empirical analysis based on this calculation method, one of the things he wanted to say in "Agricultural Administration," which he wrote while ill and under medical care, was the "objectivity" of "reasonableness." In his autobiography, he states as follows.

> Reasonable values and reasonable practices were entirely new words introduced into the theories of political economy. Often my students and sometimes my economist critics said that "reasonable" was something purely subjective, and there were as many meanings of reasonableness as there were individuals. Such a term placed the determination of reasonableness in the arbitrary mind of whatever individual happened to be in authority. But I considered this objection to be an inheritance from the subjective individualism of preceding economic theorists. A collectivistic theory of value derived from existing best practices, from custom, the common law, and the decision of courts, could make reasonableness "objective" and therefore capable of investigation and testimony, leading to the formation of working rules for collective action in control of individual action.
>
> (Commons, 1934b, p. 156)

The Agricultural Adjustment Act (AAA) and the National Industrial Recovery Act (NIRA) were ruled unconstitutional, and NIRA disappeared. However, AAA was revived in 1938 as the "Second Agricultural Adjustment Act," taking over its purpose as the "Soil Conservation and Domestic Allotment Act. As Nishikawa (1999) noted, AAA indicated that the government intervention in the economy was possible to the extent the U.S. Supreme Court permitted. What is important in discussing administrative commissions is not the constitutional or unconstitutional outcome but the policymaking process. Court decisions have an important function as the "visible hand," but as we can see from the above examples and the change in the concept of property, they change in response to the conventions of the time. The presentation of objective indicators of "reasonableness" through statistical surveys, conducting public hearings attended by interested parties, and drafting of legislation through the "due process of law" are the role of the administrative board as the fourth branch of governance.

## Labor policy of Commons

America's first workers' compensation law was a Wisconsin law passed in 1911, while America's first unemployment compensation law was also a Wisconsin law passed in 1932. These laws eventually influenced the passage of the federal Social Security Act of 1935 during the second phase of the New Deal. The Wisconsin School's labor policy theory, led by Commons, significantly influenced Wisconsin legislation.

Wisconsin's unemployment compensation law is characterized by prevention rather than compensation, taking advantage of the profit motive of management and minimizing the redistribution of income. Each company is responsible only for the unemployment of its employees and contributes a portion of its total payroll to the state fund to set up a separate company account, which provides a percentage of weekly wages in case of employee layoffs. This system differs from the other system that emphasizes income redistribution by the government. In the United States, this Wisconsin system spread to other states and eventually led to the establishment of the U.S. unemployment insurance system.

To review previous research on the topic of this section, Gruchy (1947) points out that Commons after the Great Depression of 1929 changed from a theory about "class collaboration" that assumed labor and management to a broader theory of "reasonable capitalism" (Gruchy, 1947, p. 189).[7] Nelson (1969) introduced that Commons proposed to base the effort to prevent unemployment on the adjustment of the employers' payments (Nelson, 1969, p. 109).[8] Kato (2006) points out that instead of limiting the "liberty" of employers and workers to acquire current benefits, group insurance provides stable employment for workers, which simultaneously satisfies the interests of both employers and workers, resulting in more wondrous "liberty" for both. It indirectly points to a connection to Commons' concept of institutions as "collective action in restraint, liberation, and expansion of individual action" (Commons, 1934a, p. 73).

In light of these previous studies, we will reiterate and reorganize the characteristics of Commons' labor policy theory, which has much to do with Wisconsin's unemployment compensation law and earlier workers' compensation law. After that, we will examine how it connects to the theoretical elements of *Institutional Economics*, particularly pricing theory, business cycle theory, and, ultimately, the theory of reasonable value.

### *How to capture workers' compensation and unemployment compensation*

#### *Purpose and operation of workers' compensation*

Wisconsin's Workers' Compensation Law was established in 1911, and, according to Commons, its purpose is twofold. The first is to restore the workers' earning power as quickly as possible so that society will not be burdened with disabled human beings. The second is to provide for the support of the family while the surgical and medical treatment is being given (Commons & Andrews, 1916 (1936), p. 244). The purpose is to ensure that the worker has money for medical treatment in the event of injury and for support for his or her family.

On the other hand, there are two ways to administer the Workers' Accident Compensation Law. One is to establish an administrative bureau or commission with a general authority over the enforcement of the law and to administer the law mainly through this administrative body. The other is to have the courts resolve any problems that arise. According to various studies, an administrative committee's operation is better than a court of law. This is due to the following disadvantages in the case of a trial. First, court proceedings are delayed; second, court proceedings are expensive; and third, courts are unsuitable for resolving compensation claims. According to Commons, in order to achieve the kind of relief that the law intended to provide, it would be important to give prompt, honest, and full compensation and necessary medical aid (Commons & Andrews, 1916 (1936), p. 252), and he believed that it would be better to establish an administrative commission than to hold a trial every time.

Whether an industry is responsible or not is determined by the administrative commission on a case-by-case basis in each case. If a list is prepared in advance and the responsibility is determined on the basis of that list, the list quickly becomes unstable because industrial processes are constantly changing. As a result, it is necessary to constantly amend the law, which is extremely difficult (Commons & Andrews, 1916 (1936), p. 244).

As described earlier, Commons developed his theory of workers' compensation in *Principles of Labor Legislation*. As pointed out in previous studies, in the book, he argues that the industry is responsible for the risks to workers' lives in general and that the industry needs to protect workers (Kato, 2009, p. 40). The following section condenses Commons' ideas on workers' compensation.

> [E]mployer receives credit for conditions tending to reduce or prevent accidents, conversely, he is charged for conditions conductive to accidents. The feature of accident prevention just alluded to is too often underestimated when discussing compensation law. After all, to prevent the injury is of greater significance than to provide compensation for it; accident prevention is the greatest feature of a comprehensive accident indemnity plan.
>
> (Commons & Andrews, 1916 (1936), pp. 255–256)

A characteristic of the idea of Commons is that it emphasizes the "prevention" of disasters more than "compensation" for disasters. Furthermore, the place where this is put into operation is the administrative commission. In the case of Commons' direct involvement, the industrial commission in Wisconsin, of which he was a member, asked the State Manufacturers' Association and the State Federation of Labor to select these advisory committees to represent employers and workers. The industrial commission, including the selected advisory committees, then proceeded to legislate accident prevention, minimum wages, child labor, and regulation of employment offices and finally extended unemployment compensation after enacting legislation in 1932 (Commons, 1950, pp. 275–276).

### *Purpose and operation of unemployment compensation*

In 1931, at the suggestion of Franklin Roosevelt, then still governor of New York, an interstate commission representing the governors of the six leading industrial states was established to recommend action on unemployment compensation issues. In February 1932, the commission recommended that state legislation be enacted along the same lines as the first unemployment compensation law in the United States, which had passed the Wisconsin legislature in January 1932 (Commons & Andrews, 1916 (1936), pp. 298–299). Although some states faced persistent opposition at the time on the grounds that they would be at a disadvantage in industrial competition with states that did not have unemployment compensation laws, the controversy was finally ended with the federal Social Security Act of 1935. Thus, the Wisconsin law significantly impacted unemployment compensation in the United States.

Its Wisconsin unemployment compensation law states that each company is responsible only for the unemployment of its employees, that it contributes 2% of its total payroll to the state fund to establish a company-specific account, and that if a company fires an employee, it provides 50% of his weekly salary after a two-week waiting period.[9] Thus, the state fund account set up by the employer would not compensate employees of other employers, since it would only compensate his employees (Commons & Andrews, 1916 (1936), p. 308). While this allows a company to be responsible for one's employees' employment, it also gives compensation from the reserve fund if a company is no longer employable. So, a laid-off worker could miss unemployment benefits if the employer's reserve fund had been used up. This is Wisconsin's unemployment compensation law.

According to Commons, of the 13 U.S. unemployment compensation laws adopted through May 1, 1936, 5 provide for contributions by employers only, 7 for contributions by employers and employees, and 1 for contributions by employers and general taxpayers (Commons & Andrews, 1916 (1936), pp. 304–305). However, many states eventually adopted the Wisconsin law based on capitalists' profit motive and minimizing the income redistribution function as the "standard" (Sato, 2008, p. 78).[10] In addition, each of the U.S. unemployment compensation laws is consistent in providing for state administration of unemployment compensation funds and completely shutting out private insurance companies from this field. The exclusion of private insurance is in marked contrast to the case of accident compensation (Commons &

Andrews, 1916 (1936), p. 307). Despite these differences, the basic concept is the same as workers' compensation. That is, the emphasis is on "prevention" rather than "compensation." The following explanation by Commons in *Principles of Labor Legislation* is vital.

> The employer reserve system provides a basis for the simplest and most thoroughgoing system of merit rating, for the employer's contribution rate is made to depend on the size of his reserve account. If he avoids lay-offs and compensation payments, his reserve accumulates. When it reaches a certain point he is permitted to reduce his contributions; when it reaches a higher point he may suspend his payments entirely. If, on the other hand, he provides irregular employment, his reserve will tend toward depletion and his contribution rate will be raised.
>
> (Commons & Andrews, 1916 (1936), p. 309)

This is in common with the previous section, where the prevention of work-related accidents is the main focus of a comprehensive accident compensation plan. That is, the prevention of unemployment is the main focus of a comprehensive unemployment compensation plan. Furthermore, to prevent unemployment, the system is designed to make good use of companies' profit motive, which will be discussed later in this chapter.

In *Institutional Economics*, Commons noted that the Wisconsin law attempts to bring home this distress positively to the employers who can, in the first instance, be made responsible for unemployment. "It endeavors, by administration, to create the 'employment spirit'" (Commons, 1934a, p. 858). Thus, as noted in a previous study, "Commons and others were interested in 'preventing' unemployment itself, rather than 'relieving' the lives of impoverished workers through government-led public works" (Kato, 2009, p. 42). Therefore, the significance lies in the design of a system to prevent unemployment.

On the other hand, to touch on the disadvantages of this approach, as Commons himself points out, under the Wisconsin unemployment compensation law, employers' contributions to premiums are inversely proportional to their ability to pay. For example, an employer providing 52 weeks of employment per worker per year pays no premiums or benefits. In comparison, an employer providing only 26 weeks of employment per worker per year pays 26 weeks of premiums in proportion to the total payroll. This is a regressive method of taxation because it increases as the ability to pay decreases. In this regard, however, Commons states that this is an exercise of "police power" that imposes heavy pressure on those of low social spirit who do not act voluntarily to improve the common welfare and not an exercise of "taxing power." He explains, "[i]t is not based on ability to pay in support of government; it is based on inducement to stabilize employment" (Commons, 1934a, p. 873).

As described earlier, the system design of regressive premium rates in response to the length of time that employers employ workers provides incentives for employers to stabilize employment, and the emphasis on "prevention" rather than "compensation" is a characteristic of the unemployment compensation system of Commons.

## *Goodwill formation and labor policy*

### *Economic impact of prevention systems*

Regarding Commons' idea of work accident and unemployment compensation, previous research has shown that just as the work accident compensation law in Wisconsin generated the "safety first" movement that alerted both labor and management to prevent work accidents from occurring in the first place, it provides a financial incentive for employers to prevent unemployment (Kato, 2009, p. 43). Also, as introduced in previous section, Kato (2006) points out that instead of limiting the "liberty" of employers and workers to earn their current profits, the group insurance system provides stable employment for workers, which simultaneously satisfies the interests of both employers and workers, resulting in greater "liberty" for both.[11] We confirmed that this indirectly points to Commons' concept of institutions as institutions are "collective action in restraint, liberation, and expansion of individual action" (Commons, 1934a, p. 73). In addition, Commons' emphasis on "prevention" rather than "compensation" has four other possible effects on the economy.[12]

First, for employers, even if maintaining employment increases labor costs in the short run, in the long run, it leads to lower insurance premium rates, fewer workplace accidents, and lower costs for training new employees, which in turn leads to higher expected profits. Second, for workers, the maintenance of employment will help them maintain their earning capacity, which will lead to the maintenance of their consumption capacity, thereby supporting demand. Third, for the government, preventing work-related accidents and unemployment will reduce social security costs for work-related accident compensation and unemployment compensation, thus reducing the tax burden and allowing the tax to be used for other purposes. Fourth, when viewed on a country-wide basis, the suppression of government social security spending, as pointed out in the third point, would contribute to the suppression of the role of government, that is, too big government, which actively intervenes in economic activities. That was not a significant issue at the time when Commons was around. These are the effects on the economy of a system that prefers "prevention" rather than "compensation."

### *Goodwill arising from prevention systems*

Looking at the impact of this system on the company, particularly on labor–management relations within the company, as we saw in the previous section, Commons viewed "mutual concession" and "beneficial reciprocity of wills" between labor and management as "goodwill" that constitutes intangible property (Commons, 1919, p. 5). Behind his conception was the recognition that "the laborer is not only a productive machine, he is a customer" (Commons, 1919, p. 18).

As we saw in Chapter 5, Commons, unlike Keynes, does not see workers as a "working class" but as "the public" who are also consumers. These individuals, who are also workers, consumers, and the public, belong to a variety of going concerns, including companies, families, communities, and the state. Among them, "goodwill" is an essential factor in the continuity of a company as a going concern because, as we have previously confirmed, Commons thought goodwill was an intangible asset of business more valuable than tangible properties (Commons, 1919, p. 25). In *Industrial Goodwill* (1919), he gave the example of the major automobile company Ford, which at one time doubled its wages but increased its profits by reducing the cost of labor migration, and stated that "the intangible goodwill of labor may be as profitable as the scientific management of labor" (Commons, 1919, p. 18), noting that even at this time, beneficial interrelations between labor and management were fundamental to the company as the going concern.

This is both a change in the consciousness of management and a change in the nature of capitalism. Commons, in his *Principles of Labor Legislation*, states that whereas previously, the health of the consumer, not the health of the worker, was the public benefit, today, "the health of the laborer as a producer is considered to be as much a public benefit as the health of the consumer of his product" (Commons & Andrews, 1916 (1936), pp. 526–527). In *Industrial Goodwill*, he also states that "[g]oodwill is the expectation of future profit" and "without goodwill, the tangible property is a liability rather than an asset" (Commons, 1919, p. 26), leading to the recognition that goodwill is an essential element of profit-seeking corporate activities. In his last book, *The Economics of Collective Action*, he wrote about industrial accidents.

> [I]f you know that you yourself must pay your own losses then you will take extra precaution to prevent the fire or accident. This is human nature. . . . I have seen human nature actually change in the state of Wisconsin. . . . This change in human nature has not abolished the profit motive. It has changed the motive from making profit out of injuries to their employees to making profit out of the prevention of those injuries. . . . Human nature, in this case, has been changed by changing the direction in which capitalistic profit can be made.
>
> (Commons, 1950, pp. 277–278)

This points to a change from the style of the 19th century, in which managers earned profits by inflicting hard labor on workers and hurting them, to the one in which managers made profits by increasing labor productivity through injury prevention. It is also reflected in the experts who checked safety in factories. Factory inspectors looked around for disregard of the law by employers, but the inspectors themselves did not like their jobs. However, when Commons changed the role of the inspectors to that of "safety engineers," specialists who worked with employers to prevent disasters, they were pleased with the change (Commons, 1950, p. 281).

In other words, he pointed out the significance of the shift from production activities based on management's orders and workers' hard labor under the supervision of factory inspectors to production activities based on goodwill and beneficial mutual relations between management and workers based on the advice of a safety engineer – an expert. Thus, Commons pointed out quite early on that goodwill is an essential element for a company to continue (going) as a going concern, that is, to secure profit.[13]

### *Labor policy to induce goodwill*

So what can be done to form goodwill? The Ford example pointed out earlier by Commons may have been possible only because it was a large company. Companies with limited financial resources, such as small- and medium-sized enterprises, cannot practice what Ford did, even if they wanted to. This naturally leads to the idea that the state should improve working conditions. As Commons himself stated, "[t]he protection of labor becomes public purpose" (Commons & Andrews, 1916 (1936), p. 527); it becomes necessary to proceed as a state policy.

As noted in previous studies, one of the early members of the American Association for Labor Legislation (AALL), which was the precursor to what later became known as the Ohio Plan, was Issac M. Rubinow, a doctor and social worker in the American Medical Association. He advocated a system in which both labor and management would be forced to accumulate contributions to take advantage of the risk-sharing benefits of the insurance principle, and, in addition, a national or local public agency would provide financial assistance. This was a proposal for compulsory subsidized unemployment insurance that used statistical methods to emphasize the benefits of the "insurance principle" to spread the loss of unemployment (Kato, 2009, pp. 47–49).

On the other hand, as mentioned earlier, Commons and his student, Andrews, advocated mandatory unemployment insurance as labor legislation to prevent unemployment by shifting the risk of unemployment to the employer, which later became the Wisconsin Plan (Kato, 2009, pp. 49–50).[14] Rubinow's, Commons', and Andrews' ideas would later be confronted as the Ohio and Wisconsin Plans, and both would significantly impact social security policy during the New Deal. The question here is why Commons insisted on employer contributions and the determination of coverage through a commission system when Rubinow's idea was more broadly applicable and enforceable regarding the need for the state to promote the policy.

As for the burden placed by the employer, it was because, as noted earlier, it was necessary to set up inducements to stabilize employment and to make management directly responsible for the employment of its employees, and because making this happen would lead to the formation of goodwill and beneficial relations between labor and management. On the other hand, the commission system is mainly due to Commons' experience with labor–management mediation. In an earlier study, Gonce (2002) wrote,

> The economic doctrines he constructed during his Five Big Years suggested not a breakup of monopoly power but the creation of counterbalancing power. Such a policy, it would seem, would call for an ongoing legal effort to maintain the counterbalancing.
>
> (Gonce, 2002, p. 768)

He mentioned the need for the existence of what John K. Galbraith calls "countervailing power." Also, Chasse (2017) states, "Workers can correct this bargaining disadvantage only by bargaining as a group organized in a trade union. This argument was perhaps the most influential result of John R's participation in 'collective activity' on the staff of the USIC" (United States Industrial Commission) (Chasse, 2017, p. 78), and his experience supports that claim.[15]

What can be said from the above is that it is necessary to promote institutional design that stabilizes the working environment and forms goodwill through direct negotiations between labor and management, both parties concerned, giving management inducements to maintain employment and to negotiate directly with workers, without relying too much on the government. Thus, as Kato (2013) points out,

> What Commons emphasized in establishing each system of work injury and unemployment compensation was a mechanism to expand private goodwill between labor and management as a public issue in order to support the stable and self-sustaining maintenance and development of the industry as a whole, and an idea to expand it to other industries through the compulsory means of legislation.
>
> (Kato, 2013, p. 46)

The above is the policy theory that Commons emphasized to promote the formation of goodwill between labor and management. However, much has been pointed out in previous studies up to this point. We will, therefore, explain in the subsequent sections that this policy theory is closely related to the core of his institutional economic theory.

## *Labor policy and institutional economics of Commons*

### *Relations between labor policy and pricing*

How does the labor policy connect to the pricing theory we have dealt with in Chapter 3? In *Institutional Economics*, Commons discusses raising the standard of living for workers and consumers. He asks whether workers should achieve a higher standard of living as producers through higher wages or as consumers through lower prices. At the time, the American Federation of Labor (AFL) demanded higher wages as producers and lower prices as consumers, and Commons answers this question as follows.

> [O]n the average, the prices of commodities should be stable, and labor should get its higher standards of living as *producers* at higher wages, shorter hours, and steady employment through the year, rather than as *consumers* at lower prices and unemployment.
>
> (Commons, 1934a, p. 793)

Low prices lead to unemployment through poor company performance. High hour wages without reducing working hours also lead to layoffs of some workers due to rising labor costs. Commons emphasized its position as a "producer" against the public supported improving living standards through high wages and stable employment. This leads to a labor policy theory emphasizing the prevention of work accidents and unemployment. In other words, a high standard of living can be achieved when workers earn stable wages in a stable employment environment without injury and consume at stable commodity prices. However, "stabilization" of commodity prices is desirable not only from the perspective of worker protection but also from the perspective of company management and a country's economy, as we will see next.

### *Relations between labor policy and the business cycle*

According to Commons' business cycle theory, if the expected profit rate (%) is relatively above the market interest rate (%), it will tend to raise the average commodity prices. Conversely, if the expected profit rate (%) is relatively below the market interest rate (%), it will tend to lower commodity prices. The level of expected profit rate will be significant here. The formation of goodwill, the beneficial reciprocity between labor and management through workers' compensation and unemployment compensation, will improve the company's production efficiency, increasing company performance and thus contributing to an increase in the expected profit rate. At this point, labor issues of workers' compensation and unemployment compensation become relevant to the business cycle.

As explained in detail in Shibata (2021), it should be noted that when the expected profit rate exceeds the market interest rate, the will to invest, which depends on debt, is stimulated, credit is extended, and incorporeal property increases. However, debt, which is incorporeal property, does not change in repayment (nominal value), but intangible property, which is expected profit (expected capital yields), changes in nominal value, resulting in a boom or depression.[16]

This provision of "credit" is also tied to labor issues. Before Commons wrote *Institutional Economics*, he had dealt with the relations between credit and labor problems. In his 1921 article "Unemployment: Compensation and

Prevention," he wrote: "The credit problem is our biggest labor problem, because it lies at the bottom of the question of unemployment that question is the point of bitterest contact between capital and labor today" (Commons, 1921 (1996), p. 288). In other words, the "stabilization" of prices and employment in the era of banker capitalism depends on the successful control of credit. Furthermore, he states the following in the same paper:

> [T]he business man and the banker together are the controllers of credit, and it is the control of credit which can stabilize business. The over-expansion of credit is the cause of unemployment, and to prevent the over-expansion of credit you place an insurance liability on the business man against the day when he lays off the workmen.
>
> (Commons, 1921 (1996), p. 291)

Thus, workers' compensation and unemployment compensation for business liability have an increasing "expected profit" through the formation of goodwill and a "stabilizing" function to "control the expansion of credit" in addition to "compensation" and "prevention" of work accidents and unemployment.

Commons was conscious of this point until late in his life. In his last book, *The Economics of Collective Action*, he wrote:

> [T]he cooperation of plain, ordinary people in the prevention of accidents raises all of them to a high level of promoting the public welfare, and starts them devising remedies for the former weakest spot of the

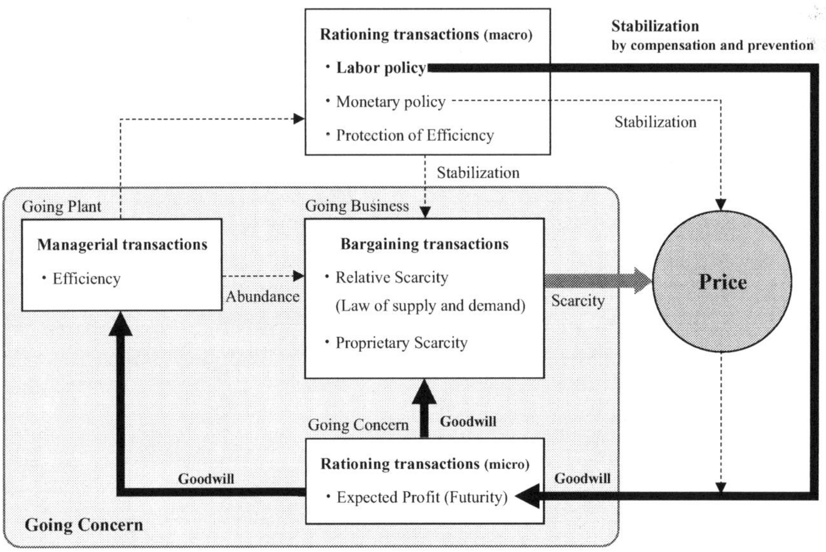


*Figure 6.1* Impact of labor policy. Compiled by the author.

> capitalist civilization. This weakest spot was then accidents to employees. The weakest spot remaining is unemployment and insecurity.
>
> (Commons, 1950, p. 285)

He saw overcoming "unemployment" and "instability" as the most significant challenges of capitalism.

## Conclusion

To summarize the above, as seen in Figure 6.1, Commons' labor policy theory forms an intangible property, goodwill, between labor and management by utilizing management's profit motive for social security programs and emphasizing workers' compensation and unemployment compensation, especially the prevention of both. These beneficial relations between labor and management lead to higher production efficiency and higher "expected profits." These lead to the business cycle theory of Commons, developed by expected profit in *Institutional Economics*. In this context, unemployment compensation is connected to the book's content, which states that workers, as producers, should obtain a high standard of living through stable employment throughout the year. Furthermore, business liability insurance is characterized by its ability to stabilize the economy, preventing credit expansion. In realizing these policies, the parties' collective bargaining agreement is essential in the administrative commission system.

Unemployment compensation in the United States began with the Wisconsin Unemployment Compensation Act (1932) to which Commons contributed. Later, the "unemployment insurance system" became popular to spread the risk of paying unemployment compensation, but the idea of making employers assume a certain level of responsibility remained, which has become the unemployment insurance system with an experience rate system.[17] Today, with the increasing financial burden of big government and the weakening of labor unions, Commons' theory of labor policy represents one helpful way to think about labor–management relations and institutional economic theory in the future of capitalism.

## Notes

1 For a detailed study of the Wisconsin School, see Kobayashi (1988). It does not deal with the economics of Commons but begins his analysis with the theory of Commons as the founder of the Wisconsin School and then examines the American labor union movement in the postwar period.

2 Commons states in the introduction to the first volume of American Labor History that the labor movement in the United States arose from circumstances peculiarly American (Commons & Associates, 1918, p. 3), and he cautions that what he discusses in the Shoemaker paper does not apply to everything else.

3 For a detailed study of Commons' "goodwill," see Kato (2006). Kato (2006) discusses Commons' proposal of a federal public employment agency as a solution to the problem of labor migration.

4 The first edition of *Principles of Labor Legislation* was published in 1916, followed by a second edition in 1920, a third edition in 1927, a fourth edition in 1936, and

a second printing of the fourth edition with further additions. This chapter is also based on the second printing of the fourth edition, in which the New Deal period was considered, and the various concepts were organized.

5 This was already written in his 1942 article "Legislative and Administrative Reasoning in Economics" (Commons, 1942).

6 At the time, Tugwell, the Undersecretary of Agriculture, was a substantive policymaker for the New Deal. For details on Tugwell's relations with the New Deal, see Nishikawa (1999).

7 Gruchy also notes just prior to this that a change in Commons' theoretical interests in the 1920s transformed his labor economics into "collective economics" (Gruchy, 1947, p. 189).

8 Other, Ito (1975) introduced that Commons said, "[a]bolish liberty, but substitute inducement" in the new public policy at the 1918 American Economic Association (Ito, 1975, p. 203). This means using company incentives in policy. Imoto (1982) introduced Nelson (1969) concerning Commons' idea of unemployment compensation.

9 For a detailed description of Wisconsin's unemployment compensation law and the process of its passage, see Sato (2008).

10 Sato said only Nebraska enacted a law precisely like Wisconsin's unemployment compensation law based on company-specific accounts. However, most states introduced experience rates, and many used the Wisconsin law as the standard concerning the employer's sole contribution and setting contribution rates, benefit amounts and duration, and eligibility (Sato, 2008, p. 78).

11 In addition to this, Kaufman (2003) analyzes that Commons and his associates recognized that employment relations were fraught with conflicts of interest but that with the appropriate incentives and practices, employers could build a significant harmony of interest with their workers (Kaufman, 2003, p. 26).

12 The impact on prices and the business cycle will be discussed in detail in the next section.

13 Kaufman (1998) points out that Commons recognized employees as "human resources" in *Industrial Goodwill* (Commons, 1919) and that the use of proactive management practices that foster goodwill and alignment of interests between employers and employees would strengthen workers' commitment to their work and increase their efficiency.

14 For a detailed comparison of Commons, Andrews, and Rubinow, see Kato (2009).

15 Elsewhere, Kobayashi (1988) analyzed that for Commons, unionism was the reaction of workers to the changes in labor–management relations caused by economic development through market expansion (Kobayashi, 1988, p. 20).

16 For details, see Shibata (2021), especially Chapter 3, "Evolution of the Private Property System," and Chapter 4, "Business Cycle Theory of Commons." In this book, the unemployment insurance system of Commons is treated as protecting intangible property that stabilizes capitalism, which is consistent with the purpose of this chapter. For details, see Chapter 5, "Stabilization Theory of Commons," in the book.

17 The current unemployment insurance system in the United States is examined in detail by Jigami (2016).

## References

### *English*

Chasse, John D. (2017). *A Worker's Economist: John R. Commons and His Legacy from Progressivism to the War on Poverty*. London and New York: Routledge.

Commons, John R. (1909) 1913. "American Shoemakers, 1648–1895," *Quarterly Journal of Economics*, 24 (November). Reprinted in Commons (1913), 219–266.

———. (1913). *Labor and Administration*. New York: Macmillan.

———. (1919). *Industrial Goodwill.* New York: McGraw-Hill.
———. (1921) 1996. "Unemployment: Compensation and Prevention," *The Survey*, 42 (October). Reprinted in Commons (1996), 288–298.
———. (1925) 1996. "Marx Today: Capitalism and Socialism," *Atlantic Monthly*, 136 (November). Reprinted in Commons (1996), 371–385.
———. (1934a). *Institutional Economics: Its Place in Political Economy.* New York: Macmillan.
———. (1934b). *Myself.* New York: Macmillan.
———. (1936). "Institutional Economics," *American Economic Review*, 26 (March), 237–249.
———. (1942). "Legislative and Administrative Reasoning in Economics," *Journal of Farm Economics*, 24 (May), 369–391.
———. (1950). *The Economics of Collective Action.* New York: Macmillan.
———. (1996). *John R. Commons: Selected Essays*, eds. by Rutherford, Malcom, & Warren J. Samuels. London and New York: Routledge.
Commons, John R., & John B. Andrews. (1916). *Principles of Labor Legislation.* New York and London: Harper and Brothers. second revised ed. 1920; third revised ed. 1927; fourth revised ed. 1936.
Commons, John R., & Associates. (1918) 1966. *History of Labor in the United States* (Volume 1). New York: A. M. Kelley.
Gonce, Richard A. (2002). "John R. Commons's 'Five Big Years': 1899–1904," *American Journal of Economics and Sociology*, 61, 755–777.
Gruchy, Allan G. (1947). *Modern Economic Thought: The American Contribution.* New York: Prentice-Hall.
Kaufman, Bruce E. (1998). "John R Commons. His Contributions to the Founding and Early Development of the Field of Personnel/HRM," Industrial Relations Research Association, Conference Paper, 328–341.
———. (2003). "John R. Commons and the Wisconsin School on Industrial Relations Strategy and Policy," *Industrial and Labor Relations Review*, 57 (1), 3–30.
Nelson, Daniel. (1969). *Unemployment Insurance: The American Experience, 1915–1935.* Madison: University of Wisconsin Press.

### *Japanese*

Imoto, Masato. (1982). "America ni okeru Shitsugyō Hoken Seido no Seiritsu: Shakai Hoshō Zaisei no Seiritsu Katei no Bunseki" (The Formation of Unemployment Insurance in the United States), *Keizai-Ronso* (The Economic Review), 129 (1–2), 41–67.
Ito, Fumio. (1975). *Commons Kenkyū: Sangyo Minshu-shugi e no Michi* (A Study of Commons: The Road to Industrial Democracy). Tokyo: Dōbun-kan.
Jigami, Ryosuke. (2016). *Shiyō-sha no Koyō Hoshō Sekinin to Shitsugyō Hoken: America Shitsugyō Hoken Seido ni okeru Keiken Ryō-ritsu-sei no Hō-teki Kentō* (Individual Employer's Liability for Employment Security and Unemployment Insurance: The Legal Analysis of Experience Rating System in the State UI Laws), *Hikone-Ronso* (Shiga University), 407, 90–107.
Kato, Ken. (2006). "J. R. Commons ni okeru Koyō Mondai to Rōshi kan no Goodwill" (J. R. Commons on the Problem of Employment and Industrial Goodwill), *Keizai-gakushi Kenkyū* (The History of Economic Thought), 48 (1), 32–45.
———. (2009). "America 1910 nendai ni okeru Shitsugyō Hoken no Kōsō: Commons, Andrews, Rubinow" (American Unemployment Insurance Schemes of the 1910s: J. R. Commons, J. B. Andrews, and I. M. Rubinow), *Keizai-gakushi Kenkyū* (The History of Economic Thought), 50 (2), 38–55.
———. (2013). "J. R. Commons no Keizai Shisō to America ni okeru Welfare no Jitsugen" (The Economic Thought of John R. Commons: The Fruition of Welfare in the United States), *Keizai Ronsō* (Kyoto University), 187 (1), 35–49.

Kobayashi, Hideo. (1988). *America Rōdō Undō Shi Ron: Wisconsin Gakuha no Kenkyū* (American Labor History: A Study of the Wisconsin School). Osaka: Kansai University Press.

Nishikawa, Junko. (1999). "Tugwell to New Deal" (Tugwell and New Deal), in Tanaka (1999), Chapter 8.

Sato, Chitose. (2008). "1932 nen Wisconsin-shū Shitsugyō Hoshō-hō to New Deal: 'Wisconshin-ha' no Shisō to La Follette Chiji ni yoru Shū Seiji wo Chūshin ni" (The Wisconsin Unemployment Compensation Act of 1932 and the New Deal: Focusing on the Thought of 'Wisconsin School" and State Politics by Governor La Follette), *Shakai-Keizaishi-Gaku* (The Socio-Economic History Society), 73 (6), 57–78.

Shibata, Tokutaro. (2021). *J. R. Commons no Seido-teki Keizaigaku* (Institutional Economics of J. R. Commons). Tokyo: Nihon-Keizai-Hyōronsha.

Tanaka, Toshihiro. (Ed.). (1999). *America-jin no Keizai Shisō: Sono Rekishi teki Tenkai* (American Economic Thought: Its Historical Development). Tokyo: Nihon-Keizai-Hyōronsha.

# Part IV

# Reasonable capitalism

# 7 Theory of reasonable value

## Rationing transactions and institutional adjustment

In this part, we will examine capitalism's state regarding the relations between Commons' theory of reasonable value and the concept of transactions.

Commons' theory of reasonable value includes two parts, one concerning reasonable prices and the other concerning reasonable policy formation. Until now, we have treated the two without distinguishing between them. Since 1929, however, Commons has changed the content of reasonable value from price to policy formation. Therefore, this chapter begins our discussion by distinguishing reasonable value into "reasonable price" and "reasonable value" concerning policy formation. In doing so, we will consider reasonable value related to "reasonable price" in connection with his theory of price formation and reasonable value related to reasonable policy formation in connection with his theory of labor policy. In these discussions, we will use the drafts of *Institutional Economics* to reflect results from previous studies.

On the other hand, the name and meaning of "rationing transactions," one of the transaction concepts of Commons, have been changed several times before reaching *Institutional Economics*. However, the final "rationing transaction" includes several transactions of different natures, including those characteristics of fascism and communism, for which Commons was critical. In this chapter, we reclassify rationing transactions into those that create reasonable value for policy formation, which Commons considered desirable and those that do not, to clarify what kind of rationing transactions should be practiced to create reasonable value. By rearranging the above multifaceted reasonable value and rationing transactions, we will clarify the connections among the difficult-to-understand parts of Commons institutional economic theory.

### Reasonable price and reasonable value[1]

#### *Reasonable value in the broad sense used by Commons*

Commons did not deny the law of supply and demand in the market but believed that the state should control the law of supply and demand by law so that producers can gain from their efficiency for a certain period. This is

DOI: 10.4324/9781032701394-12

because if it did not, producers and consumers would be disadvantaged due to differences in bargaining power and unfair competition. In other words, stabilizing prices in this way means realizing "reasonable prices." A "reasonable price" is defined as "gradually constructed, in the minds of successive courts, on the three prerequisites of Equal Opportunity, Fair Competition, and Equality of Bargaining Power" (Commons, 1934a, p. 63). In other words, the price would be achieved if the bargaining transactions function soundly. However, if it is unreasonable, institutional adjustments, such as competition policy through rationing transactions, are necessary.

True "reasonable value," on the other hand, is defined as "as formed in the practices of courts, juries, commissions, arbitration arrangements, and so on, is a concept of collective action in terms of money, arrived at by consensus of opinion of reasonable men – "reasonable" in that they are men who conform to the dominant practice of the time" (Commons, 1934a, pp. 206–207). This can be said to refer to policies and rules agreed upon through a due process of rationing transactions.

As Commons titled his book "Reasonable Value" in the drafting stage of *Institutional Economics*, he uses the term "reasonable value" as a keyword in constructing his economic theory.[2] However, there are times when he uses the term "reasonable value" when explaining reasonable prices. The following explanation in *Institutional Economics* is an example.

> Reasonable value of service is what other *buyers*, similarly situated, would pay for the service rendered. A reasonable cost of service is what other *sellers*, similarly situated, would receive in compensation for service rendered. Marshall's problem of *free* competition and his equilibrium margin of utility or profitableness, which, however, may be destructive, extortionate, or discriminatory in actual practice, give way to the problem of *fair* competition, *equal* opportunity, and *reasonable* value.
>
> (Commons, 1934a, p. 230)

In the above example, "reasonable value" appears alongside fair competition and equal opportunity, referring to "reasonable price" as the just price realized from fair competition and equal opportunity in the market. We use the two separately in support of Uni (2022) that the two concepts are strictly different. Uni (2022) states,

> In the drafting stage up to 1929, Commons regarded the theory of reasonable price as the content of Reasonableness. Ultimately, however, the main content of the theory of reasonable value was replaced by the theory of the formation of reasonable institutions and policy. In other words, between 1929–34, Commons significantly changed the content of the book's most important subject, reasonable value.
>
> (Uni, 2022, p. 84)

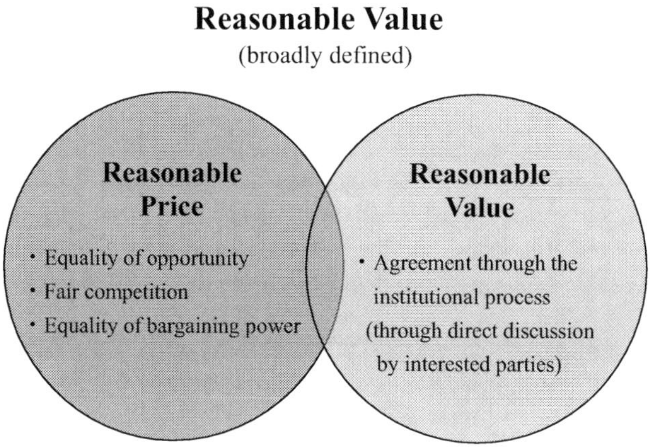


*Figure 7.1* Reasonable price and reasonable value. Compiled by the author.

Uni also explains that by the time he was writing the manuscript of *Institutional Economics* in 1927–1929, Commons was working to give ethics a quantitative meaning compatible with value as an economic quantity. We support this explanation.

However, we adopt the interpretation that, in some cases, there will be some overlap between the two. This is because, in some cases, a reasonable price can be achieved through institutional adjustment by rationing transactions through agreements by the right people (Figure 7.1).

### *Creating reasonable "value" in labor policy*

We have seen that Commons' labor policy theory impacts price determination and business cycles. However, these policy theories eventually yielded true "reasonable value," not a reasonable price. Commons called "reasonable value" an "objective, measurable in money, and compulsory" value determined by "court's decision" rather than individual opinion (Commons, 1936, p. 244). However, as we saw in the previous section, he divided reasonable value into two categories: micro regarding prices and macro (social) policy formation discussed in *Institutional Economics*, Chapter 10, "Reasonable Value," as follows:

> [O]ur idea of reasonable value is the consensual idealism of those who work together and are dependent one upon another for the continuance of their cooperation. It is not what "I think" ought to be, but what "we think" ought to and can be attained, as a going concern.
>
> (Commons, 1934a, p. 743)

By "those who work together and are dependent one upon another," we mean not only labor–management bargaining agreements in companies as going concerns but also labor unions and management associations that pit their respective interests against each other at the collective bargaining table of an administrative commission, where the agreements that emerge create true reasonable value. Furthermore, goodwill, a mutually beneficial relationship, will be formed if the agreement enriches both parties.

The phrase "not what I think ought to be" implies that it is not a matter of putting into practice what the top management of a country or a company thinks is good. In this sense, workers' compensation, promoted by Commons and the Wisconsin School, is a method that can generate true reasonable value in the sense that compensation is reviewed by an industrial committee consisting of representatives of labor and management.

On the other hand, concerning the unemployment compensation system, the position that unemployment is society's responsibility gives rise to the idea that workers, employers, and the state contribute to the compensation. However, Commons has promoted a system that makes companies responsible for unemployment. Depending on one's point of view, this is class legislation that only bails out the workers. However, if inequality exists, the courts will recognize that it is class legislation. Commons does not reject this idea but argues in *Principle of Labor Legislation* that the idea progresses from class legislation to reasonable classification.

> It is by recognizing this inequality of bargaining power, coupled with a public purpose, that the courts pass over, in any particular case, from the theory of *class legislation* to the theory of *reasonable classification*. . . . "Reasonable" classification benefits or burdens a class where there is real inequality to be overcome and a public benefit to be attained. That which is class legislation at one time may become reasonable classification at a later time, if the court perceives that what it once thought was equality is really inequality, and what it once thought was merely private benefit is also public benefit.
>
> (Commons & Andrews, 1916 (1936), pp. 529–530)

Suppose workers' compensation and unemployment compensation are realized through collective bargaining agreements. In that case, goodwill will be formed within companies by building trust between the two, and production efficiency will increase. If this contributes to boosting the economy through higher expected profits, workers' compensation and unemployment compensation laws will evolve from class legislation to reasonable classification for the public good. A distinctive feature of Commons' thinking on workers' compensation and unemployment compensation is the successful use of the pursuit of private company interests to serve the public good. The following sections of *Institutional Economics* reflect this idea of guiding society in a more positive direction.

> If the profit-motive, in the field of economics, can be enlisted in the program of social welfare, then a dynamic factor, more constructive than

> all others, is enlisted. It is an appeal to the business man to get rich by making others rich, and if he does not respond, then to appeal to collective action.
>
> (Commons, 1934a, p. 875)

Thus, the idea of workers' compensation and unemployment compensation espoused by Commons links the private profit-seeking motive of a company to the public interest of preventing work-related accidents and unemployment. By incorporating proper collective bargaining between labor and management into this process, the policy theory creates reasonable values of macro and social dimensions that lead society to stability.

## Classification of rationing transactions by Commons

### *Background to the rationing transaction*

Commons renamed "rationing transactions" several times leading up to *Institutional Economics*. First, in *Legal Foundations of Capitalism* (1924), he named it "authoritative transaction." Here,

> We have seen that unauthorized transactions are likely to fail in the two respects of lack of correlation and insecurity of expectations. For this reason a government or judiciary, with its rules regarding transactions, is needed to intervene with double purpose of correlating rights, exposures, liberties, duties, and of maintaining the correlation even if the parties prove false or change their minds.
>
> (Commons, 1924, p. 107)

Moreover, "[t]here is no bargaining between citizen and official, no power to withhold service or property, the psychological aspect of the transaction being that of command and obedience" (Commons, 1924, p. 107).[3]

In subsequent manuscripts of *Institutional Economics*, first in the 1925 manuscript (Commons, 1925), the three types of transaction concepts did not appear. In the following 1927–1929 manuscript, the first chapter, "Methods," used the name "judicial transaction" and stated that "[m]anagerial and judicial transactions employ the social psychology of command and obedience.... The distinguishing mark of these managerial and judicial transactions is absence of alternatives" (Commons, 1927–29, s.12).[4] The meaning can be said to be the same as the "authoritative transactions" mentioned earlier, but the name has been changed.

The name "rationing transaction" appeared in *Institutional Economics* (1934). Rationing transactions "apportion the burdens and benefits of wealth creation by the *dictation* of legal superiors" and are "the negotiations of reaching an agreement among several participants." Commons also explains on the note that "there may be arguments and pleadings, but these are not bargaining" (Commons, 1934a, pp. 67–68). In other words, as Uni (2014) pointed out, Commons expanded the concept of rationing transactions at this stage to include not only unilateral command–obedience relations but also arguments, pleadings, and negotiation.

### *Classification of rationing transactions in Institutional Economics*

In *Institutional Economics*, Chapter 10, "Reasonable Value," Commons classifies rationing transactions in terms of a process into five categories (Commons, 1934a, pp. 754–760) as explained in the next sections:

#### *Log-rolling*

Log-rolling is the process by which equals cooperate and reach voluntary agreements. It is democratic as a process of rationing benefits and burdens, although its meaning has been extended to legislative "trading vote." Commons explains that this process is universal but not universally good because its objectives vary, and it is inefficient because it takes time to make decisions.

#### *Dictatorship*

Dictatorship refers to fascism or government by a dictator. Commons explains that this approach is efficient in consensus building but not good because a higher authority coerces consensus. The will of the individual is ignored. In other words, it is an autocratic process against a democratic process of mutual aid.

#### *Cooperation*

Cooperation is a way of doing things, such as cooperativism. Commons describes this approach, along with "collective bargaining" below, as an action that falls somewhere between "log-rolling" and "dictatorship." Cooperation is characterized by working together instead of competing, but it has two poles: anarchism, which is voluntary cooperation, and communism, which is compulsory cooperation. He pointed out that these attempts remain to this day, but that cooperation, especially by workers, lacks the ability to elect their bosses in the workplace, which eventually leads to decision-making by "log-rolling" or "dictatorship" by workers and sharing these problems.

#### *Collective bargaining*

Collective bargaining is a joint agreement by representatives of interested parties, which Commons recommends. He recommends this because both parties are equally organized, and joint agreements govern individual contracts. In labor issues, each individual labor contract between an individual employer and an individual worker is made on the basis of joint agreements on labor rules. This is the working rule of the collective agreement, which fits the rationing transactions' definition of "the negotiations of reaching an agreement among several participants."

*Arbitration*

Arbitration is a judicial decision equivalent to a judicial rationing of wealth. The advantage of this is that it is not a dictatorship because it is bound by codified law, custom, and precedent. It does not have to rely on log-rolling because the arbitrators and judges are superior to the disputants. The arbitrators also hear the arguments and pleadings of the parties' representatives during the arbitration process.

These are the categories of rationing transactions. From the relevant section of *Institutional Economics*, the advantages of "collective bargaining" and "arbitration" are mentioned among these five, but in Commons' "Autobiography" (Commons, 1934b), published in the same year as *Institutional Economics*, the following statement, introduced in the previous chapter, was made.

> The essential point, as I learned in 1900 at the miners' joint conference, was the elimination, as far as possible, of a third party, the arbitrator – whether King, legislature, governor or dictator, handing down rules and regulations from above – and substitution of rules agreed upon collectively, by conciliation. . .. It is not revolutions and strikes that we want, but collective bargaining on something like an organized equilibrium of equality. This I take it, was the social philosophy of Samuel Gompers. It seems to me the only way to save us from Communism, Fascism, or Nazism.
>
> (Commons, 1934b, pp. 72–73)

What can be read from these is that, among the rationing transactions expanded in *Institutional Economics*, Commons particularly emphasizes the rationing of benefits and burdens through the process of "collective bargaining" and conversely that communism and fascism are methods to be avoided even in the same rationing transactions. It also points out that in some cases, forced arbitration is also undesirable.

Therefore, to understand the institutional economic theory of Commons and the theory of reasonable value, rationing transactions must be reclassified. We will present that classification in the next section.

## Reclassification of rationing transactions and creation of reasonable value

### *Three types of rationing transactions*

In the analysis up to the previous section, we confirmed that Commons, in *Institutional Economics*, divided rationing transactions into five types in terms

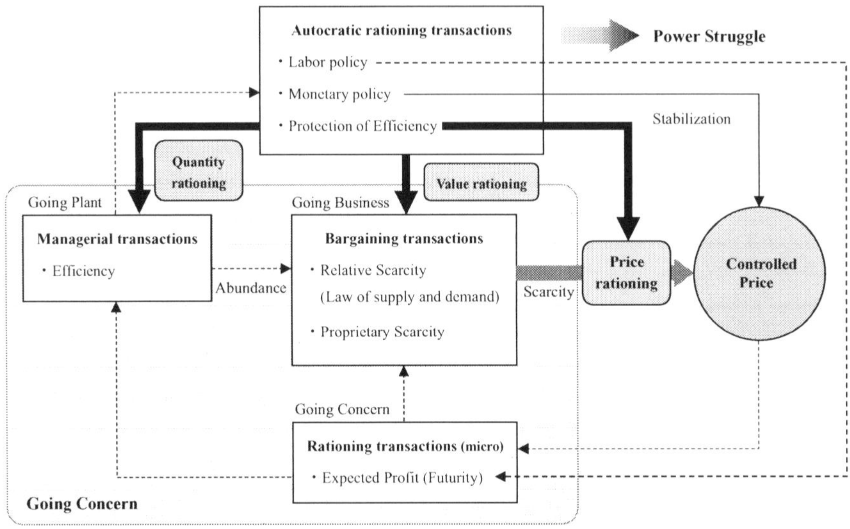


*Figure 7.2* "Autocratic" rationing transactions. Compiled by the author.

of process: "log-rolling," "dictatorship," "cooperation," "collective bargaining," and "arbitration." We propose to reclassify these into three categories: "autocratic" rationing transactions, "democratic" rationing transactions, and "reasonable" rationing transactions.

### *"Autocratic" rationing transactions*

This corresponds to the "dictatorship" referred to in the previous section, which at that time was communism or fascism. It also applies to the cases in which "cooperation" becomes forced cooperation, resulting in a workers' dictatorship, and cases in which the legally superior party fails to comply with custom and precedent in "arbitration." These are ways of emphasizing the duty to collective action over the right to individual action.

As explained in Figure 7.2, which expands on the pricing theory, the characteristics of an "autocratic" rationing transaction are "quantity rationing" when applied to a going plant, a production organization; "value rationing" when the tax is applied to a going business, a business organization; and "price rationing" when applied directly against the market price and would create a controlled price. The biggest problem with this approach was that it concentrated immense power in the government departments that had jurisdiction over "autocratic" rationing transactions at the macro-level, and Commons was concerned that this would eventually lead to a power struggle.

### *"Democratic" rationing transactions*

This applies to "log-rolling" and "cooperation," respecting rights rather than duties imposed on individual behavior. If equals can cooperate with each other in this manner and allocate benefits and burdens by voluntary agreement, it is possible to generate reasonable prices in the marketplace. However, as we saw in the previous section, while the process is democratic and meaningful, if vote trading in Congress escalates, if the bosses come to power in voluntary cooperative associations, or if too much power is given to certain persons to correct decision-making inefficiencies, the process shifts to "autocratic" rationing transactions.

### *"Reasonable" rationing transactions*

This is "collective bargaining" and "arbitration," but it is particularly applicable to "collective bargaining." Commons specifically envisioned policy formation through the administrative commission. In the case of the worker's compensation system, in which Commons was deeply involved, the administrative commission, attended by both workers and managers, decides what kind of compensation should be provided in the event of an industrial accident. In the case of this system, the content was designed to require companies to take responsibility and provide incentives so that the emphasis would be placed on preventing work-related accidents rather than on compensating for them in the first place. Such rules create obligations on the part of both companies and workers to abide by the rules and work to curb individual behavior. At the same time, however, the rules allow workers to continue to work with the promise of compensation in the event of work-related accidents. At the same time, they allow companies to increase expected profits by reducing extra labor costs, such as training costs for new employees to replace those who retire due to injury, thereby allowing companies to continue to conduct business activities. In other words, it conforms to the institutional concept of Commons, which is "collective action in restraint, liberation, and expansion of individual action" (Commons, 1934a, p. 73).

This is most applicable to the definition of reasonable value identified earlier, "[r]easonable value, as formed in the practices of courts, juries, commissions, arbitration arrangements, and so on, is a concept of collective action in terms of money, arrived at by consensus of opinion of reasonable men – 'reasonable' in that they are men who conform to the dominant practice of the time" (Commons, 1934a, pp. 206–207). Thus, it can be said that reasonable value is created from these "reasonable" rationing transactions among rationing transactions.

## "Reasonable" rationing transactions and reasonable value

While Figure 7.2 describes the case of an "autocratic" rationing transaction, Figure 7.3 describes the case of a "reasonable" rationing transaction. When rationing transactions in the macro dimension become "reasonable" rationing transactions, reasonable value is created through an institutional process in which interested parties directly discuss and reach an agreement at administrative commissions. Suppose efficiency protections such as patents and trademarks are determined similarly. In that case, achieving reasonable prices

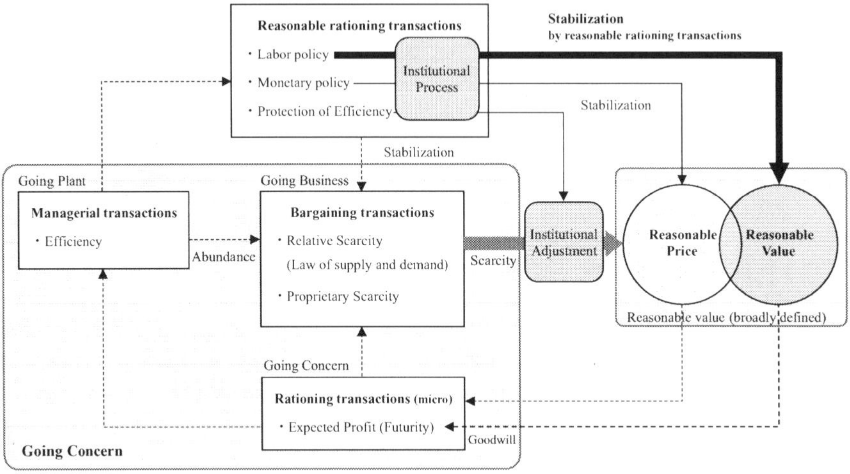


*Figure 7.3* "Reasonable" rationing transactions and creation of reasonable value. Compiled by the author.

created from "equality of opportunity, fair competition, and equality of bargaining power" will be possible through institutional adjustments.

Reasonable value resulting from "reasonable" rationing transactions can build goodwill, which is a beneficial interrelationship between labor and management, for example, by realizing proper workers' compensation and unemployment compensation in individual companies. Commons states that goodwill is an intangible property, "the expectation of future profit" (Commons, 1919, p. 26).

When the expected profit in the micro dimension increases in this way, the going plant, the production organization, will be directed to produce aggressively, creating a virtuous cycle in the economy. In other words, reasonable capitalism based on the reasonable value of good rules will be realized.

How can we explain the overlap between reasonable value and reasonable price in Figure 7.3? In the previous section (Figure 7.1), we confirmed that this is a case where a reasonable price can be achieved through institutional adjustment by rationing transactions through agreement by the right people. Another way of looking at it is that what is generated by reasonable process and objectively measured in money also falls under this category. In *The Economics of Collective Action*, Commons describes the Agricultural Adjustment Act (AAA) in 1933 as follows, though we partially confirmed it in previous sections.

> In the case of the Agricultural Adjustment Act, if we set up the actual liberty gained by farmers, which is freedom from coercion of prices and wages received or paid by them during the emergency, over against the economic liberty lost by other members of society and by themselves

> during the emergency, we should have a fair measure of the balanced equilibrium of public welfare intended to be brought about by the statute.
>
> (Commons, 1950, p. 237)

Economic agents with conflicting interests directly exchange opinions in an administrative committee when formulating policies. At that time, if the research department can obtain statistical data on the liberties gained and losses incurred by each economic entity due to the policy, it is possible to determine whether the economic gains and losses are not biased in favor of a particular economic entity. This is the calculable true "reasonable value." It is "reasonable price" as a just price and "reasonable value" agreed upon through the proper participation of both parties in the policy formation process. This is one interpretation of the overlap between reasonable price and reasonable value shown in Figure 7.3.

Thus, regarding the New Deal, the Agricultural Adjustment Act and the National Industrial Recovery Act (NIRA) in 1933 were both ambitious attempts, but both experiments were ruled unconstitutional. However, the Securities Exchange Act (1934) was a similar experiment, but it was not ruled unconstitutional. According to Commons, the reason is that the regulation by the Securities and Exchange Commission is a general regulation imposed on all industries. However, the AAA and NIRA were problematic because the regulations were specific. That is, they were unreasonable because they were burdensome and unjust to certain economic actors and because the courts found that the policymaking process did not reflect the interests of those economic actors, thus creating an unreasonable price and an unreasonable value.

## Conclusion

Elucidated earlier were the relations between rationing transactions and the creation of reasonable value of Commons. To summarize what we have attempted to do in this chapter, "reasonable value," which Commons used, in fact, includes two meanings: reasonable price and reasonable value. This is one of the reasons why Commons' institutional economic theory is difficult to understand. "Reasonable price" is constructed on the basis of three preconditions: equality of opportunity, fair competition, and equality of bargaining power. "Reasonable value" other than reasonable price is created from agreements reached through direct discussion by interested parties in the institutional coordination process.

Rationing transactions generate reasonable prices and values. However, his rationing transactions also include some kinds of meaning, which is another reason why Commons' institutional economic theory is difficult to understand. Rationing transactions create reasonable value, especially from the five process-based rationing transactions: log-rolling, dictatorship, cooperation, collective bargaining, and arbitration, which Commons classified in

*Institutional Economics*. They can be reclassified into three categories: "autocratic" rationing transactions, "democratic" rationing transactions, and "reasonable" rationing transactions.

While "autocratic" rationing transactions are efficient in their decision-making, they result in too much power being concentrated in the government, leading capitalism into a power struggle. "Democratic" rationing transactions, while being meaningful in their method, are inefficient in their decision-making, and if the leaders are chosen incorrectly, they can lead to "autocratic" rationing transactions. On the other hand, "reasonable" rationing transactions may lead capitalism to reasonable capitalism by creating reasonable value through an institutional process in which interested parties can directly discuss and reach an agreement. By the above, we can understand the essence of the institutional economic theory of Commons by sorting out the multiple senses of "reasonable value" and "rationing transactions."

## Notes

1 For the distinction between reasonable price and reasonable value, we refer to Uni (2022). Uni conducted his research using the manuscript of *Institutional Economics* of Commons. In Uni (2014), he addressed the importance of "proprietary scarcity" in the manuscript. It emphasized the importance of sellers artificially limiting or withholding goods from the market to maintain prices. According to his analysis, this concept was expanded in 1934 as a control not only on the supply but also on the demand side. Uni also clarified that the concept of rationing transactions, which is also dealt with in this and later chapters, was "judicial transactions" at the micro level in the manuscript. However, in 1934, the concept was expanded to "rationing transactions" at the macro level. Furthermore, Uni (2022) reveals that Commons' theory of "reasonable value" expanded its meaning to the reasonable "policy process" between 1929 and 1934, whereas until 1929, it meant the reasonable "price," as presented in this chapter. This study is based on these results.

2 The title of Commons (1925), a manuscript of *Institutional Economics*, was *Reasonable Value*, and the title of the subsequent Commons (1927–29) manuscript was *Reasonable Value: A Theory of Volitional Economics*.

3 "Authoritative transaction" in *Legal Foundation of Capitalism* is discussed in detail in Chapter 9.

4 For quotations from the 1927–1929 manuscript, sheet numbers are given after "s." in this book.

## References

### *English*

Commons, John R. (1919). *Industrial Goodwill*. New York: McGraw-Hill.

———. (1924) 1995. *Legal Foundations of Capitalism*. New Brunswick and London: Transaction Publishers.

———. (1925). *Reasonable Value*. Manuscript.

———. (1927–29). *Reasonable Value: A Theory of Volitional Economics*. Manuscript. (Collection of the National Agricultural Library. NAL call number: HB501 C66 1927, Identifier: CAT10844889001 and CAT10844889002).

———. (1934a). *Institutional Economics: Its Place in Political Economy*. New York: Macmillan.

———. (1934b). *Myself.* New York: Macmillan.
———. (1936). "Institutional Economics," *American Economic Review*, 26 (March), 237–249.
———. (1950). *The Economics of Collective Action.* New York: Macmillan.
Commons, John R., & John B. Andrews. (1916). *Principles of Labor Legislation.* New York and London: Harper and Brothers. second revised ed. 1920; third revised ed. 1927; fourth revised ed. 1936.

### *Japanese*

Uni, Hiroyuki. (2014). "J. R. Commons no Ruisekiteki Inga Renkan Ron: *Seido Keizaigaku* to 1927 nen Sōko no Hikaku Bunseki" (J. R. Commons' Theory of Cumulative Causation: A Comparative Analysis of *Institutional Economics* and Its Manuscript in 1927), *Kikan-Keizai-Riron* (Political Economy Quarterly), 51 (2), 77–88.
———. (2022). "J. R. Commons no Tekisei Kakaku Ron to Tekisei Kachi Ron" (John. R. Commons's Reasonable Price and Reasonable Value), *Kikan-Keizai-Riron* (Political Economy Quarterly), 59 (3), 84–95.

# 8 Commons' transaction economics and new institutional economics

## Markets, organizations, and state

In the previous chapters, we have grasped the overall picture and systematics of Commons' theory of institutional economics as transaction economics centered on the concept of transactions. This chapter will highlight the characteristics of Commons' theory by comparing it with other theories and ideas in close proximity. Specifically, we will compare Commons' transaction economics with Oliver E. Williamson's transaction cost economics, Mancur Olson's logic of collective action, Richard A. Posner's law and economics, and Douglass C. North's institutional evolution.

### Transaction cost economics of O.E. Williamson and transaction economics of Commons

Here, we examine the uniqueness of transaction economics by comparing Commons' transaction economics with Oliver E. Williamson's transaction cost economics. Williamson is strongly influenced directly by Ronald H. Coase, but as he states, he is also strongly influenced by Commons.

> The emphasis on transactions favored here bears a similarity, which is sometimes quite close, to John R. Commons' study of institutional economics in the 1930s. Thus I, like Commons, regard the transaction as "the ultimate unit of economic investigation.
>
> (Williamson, 1975, p. 254)

While it is true that there are similarities between the two in terms of viewing transactions as the fundamental unit of study and in terms of distinguishing between markets and business organizations, their content differs in fundamental ways.[1] This difference is because Williamson's transaction cost economics develops a "new institutional economics" on top of the achievements of traditional microeconomics. His transaction cost economics takes transactions as the basic unit of analysis, examines contract problems from the perspective of "saving transaction costs," and conducts a comparative institutional analysis of markets and business organizations. The critical point is that it deals with the institutionalization of private ordering using the recognition based

DOI: 10.4324/9781032701394-13

on "bounded rationality" (exclusion of comprehensive planning), the pursuit of self-interest through "opportunism" (limitation of promises), and bilateral relations through "asset specificity" (limitation of the effectiveness of competition) (Williamson, 1986, pp. 177–181). The key issues are "economic agents" assuming bounded rationality and opportunism, the difference of "market and organization," and forming private "order." This section will focus on these three issues and compare Williamson's transaction cost economics with Commons' transaction economics.

### *Economic agents*

Concerning the economic agents, Williamson's "bounded rationality" is mainly concerned with calculating transaction costs, and its driving force is efficiency-based selection behavior. The assumption of "opportunism" emphasizes human beings' selfish and calculating aspects. In both cases, the index of action is based on objectively measurable monetary costs. Therefore, Williamson's assumption does not emphasize the volitional aspect of the parties to the transaction, such as "forbearing" their actions through the psychology of bargaining with the other party. On the other hand, Commons emphasizes the social nature of economic agents by this "forbearance." The reason is that "(i) t is from forbearance that the doctrine of reasonableness arises" (Commons, 1931, p. 654) and because "forbearance" allows each individual in society to modify his behavior to a greater or lesser degree by the behavior of others (Commons, 1931, p. 655). Therefore, Williamson's economic agents are fundamentally different from the economic agents who "perform," "avoid," and "forbear" themselves based on the "will-in-action" as Commons conceives. The individual with a "willingness" envisioned by Commons is an entity that gives "meaning" to objects. In contrast, the individual envisioned by Williamson is an entity that passively and mechanically makes decisions based on interests. In other words, the fundamental difference between the two is that Commons set up a volitional individual in social relations, whereas Williamson set up a passive individual in economic relations.

### *Market and organization*

Commons and Williamson share the same distinction between market transactions and intra-organizational transactions. However, in Williamson's case, whether transactions occur in the market or within an organization, the focus is only on economic "exchange" based on efficiency. This exchange is the equivalent of what Commons calls "bargaining transactions." Thus, as Taka points out, Williamson's transactions do not take into account legal relations, such as Commons' "managerial transactions" and "rationing transactions," but only "bargaining transactions" in common (Taka, 1998, p. 68). Strictly speaking, however, even "bargaining transactions" differ because of the fundamentally different conceptions of economic agents. Transaction cost economics internalizes transactions in business organizations based on efficiency to save transaction costs. In Commons' transaction economics, "managerial transactions," which are intra-business transactions, are also based on efficiency. However, the unit of measurement is still different in that it is based on "man-hour," the ratio of output per hour (physical use-values) to input per hour rather than monetary costs. The most significant difference between Commons and Williamson is that, as Ramstad notes, Williamson does not take the perspective of "rationing transactions" (Ramstad, 1996, p. 415).[2]

### *Order*

In Williamson's "transaction cost economics," losses due to inefficient transaction costs are a problem, but "conflict" and "dependence" among people are not the main problem. The reason is that Williamson focuses on forming a private order in the market based on selfish individuals. On the other hand, Commons focuses on forming order through "due process of law" by collective organizations with legal relations. He showed that "the visible hand of the court" (Commons, 1924, p. 204) performed an "artificial selection" (Commons, 1934, p. 45) of customs and that the evolution of society was associated with the evolution of law. The court plays a vital role because it acts by the "due process of law" outlined in the U.S. Constitution. The courts perform an "artificial selection" of customs while being constrained by naturally occurring customs. This fifth person finally decides whether it is "reasonable" or not by checking the rights–duties relations of the disputants. This process is order formation through the due process of law, which Commons thinks. Williamson, however, does not have this kind of artificial order formation based on custom.

Thus, Williamson's transaction cost economics and Commons' transaction economics share only a problematic awareness of the importance of institutions and a rough commonality in general market transactions. Thus, as Ramstad puts it, "the concept of a transaction does *not* appear to intertwine the OIE (Old Institutional Economics) and the NIE (new institutional economics)" (Ramstad, 1996, p. 422, "()" are by the author). This remark is evident from the fact that Williamson himself follows traditional microeconomic methods.

> Unlike the earlier institutionalists, however, the current group is inclined to be eclectic. The new institutional economists both draw on microtheory and, for the most part, regard what they are doing as complementary to, rather than a substitute for, conventional analysis.
>
> (Williamson, 1975, p. 1)[3]

Although Commons and Williamson have focused on the concept of transaction, based on previous discussions, Williamson's transaction represents a traditional economic "exchange" in that it is based on an objective cost analysis. In contrast, Commons' transaction represents a social "transaction" that considers the will of the parties and their legal relations.

## The theory of organization: comparison with M. Olson and others

### *M. Olson and free riders*

Next, we explore the characteristics of the going concern theory of Commons through comparisons with theories on groups and organizations.[4] First, Commons' going concern theory assumes individuals can act actively for the collective good, but M. Olson criticizes this.

> Bentley, Truman, Commons, Latham, and many of the pluralist and corporatist thinkers are fully as guilty of the "anarchistic fallacy" as the anarchists themselves. The anarchists supposed that the need or incentive for organized or coordinated cooperation after the state was overthrown would ensure that the necessary organization and group action would be forthcoming. Is the view that workers will voluntarily support a trade union, and that any large group will organize a pressure-group lobby to ensure that its interests are protected by the government, any more plausible?
>
> (Olson, 1965 (1971), p. 131)

Olson points out that in large groups, rational individuals do not act uniformly in the group's interest and that there are "free riders" who seek only to enjoy the benefits. He says the following.

> It does *not* follow because all of the individuals in a group would gain if they achieved their group objective, that they would act to achieve that objective, even if they were all rational and self-interested. Indeed, unless the number of individuals in a group is quite small, or unless there is coercion or some other special device to make individuals act it their common interests, *rational, self-interested individuals will not act to achieve their common or group interests.*
>
> (Olson, 1965 (1971), p. 2)

As Olson points out, it is true that the larger the group, the more free riders will appear. Taking the example of labor unions, employees of companies with large labor unions can benefit from them without having to join the movement. Although Commons positively evaluated the organized behavior of labor unions, he did not fully consider the issue of free riders since he assumed that their members were individuals with willingness. However, Olson's argument, as he admits, does not apply as it does to small groups. Olson said, "the small, or 'privileged,' group is in a more advantageous position from the beginning, for some or all of its members will have an incentive to see that it does not fail" (Olson, 1965 (1971), p. 57).

In this respect, Commons' assertion that individual initiative is closely linked to going concerns is not erroneous. Furthermore, concerning the problem of large groups, if the number of free riders in a group grows too large, the group itself will begin to decline. In such a case, what will the purposeful individuals do? Albert O. Hirschman has an instructive discussion of this question.

### *A.O. Hirschman and expectation*

Hirschman, like Olson, not only assumes a "rational individual," but he also addresses the issue of revitalizing a group that is in decline. His approach is based on the keywords "exit," "voice," and "loyalty" (Hirschman, 1970). This approach means that individuals in a declining group have the choice of remaining loyal to the group's upper management, speaking out (protest) and seeking remedial measures, or leaving the group. Whether it is a company or a labor union, when the group to which one belongs begins to decline, the individual is forced to take some action. If they have a reliance on the organization, they will be "loyal." If not, they may choose to "leave." If the group members find it difficult to leave, they may first choose to "speak out" (protest). This idea suggests that the going concern to which one belongs may improve and survive or decline and perish, depending on the active actions of individuals with the willingness. This idea is related to the freedom pointed out by Commons. Also, concerning "loyalty," Hirschman said,

> [T]he expectation that, over a period of time, the right turns will more than balance the wrong ones, profoundly distinguishes loyalty from faith. (t)he expectation that, over time, what is right should outweigh what is wrong is what makes loyalty so different from faith.
>
> (Hirschman, 1970, p. 78)

Although Hirschman's theory is used here in the sense that individual "expectation" postpones organizational decline, it also has something in common with the going concern theory in that it shows the relations between "expectation" and organizational sustainability. However, Hirschman's theory, like Olson's, is developed as a choice behavior of rational individuals. The idea that, in choosing between "exit" and "voice," individuals conclude from a cost analysis that considers the cost of entering the organization and the cost of leaving the organization is very different from Commons' view of economic agents, which rejects invariant rationality. This difference is also actual for O.E. Williamson.

As discussed in the previous section, Williamson's "transaction cost economics" adopts "bounded rationality" under the influence of Herbert A. Simon and, at the same time, assumes an "opportunistic" economic agent that strategically pursues its interests.[5] Williamson also considers "markets and hierarchies are regarded as alternative contracting modes" (Williamson, 1975, p. 253). On the other hand, the pluralistic economic agents of Commons may participate in market transactions (bargaining transactions) as consumers, engage in production activities under the orders of their superiors as members of a company (managerial transactions), bear taxes as members of the state (rationing transactions), or enjoy their leisure time as members of cultural circles. In other words, they are economic agents with a will as members of various going concerns and are not computational agents for whom transaction "costs" analysis is central.

### *Nonprofit organization*

Therefore, the going concern theory of Commons is characterized by its scope of application, which can include both market and nonmarket entities. When we consider the problems of nonmarket and nonprofit organizations, such as political and cultural groups, the going concern theory takes on a new meaning. It is because the role of nonprofit organizations, such as volunteer organizations, in addressing global environmental, poverty, and disaster issues is essential when analyzing economic society. However, the activities conducted by these groups have been excluded from analysis because they are unproductive in an economic sense. According to Commons' interpretation, productivity issue of economic agent origins stem from Adam Smith's distinction between productive and unproductive labor.

> Smith and his followers contented themselves by distinguishing "productive" from "unproductive" labor. The physician or surgeon, the lawyer, statesman or politician, the minister or priest, the teacher, the musician or actor, the scientist, the domestic servant, the housewife, were "unproductive" because the usefulness of their labor did not appear in a commodity which could be saved and sold on the markets, or exchanged directly for other commodities or for the labor of others.
>
> (Commons, 1934, p. 180)

The value produced by those who perform unproductive labor is undoubtedly great, but no direct means of measuring it exists. Commons saw these scarcity values as measurable using money but not their use value because they are intangible. In other words, his understanding is that economics has excluded those who produce intangible values from its analysis because it has made tangible goods the basis of its analysis. Commons recognized this as a problem, and when he defined the going concern, he included industrial concerns that produce tangible goods and political and cultural concerns in his concept.

Today, nonprofit organizations and volunteer organizations that perform unproductive labor are composed of individuals with what Commons calls willingness. Since these organizations are usually small, as Olson pointed out, they are less likely to have free riders. This situation combines objectives and expectations, and the result is a going concern as a collective will.

### *E. Ostrom and common pool resources*

That has something in common with the argument of Elinor Ostrom, who developed the theory of common pool resources. Based on the results of experimental studies on common pool resources in various regions, Ostrom presented the design principle. Design principles are institutions' successful elements or conditions regarding the maintenance of common pool resources and the adherence to rules by generations of users (Ostrom, 1990, p. 90). In this context, Ostrom argues that in a strong institution where shared resources can be managed over the long term, monitoring and sanctioning are not done by an external power but by the participants themselves (Ostrom, 1990, p. 94).

Ostrom emphasized the importance of "quasi-voluntary compliance" by individuals when coercive power operates within an organization that manages common pool resources. She further states that the mechanisms for resolving conflict are sometimes entirely informal, with those chosen as leaders also being the basic handlers of conflict (Ostrom, 1990, p. 101). Although Ostrom's argument is about the management of common resources, her analysis is similar to that of the going concern theory, which emphasizes individual initiative, especially in its focus on sustainable institutions.

In summary, the going concern theory of Commons includes the free rider problem pointed out by Olson when the organization is enormous. When the organization is small, Hirschman's idea that individual "expectations" sustain the organization has some commonality with the individuals with willingness by Commons. However, Hirschman's theory, like Olson's, differs significantly from Commons in that it is developed as the cost-selection behavior of rational individuals. On the other hand, Ostrom's theory of organizations that can manage common pool resources and Commons' going concern theory have much in common regarding individual spontaneity and organization continuity.

From the above comparison, the contemporary significance of Commons' going concern theory is threefold. First, he regards organizations as continuous "going concerns," not limited to companies but including nonprofit organizations. At this point, Commons' going concern differs from Veblen's going concern and Williamson's hierarchical organization.[6] The second is that the willingness of individuals belonging to the going concern is the foundation, and it plays a significant role in the organization's continuity. It is also significant that individuals do "performance," "avoidance," and "forbearance" based on their "will-in-action," and especially that organizational order is maintained through "forbearance." That is because "(i)t is from forbearance that the doctrine of reasonableness arises" (Commons, 1931, p. 654) and because "forbearance" allows each individual in society to modify his behavior to a greater or lesser degree by the behavior of others (Commons, 1931, p. 655). The third is the importance of the going concern in capitalism. As we have seen so far, Commons idealized an economy with a balance of three types of transactions (bargaining, managerial, and rationing). The aggregate of transactions is the going concern – the institution. It is based on the willingness of individuals and is sustained by individual "forbearance" and working rules. Therefore, Commons, who emphasized the role of the going concern in capitalism, said, "Capitalism begins, not with Adam Smith, but with going concern" (Commons, 1934, p. 881).

## Law and economics: R.A. Posner and Commons

Modern law and economics" is a relatively new discipline in the United States. It began with Ronald H. Coase's "The Problem of Social Costs" (Coase, 1960). It was followed by Guido Calabresi's *The Costs of Accidents: A Legal and Economic Analysis* (Calabresi, 1970) and Richard A. Posner's *Economic Analysis of Law* (Posner, 1973). However, the study of law and economics in the United States had been discussed differently before this.

Commons' "law and economics" is one such example. The content of his work is an analysis of collective action using juristic concepts, and as can be seen from the title of his *Legal Foundations of Capitalism* (1924) and his article "law and economics" (1925), he researched law and economics. In this section, we will examine Commons' study of "law and economics" to determine how it differs from Posner's contemporary "law and economics" in particular.[7]

### *Posner's "law and economics"*

#### *Economic analysis of law: Hand's formula*

The main feature of modern "law and economics" is the application of economics methods to the analysis of law and the use of neoclassical microeconomic theory based on "rationality" and "efficiency." A vocal advocate of the effectiveness of this approach is Posner, who teaches at the University of Chicago Law School and served as a federal appellate judge on the U.S. Court of Appeals for the Seventh Circuit. He asserts that "the law and economics movement is just economics too" (Posner, 1993, p. 85) and takes for granted that rational individuals maximize utility as follows.

> So if I am offered a choice between 3 and 2 I will prefer 3. But what if I have another opportunity, worth 4? Then I will prefer it, because I prefer more to less. Well, but what if I have still another opportunity, worth 5? I will choose that. And so on until I have – maximized my utility.
>
> (Posner, 1993, p. 85)

Posner argues that the "new institutional economics" of Coase, North, Williamson, and others overlaps in many respects with "law and economics" and that the only differences between the two are matters of emphasis and vocabulary (Posner, 1993, p. 73).[8]

Without going into both issues here, we would like to note that "law and economics" is also used in real-life decisions in the United States. A typical example is the "Hand formula" for discerning whether there is negligence liability in an accident. The formula compares the expected amount of damage from an accident (= the probability of loss (P) × the gravity of loss (L)) with the burden (cost) of adequate precautions of an accident (B). If $P \times L > B$, the party is considered negligent because he/she could have avoided the accident at a lower cost but did not. On the other hand, if $P \times L < B$, the party is not negligent because the cost of avoiding the accident would have been too high. The assumption is that a reasonable actor would choose the less expensive option.

This idea is representative of modern "law and economics." The judge, Posner himself, based his rulings on it.[9] For example, there was a case in which the negligence of a ship's owner was questioned after a longshoreman was killed when he fell through a hatch of a ship that had been left open and into the hold.[10] Applying Hand's formula to this case, the accident could have been prevented if the ship's crew had closed the hatch after the dockworker's work. However, this would have forced the crew to work overtime, which would have increased labor costs. To begin with, the ship's crew should open and close the hatches each time, but there was a general practice of leaving the hatches of the holds open to facilitate cargo loading and unloading. Therefore, the cost of preventing or avoiding accidents (B) is not low since closing the hatches after hours is necessary to avoid accidents. Second, Posner determined that the probability of an accident (P) was not high. The reason was that most of the workers had finished their work and were ready to leave, but only the longshoreman who died did not, and the accident occurred. We obtain $P \times L < B$ by applying the above to the formula. Therefore, Posner ruled that the parties were not negligent because avoiding an accident would have been too expensive.

### *Efficiency in the procedure*

Next, there was a case that addressed whether a city ordinance providing for towing and moving illegally parked cars without notifying the owner in advance violated "due process of law" under the Fourteenth Amendment to the U.S. Constitution.[11] First, the Fourteenth Amendment to the U.S. Constitution states as follows.

> All persons born or naturalized in the United States, and subject to the jurisdiction thereof, are citizens of the United States and of the State wherein they reside. No State shall make or enforce any law which shall abridge the privileges or immunities of citizens of the United States; nor shall any State deprive any person of life, liberty, or property, without due process of law; nor deny to any person within its jurisdiction the equal protection of the laws.
>
> (Fourteenth Amendment to the Constitution of the United States, Section 1, approved July 9, 1868).

While the side who claimed that the city's ordinance violated constitutional rights advanced the argument that the city was taking property (automobiles) without a prior hearing with the owner, Posner ruled that the ordinance did not violate the Constitution. According to him, the legal process should aim to reduce two costs, "error costs" and "direct costs," thereby ensuring "efficiency." "Error costs" are the social costs arising from judicial system errors. On the other hand, "direct costs" are the actual costs arising from using the justice system.

Posner concluded that the error cost of introducing the ordinance would be small because the error in issuing a ticket for illegal parking is low. Concerning direct costs, he considered that it would save time and money to do things the way this ordinance would be done, rather than having to find the owner and ask him or her about each tow of illegal parking. Accordingly, for the preceding reasons, he held that the ordinance did not violate the Fourteenth Amendment to the U.S. Constitution.[12]

This idea of ensuring "efficiency" by reducing costs is an application of cost minimization in microeconomics. In its background, the objective is to obtain efficiency based on the rational behavior of economic agents and, beyond that, to increase wealth and maximize the utility of society as a whole. Posner's "law and economics" uniquely applies these economic ideas to actual judgments.

#### *Issues of "law and economics"*

The method described earlier is significant because it provides an objective standard for sentencing. The example above of illegal parking is a realistic conclusion, considering the effective use of limited budgets and personnel. It has something in common with the awareness of the problems economics face regarding how to utilize limited resources. On the other hand, however, the following limitations are pointed out.

- If human beings act rationally in terms of economics, many crimes should not occur.
- It is impossible to understand the parts rooted in human habits and morals only by economic analysis.
- Processes of procedural justice, such as "due process of law" and procedural guarantees, are often negatively evaluated by "law and economics" because they often undermine "efficiency." However, guaranteeing the opportunity to participate and speak out is also the foundation of democracy and should not be understood solely from the standpoint of "efficiency."

(Kobayashi & Kanda, 1986, pp. 191–192).[13]

Thus, modern "law and economics," as represented by Posner, treats procedural "fairness" and "justice" as secondary while assuming human "rationality" and using economic "efficiency" as the standards of analysis. In Posner's case, in particular, "efficiency" means maximization of the wealth of society as a whole, and he is unique in that he argues for the design of a legal system that will realize this. In the next section, we will analyze the doctrine of Commons again in light of these ideas and consider its significance.

### ***Commons' "law and economics"***

#### *Unity of "law" and "economics" through three measurements*

Posner's emphasis on "efficiency" is an essential element of Commons, but it is one of the five elements of understanding economic activity: "scarcity," "efficiency," "futurity," "sovereignty," and "custom." He opens his article "law and economics" (1925), published in the *Yale Law Journal*, with the following statement.

> Of the five elementary concepts or principles of economic theory, at least four are functional also to the science of law, namely, Scarcity, Futurity, Custom and Sovereignty. A fifth concept in economics, Efficiency, connects that science with the physical sciences.
>
> (Commons, 1925, p. 871)

Modern "law and economics," as represented by Posner, emphasizes this fifth concept, efficiency, which is a characteristic of an "economic analysis of law." In the case of Commons, however, as noted earlier, juristic concepts are applied to economic analysis, considering the legal system's impact on economic activity. Therefore, the units used by "law and economics" are explained below in light of the legal concept.

> Words give us theories, but numbers give us sciences. The science of economics, unlike the physical sciences, has two systems of measurements, a quantity measurement and a scarcity measurement, while the law adds the measurement of "reasonableness."
>
> (Commons, 1925, p. 381)

The first "quantity measurement" is derived from physics and applies to length, volume, weight, work, time, and so on. The second "scarcity measurement" is derived from the market and applies to demand, supply, and price, and in the case of the United States, the unit of measurement is the dollar. The measurements of "quantity" and "scarcity" are compatible, as in "50 cents a yard." On the other hand, the third measurement of reasonableness is "a unit of measurement which the people, through their representatives, had agreed upon," he explains. As we already confirmed in Chapter 7, it applies to what juries, courts, public utility commissions, arbitration boards, and legislatures have decided according to the customs of their times and places (Commons, 1925, pp. 162). Among these, the price that results from "equal opportunity," "fair competition," and "equality of bargaining power" is called a "reasonable price," as we have already confirmed. From the above, the unity of "law" and "economics," as Commons sees it, is characterized by quantity and scarcity (price), as well as "reasonableness," which emerges from the agreement of representatives in the time and place in question.

### *Application of juristic concept to economic analysis*

Commons spent many years examining the Court's decisions and recognized the legal system's economic impact. Morton J. Horwitz, a specialist in American legal history, describes Commons as follows.

> The first thinker to see the relationship between the de-physicalization of property and its abstraction into market value was the great Wisconsin

> institutional economist John R. Commons. His penetrating – though often obscure – *Legal Foundations of Capitalism* (1924) traced the late-nineteenth-century judicial shift to a market value standard. The Rate Cases, in particular, allowed Commons to appreciate that it was the guarantee of a *future* income stream that determined the *present* value of property.
>
> (Horwitz, 1992, p. 162)

In *The Legal Foundations of Capitalism*, Commons cites the decision in the first Minnesota Rate Case in 1890 as a representative rate regulation case. This involved the issue of how to assess the property of railroad companies when regulating railroad rates. In this case, the decision changed the definition of property to include not only material things but also exchange value, including expected earning power (Commons, 1924, pp. 14–17). Horwitz's point refers to the fact that Commons stated that the concept of property changed (from tangible property to incorporeal and intangible property) from case law research and that "[a]ll value is expectancy" (Commons, 1924, p. 25).

Thus, Commons' "law and economics" emphasizes the importance of "economic change by legal system" and "application of the juristic concept to economic analysis." Commons himself stated the following about this.

> I was necessarily studying hundreds of decisions, mainly of the United States Supreme Court and Commercial Arbitration tribunals, endeavoring to discover on what principles these tribunals decided disputes of conflicting interests – the Court acting under the clauses of the Constitution relating to due process of law, to the taking of property and liberty, and to equal protection of the laws. These decisions were discussed in my *Legal Foundations of Capitalism* (1924), to which the present volume is a related study of the theories of economists. I found that few of the economists had taken the point of view here developed, or had made contributions that would make it possible to fit legal institutions into economics or into this constitutional scheme of American judicial sovereignty.
>
> (Commons, 1934, p. 3)

On the other hand, modern "law and economics" is developing rapidly in recognition of the limitations indicated earlier. Thus, many of the issues may be resolved with future theoretical developments. However, it cannot be said that all the problems that have been pointed out before, such as the trade-off between "efficiency" and "fairness" or "impartiality," or how to deal with the relations with conventional jurisprudence, have been resolved. The tremendous significance of Commons' "law and economics" is that it attempts to find unity between law and economics through the "application of the juristic concept to economic analysis" and "reasonableness," unlike "law and economics," which applies economic methods to the analysis of law.

## Institutional evolution and economic development: comparison with D.C. North

Douglass C. North was one of the leading figures in new institutional economics (NIE), and Commons is one of the representative figures of Old Institutional Economics (OIE). Both were economists whose research focused on "institutions," but NIE, which attempted to integrate neoclassical economics, and OIE, a fundamental critique of neoclassical economics, differ in many respects.

However, according to Rutherford, who compares old and new institutional economics, although there are differences between Commons' approach and NIEs, Commons' tradition, which emphasizes transactions, property rights, and organization, is more linked to NIEs than the Veblen and Ayres' tradition (Rutherford, 1994, p. 2). One reason is that, as we identified in the previous section, Williamson states in his main book that the inspiration for the transaction concept came from Commons (Williamson, 1975). After that, there have been few other studies concerning the comparisons between the two, especially about North and Commons. However, a study on North and Commons (Broda, 2021) and a critical study book on North (Krul, 2018) have been published recently.

This section compares the two on the evolution of institutions and economic development. While North and Commons have in common the criticism of neoclassical economics and its emphasis on the role of institutions, their approaches are fundamentally different. We will compare their similarities and differences in light of the previous studies mentioned earlier. However, we will also seek to ascertain any similarities or differences between them other than those pointed out in the previous studies and their respective strengths and weaknesses. Furthermore, we will determine which approach can better explain the relations between institutional evolution and economic development in contemporary capitalist countries.

### *Overview of institutional change and economic development by North*[14]

#### *Institutional concept of North*

Early on, North emphasized the neoclassical approach, assuming that institutions are efficient solutions to economic problems. However, as his research progressed, he became increasingly critical of the neoclassical approach. He was particularly critical of neoclassical economics for disregarding institutions and time and neglecting the role of transaction costs, beliefs, ideology, and political processes in the economy.

Regarding the relations between institutional change and economic development in economic history, the conventional view is that countries that have been able to establish free markets have developed while others have stagnated. This leads to the conclusion that reducing government intervention and deregulation will lead to economic development. However, North points out that this is incorrect and that the role of institutions is important for economic development.

The institutions, North believes, are defined as "the rules of the game in a society" and "the humanly devised constraints" (North, 1990, p. 3). They were divided into formal constraints, such as constitutions and laws, and informal constraints, such as customs, which affect the performance of the national economy. And since changes in informal constraints take time, it was considered meaningless to introduce only formal institutions from other countries.

North viewed organizations as the game's players if institutions were the game's rules. He also believed that the institutional framework determines the type of organization and how it evolves, for example, if productive institutions can be built, productive organizations will be created. Therefore, the key is how to construct productive institutions that contribute to economic development, and the key is the state.

### *Reduction of transaction costs and economic development by the state*

Historically, when the protection of property rights (ownership) by the state is established, transaction costs in the market are reduced, and economic development occurs through the development of a market economy. North believed that this was the source of the prosperity of Western nations and pointed out the importance of the state creating rules for economic development. As a specific example, he explained that:

> It was the reduction in transaction costs due to the establishment of private property rights and competition in trade and commerce that allowed England to escape the Malthusian check[15] that both France and Spain suffered during the seventeenth century.
>
> (North, 1981, p. 157)

Summing up the above, in other words, "[o]ne gets *efficient* institutions by a policy that has built-in incentives to create and enforce efficient property rights" (North, 1990, p. 140). North believed that this would lead to efficient economic organizations, such as corporations, and economic development. On the other hand, he also pointed out the negative effects of the concentration of power: "Decline has resulted from disincentives to engage in productive activity as a consequence of centralized political control of the economy and monopoly privileges" (North, 2005, p. 134).

In his late 2005 book, North refers to "adaptive efficiency" as "the ability of some societies to flexibly adjust in the face of shocks and evolve institutions that effectively deal with an altered 'reality'" (North, 2005, p. 6); the Soviet Union, unlike the United States, lacked this adaptive efficiency and thus ended its short history.[16]

## How to capture institutional evolution and economic development

### The relations between institutional evolution and economic development

Based on the institutional economics of North, we will first refer to Philippe Broda's study (Broda, 2021) to compare how North and Commons view institutional evolution and economic development.

According to Broda, North and Commons have in common:

- The incorporation of institutions into historical dynamics.
- The primary role that institutions play in guaranteeing expectations.
- The adoption of pragmatic thinking.

A major commonality is that they both focus on institutions and emphasize the guarantee of expectations in their historical considerations. However, Broda emphasizes many differences, as shown in Table 8.1. First, while North distinguishes institutions as "rules of the game" and organizations as "players in the game," Commons defines institutions as "collective action in restraint, liberation, and expansion of individual action" (Commons, 1934, p. 73). Moreover, while Commons concretizes institutions as working rules, he also considers the continuous organizations, called the going concerns, to which working rules apply as institutions, so he does not distinguish between institutions and organizations. The difference, then, is that North was primarily concerned with how developing countries could establish an order of open access to markets similar to that established by Western capitalist countries, whereas Commons was concerned with the challenges facing the United States in the era in which he lived, namely, how to make capitalism survive.

Next, on the political side, North believed that the state's coercive power was unnecessary and that political neutrality was necessary. On the other hand, according to Broda, Commons believed that the state's coercive power was always present and rejected political neutrality. Moreover, regarding the state's role, North believed that the state should not interfere in private economic activities. However, it was essential for the state to determine how to bring a structural transformation to a situation where the market mechanism through competition could function. In the case of Commons, on the other hand, the state should reduce the intensity of competition in the market and thereby stabilize the economy. In doing so, he emphasized the role of the courts' judicial power to keep the coercive power of the state within appropriate limits. Broda compares the two above.

In his paper, Broda concludes that Europe now tries to be competitive and efficient based on what North has defined but that Commons would have considered such (rights-granting) actions with caution (Broda, 2021, p. 16).

### Critical study of North's new institutionalist economic history

We next refer to Matthijs Krul (2018), who conducted a critical study of North.[17] According to Krul, North's New Institutionalist Economic History

*Table 8.1* North and Commons: evolution of institutions and the role of the state. Prepared by the author from Broda (2021).

| | *North* | *Commons* |
|---|---|---|
| Institutions and Organization | Distinguish | Not distinguish |
| Concern | How developing countries can achieve open-access order | How advanced capitalist countries can keep capitalism alive |
| Enforcement | Unnecessary (eliminated in modern states) | Always present (still present today) |
| Political Neutrality | Necessary | Refusal |
| Pertaining to the State | Establishment of nonpersonal (objective) rules | Collective bargaining of social groups |
| State | • Should not interfere with economic activities<br>• Transition to open access with functioning market mechanism through competition. | • Should stabilize the economy<br>• Reducing the intensity of competition<br>• Emphasize the role of judicial power (the role of keeping coercion within proper bounds) |

(NIEH) focuses on the formation and change of institutions (Krul, 2018, p. 4), but why did North attempt to analyze economic history in this way? According to Krul, North was influenced by what he called "the challenge of Karl Polanyi" in a 1977 paper (North, 1977). It was, "If neoclassical economics has only a very limited range of applicability, how can institutional changes in history be explained without giving up on economic orthodoxy altogether?" (Krul, 2018, pp. 5–6). So, to answer the challenge of Polanyi, North had to retain the core of the neoclassical economic theory on which he stood, while criticizing the flawed parts.

As reviewed in the previous section, North's analysis of economic history uses economic terms such as "transaction costs," "incentives," and "games," as well as "lock-in" and "rent-seeking," especially microeconomic terms, to describe the relations between dynamic institutional change and economic outcomes in human history. For this achievement, he was awarded the Nobel Prize in Economics. However, as Krul points out earlier, the point is that North has not abandoned the core of the neoclassical economic theory such as the rational choice to obtain utility and profit and the pursuit of efficiency contained in "adaptive efficiency."

Krul said that North's methodological problem was that the subject of rational choice theory and the social institutional element were trade-offs, but North sought both, which led to a fundamental contradiction. In addition to the task of problematizing institutions and history, North also had the task of defending economics and its analytical tools. Thus, pursuing only rational choice would protect the analytical tools of economics, but it would diverge from realistic analysis. On the other hand, if he abandons his commitment to the analytical tools of economics, he can aim for integration with other social sciences, but this would increase uncertainty and break coherence. North sought these two incompatible things. Thereby, "[t]he more it seeks to incorporate social, cultural, and even psychological elements into the model as endogenous variables, the more this will cause problems of consistency with maintaining a purely instrumentally rational view of agency . . . . The consequence is that the two legs of North's NIEH end up walking in different directions" (Krul, 2018, p. 133).

Was North able to refute Polanyi's challenge? Krul's judgment was harsh: "We must therefore conclude that North's NIEH, understood as a rebuttal to Polanyi, failed in its mission" (Krul, 2018, p. 229). This is because, as noted earlier, the effort as a whole was incomplete and inconsistent. Specifically, the more it included limited rationality, incomplete information, game theory, and evolutionary approaches, the less theoretically coherent it became. In other words, according to Krul, North could not separate itself from the assumptions made by postwar mainstream economics. This was the result of a trade-off that can be said of new institutionalist theory in general, simultaneously pursuing the incompatibility of adhering to the disciplinary standards of economics, such as tractability and modeling, and integrating other sciences to revise behavioral principles (Krul, 2018, pp. 228–233).

### *Discussion of North and Commons in light of previous research*

#### *Similarities between the two*

In light of the above prior research, we would like to compare North's and Commons' ideas on the evolution of institutions and economic development. First, looking at the commonalities between the two, we can see that both focus on "institutions" and the concept of "transactions" (costs), which conventional neoclassical economics has not embraced. In addition, Broda cites the incorporation of institutions into historical transitions, the "guarantee of expectations" as the fundamental role of institutions, and pragmatism. Nevertheless, we notice the following three other similarities when comparing the two.

The first commonality is the focus on the source of active behavior of economic agents, represented by "incentives." As North states, "Incentives are the underlying determinants of economic performance" (North, 1990, p. 135), emphasizing that economic outcomes differ depending on the incentives given to economic agents. On the other hand, Commons did not consciously use the term incentive, but he repeatedly insisted on the importance of the active will connected to action, which is called willingness. He also presented a labor theory called "goodwill of labor"[18] in which the automobile company Ford doubled wages to reduce the cost of labor migration and increase profits, which is an example of incentives in practice. In addition, as we confirmed in Chapter 6, Wisconsin's unemployment compensation system provides incentives for employers to stabilize employment.

The second commonality is the focus on the impact of changes in the legal system on economic activity. They both cite the U.S. case of Munn v. Illinois (1876) as an example of a change in the treatment of property rights (North, 1981, p. 191; Commons, 1924, p. 14). In this case, the decision was that when a state government lowers the rates for services provided by a business, the resulting reduction in the exchange value of the business does not amount to a deprivation of property rights under the Fourteenth Amendment to the U.S. Constitution. North noted that the last quarter of the 19th century marked a significant shift from state regulation to federal regulation and from government encouragement and promotion of business activity to control of business activity. On the other hand, Commons focused on expanding the concept of property from tangible property to include incorporeal and intangible property, and the accompanying changes in the nature of business. Although from different perspectives, both focused on the impact of changes in the legal system or in the scope of application of law on economic activities.

A third commonality is the focus on the impact of sovereignty on institutional change and economic development or, in other words, on the power to enforce laws and contracts. North states that: "[t]his emphasis upon enforcement is another major difference between Oliver Williamson's approach to transaction costs and the one taken in this study" (North, 1990, p. 54). This is in common with Commons, who emphasizes sovereignty's role in guaranteeing expectations. Both realized the importance of sovereignty as the determiner of rules to guarantee expected profits by protecting property rights. Thus, the increase in expected profit increases the incentive for an efficient utilization of the factors of production, which in turn leads to invention and innovation. These are the similarities between the two, but the second and third similarities also explain the dynamic aspect of their analysis, unlike the static analysis of neoclassical economics.

### *Differences between the two*

Even though North does not mention Commons in any of his major works, there are similarities between the two that cannot be overlooked. On the other hand, however, there are also fundamental differences between the two. As pointed out in previous studies, North's distinction between institutions and organizations and his analysis of 10,000 years of human history are essential points of difference. However, there are also three other significant differences.

The first difference is that Commons "applies juristic concepts to economic analysis." This fundamentally differs from North's application of economic theory to historical analysis and is the most significant methodological difference. As we have already seen, the smallest unit of analysis of Commons is the "transaction concept" based on law, economics, and ethics, and the three types of transaction concepts can explain microeconomic, macroeconomic, and social activities. Managerial transactions refer to production activities based on efficiency, while bargaining transactions refer to trading activities in the market based on scarcity. The choice between these two types of transactions is the issue in North and Williamson's argument, where the choice between market or organization is the issue. However, in the case of Commons, the goal is to achieve stabilization by rationing transactions that can control them well.

The second difference is that North's new institutionalist economic history aimed for an open-access order in which the market mechanism functions through competition, while the institutional economics of Commons is a "stabilization theory that corrects the concentration of wealth and power." This is the stabilization by the state that Broda points to. While Broda points to North's lack of support for monetary policy as a difference, there are other important differences. In the case of Commons, regarding the concentration of wealth, in addition to monetary policy, the distribution of wealth can be regulated through "rationing transactions," such as the protection of intangible property such as patents and the development of labor laws, as we confirmed in the previous chapters. As for the concentration of power, Commons believes that it can be regulated by the role of the Supreme Court and the system of administrative commissions that reflect the interests of economic agents.

The third difference is the "credit money theory." Commons has developed his own theory of credit money based on the credit–debt relations. From there, he has a systematic theory of institutional economics, including a monetary policy theory that appropriately manages credit money, the concept of expected profit based on the premise of business using credit money, a business cycle theory using expected profit as a keyword, and a pricing theory based on the concept of transactions. For North, however, who is based on neoclassical economics and defends its theoretical analytical tools, there is no such unique monetary and financial theory. The importance of money and finance in the analysis of contemporary capitalism need not be pointed out, but in North's case, while the financial system, as a rule, may be the subject of historical analysis, money and finance are not the central object of institutional economic theory. This is another major difference.

These are the differences between the two. The second point is based on Broda's analysis, but the first and third differences are areas that Broda does not point out.

As Broda points out, the economies of today's developed countries are trying to be competitive and efficient, as defined by North. However, the result is manifested in the uneven distribution of wealth. Broda said that Commons would carefully consider such a practice and aim to prevent chaos in the developed countries (Broda, 2021, p. 16).

Therefore, the institutional economics of Commons as a "stabilization theory that corrects the concentration of wealth and power" has more potential to address this reality than North's analysis. Moreover, while North's theory focuses on a long-term analysis for developing countries to achieve the economic development, Commons' theory has the potential to address the problems faced by modern capitalist countries in that it is a medium to long-term analysis for advanced capitalist countries to maintain capitalism. This section compares North's and Commons' theories on the evolution of institutions

*Table 8.2* North and Commons: institutional evolution and economic development. Prepared by the author.

| | *North* | *Commons* |
|---|---|---|
| Similarity | 1. Focus on the sources of active behavior of economic agents, as represented by **incentives**<br>2. Focus on the **impact of changes in the legal system** on economic activity<br>3. Focus on the **impact of sovereignty** on institutional change and economic development (focus on the power to enforce laws and contracts) | |
| Difference | 1. Application of **economic theory** to historical analysis<br>2. Historical analysis showing the superiority of the **open-access order**<br>3. **No** original monetary theory | 1. Application of **juristic concepts** to economic analysis<br>2. **Stabilization** theory to correct the concentration of wealth and power<br>3. Unique **credit monetary** theory |

and economic development. It points out that in addition to the similarities and differences pointed out by previous studies, there are also similarities and differences shown in Table 8.2.[19] In particular, while North's theory is an application of economic theory to historical analysis, Commons' theory shows the application of juristic concepts to economic analysis, and Commons has his own theory of credit money, which North does not. The significance of such a comparison lies in the fact that North himself does not refer to Commons at all in the first place, in addition to the fact that few previous studies are comparing the two.

## Conclusion

The transaction economics of Commons and the new institutional economics are related in some respects but have some fundamental differences. Compared to Williamson's transaction cost economics, in economic agents, Williamson set up passive individuals in economic relations, whereas Commons set up active individuals in social relations. As for markets and organizations, both made distinctions, but Williamson lacked the rationing transaction perspective of Commons. Also, concerning order, Williamson is concerned with the private order formation of the market, whereas Commons is concerned with the artificial order formation of collective organizations with legal relations. In other words, Williamson's transactions represent traditional economic "exchanges" that revolve around objective cost analysis. In contrast, Commons' transactions are social "transactions" that consider the will of the parties and their legal relations.

Compared to Olson's logic of collective action, Commons' going concern theory may not consider the issue of free riders, but that is for large organizations and does not apply to small organizations. Hirschman's "exit," "voice," and "loyalty" approach has in common the fact that expectations are related to organizational sustainability, but it is based on a rational individual cost analysis of whether individuals exit organizations. It, like Williamson, is very different from the economic actors assumed by Commons. On the other hand, Ostrom's theory of common pool resources has something in common with Commons' going concern theory, which considers individual initiative, reasonableness, and restraint.

Posner's law and economics features an economic analysis of law that uses terms such as Hand's formula. It is characterized by applying economic theory to the analysis of law, which aims to ensure efficiency based on the rational behavior of economic agents and maximize the utility of society as a whole. In the case of Commons, "efficiency," which Posner emphasized, was only one of the five elements of understanding economic activity: scarcity, efficiency, futurity, sovereignty, and custom. Commons' case is characterized by applying the juristic concept to economic analysis, as exemplified by the theory of transaction economics, while simultaneously considering the legal system's impact on the economy.

North's new institutionalist economic history has much in common with Commons in new institutional economics, including the active behavior of economic agents using incentives, the impact of changes in the legal system on the economy, and the impact of sovereignty on institutional change and economic development. However, North's case, like Williamson and his colleagues, is based on the reduction of transaction costs, for example, linking the reduction of transaction costs by the state to economic development. Thus, it differs significantly from the application of legal concepts by Commons to economics, the stabilization theory that corrects the concentration of wealth and power, and the original theory of credit money. These differences represent the difference between the new institutional economic theory and transaction economics, as well as the difference between North and Commons.

Comparing the old and new institutional schools, Rutherford, at the end of his 1994 book, wrote:

> [T]he point is that OIE (Old Institutional Economics) and NIE (New Institutional Economics) could speak to each other to a much greater extent than is commonly recognized, and that there could be significant gains from such a conversation, particularly if the similarity of the problems being faced and the areas of complementarity that exist were to be the focus of discourse
>
> (Rutherford, 1994, p. 181, () is by the author),

which is exactly what is true.

## Notes

1 See Rutherford (1994, 2001) for an assertion of the commonalities between the new and old institutional schools.

2 Even if Williamson considers the role of government, the micro- and macro-level rationing transactions we have presented differ significantly from Williamson's concept of transaction cost. In particular, the "reasonable" rationing transactions that create reasonable value, which we identified in the previous chapter, are critically different.

3 Commons also noted that his institutional economics does not deny existing economics: "The problem now is not to create a different kind of economics – 'institutional' economics – divorced from preceding schools, but how to give to collective action, in all its varieties, its due place throughout economic theory" (Commons, 1934, p. 5). Veblen, a scathing critic of classical and neoclassical economics, also wrote:

> Of the achievements of the classical economists, recent and living, the science may justly be proud; but they fall short of the evolutionist's standard of adequacy, not in failing to offer a theory of process or of a developmental relation, but through conceiving their theory in terms alien to the evolutionist's habits of thought.
>
> (Veblen, 1898 (1919), p. 57)

We must remember that these are not a total rejection of mainstream economics.

4 See Moriwaki (2000) for a discussion of Olson, Hirschman, and Ostrom's argument. Moriwaki (2000) develops an argument for a public choice approach, which analyzes groups and organizations from the perspective of individuals' rationality-based choice behavior.

5 According to Forest and Mehier (2001), Simon was influenced by Commons and sees a close relationship between their ideas of rationality. However, they analyze that Simon has lost the fundamental social dimension in the transactional conception of Commons (Forest & Mehier, 2001, p. 602).

6 In the same institutional school, especially neo-institutional economist, Gunnar Myrdal's idea of an organization is closer to the idea of Commons' going concern. In *Beyond the Welfare State*, Myrdal states the following:

> The Welfare State has to devote continual vigilance to the building up and preservation of its human basis in democratic participation on the part of the people. In the countries where this problem has been tackled most seriously, and which also, on the whole, have been most successful in their strivings to keep up and widen active popular participation, a widely diversified educational campaign is continually carried on by the organizations and political parties.
>
> (Myrdal, 1960, p. 52)

7 In a previous study, Taka (1998) clarified Commons' view of "law and institutions" or "law and economics" in order to clarify his institutionalism intrinsically. In this section, we would like to show the significance of Commons' "law and economics" as an ideology and doctrine by discussing Posner's view, which contrasts with Commons' view.

8 In contrast, Coase kept his distance from Posner and was cautious about the idea of "new institutionalist economics" = "law and economics." See Posner (1993, 1995) for a discussion of Coase and Posner. See also Matsuo (2000) for a discussion of the differences between the two.

9 See Hayashida (1996, pp. 107–112). The same paper explains Posner's ideas and personality in detail and plain.

10 United States Fidelity & Guaranty Co. v. Jadranska Slobodna Plovidba, 683 F.2d 1022 (7th Cir. 1982).

11 Sutton v. City of Milwaukee, 672 F. 2d 644 (7th Cir.1982).

12 See Hayashida (1996, p. 111) for a discussion of this case.

13 Kobayashi and Kanda (1986) also introduces the point that modern "law and economics" has some answers to these issues.
14 See Chavance (2007) for a discussion of North's institutional economics and the essence of the new institutional economics.
15 Population growth and the spread of poverty.
16 At the end of the book, however, North points out that adaptive efficiency may have limits, given that previous civilizations have experienced economic decline (North, 2005, p. 169).
17 North has received many positive evaluations, especially praise for bringing about a new harmony between economics and historical analysis. On the other hand, North has received negative evaluations, such as its extension into new areas of economic imperialism in the neoclassical paradigm. Krull's study is characterized by its objective criticism based on a detailed methodological analysis, while there have been many high evaluations of North.
18 For more on Commons' labor theory, see Chapter 6.
19 The bold text emphasizes important points.

## References

### *English*

Broda, Philippe. (2021). "Institution, Economy and Politics: The Debate between Commons and North," *The European Journal of the History of Economic Thought*, 28 (3), 419–435.
Calabresi, Guido. (1970). *The Costs of Accidents: A Legal and Economic Analysis*. New Haven: Yale University Press.
Coase, Ronald H. (1960). "The Problem of Social Cost," *Journal of Law & Economics*, 3 (October), 1–44.
Commons, John R. (1924) 1995. *Legal Foundations of Capitalism*. New Brunswick and London: Transaction Publishers.
———. (1925). "Law and Economics," *Yale Law Journal*, 34 (February), 371–382.
———. (1931). "Institutional Economics," *American Economic Review*, 21 (December), 648–657.
———. (1934). *Institutional Economics: Its Place in Political Economy*. New York: Macmillan.
Forest, Joëlle, & Caroline Mehier. (2001). "John R. Commons and Herbert A. Simon on the Concept of Rationality," *Journal of Economic Issues*, 35 (3), 591–605.
Hirschman, Albert O. (1970). *Exit, Voice, and Loyalty: Responses to Decline in Firms, Organization, and States*. Cambridge, MA: Harvard University Press.
Horwitz, Morton J. (1992). *The Transformation of American Law, 1870–1960: The Crisis of Legal Orthodoxy*. New York: Oxford University Press.
Krul, Matthijs. (2018). *The New Institutionalist Economic History of Douglass C. North: A Critical Interpretation*. Cham, Switzerland: Palgrave Macmillan.
Myrdal, Gunnar. (1960). *Beyond the Welfare State*. London: Gerald Duckworth.
North, Douglass C. (1977). "Markets and Other Allocation Systems in History: The Challenge of Karl Polanyi," *Journal of European Economic History*, 6 (3), 703–716.
———. (1981). *Structure and Change in Economic History*. New York and London: W. W. Norton & Company, Inc.
———. (1990). *Institutions, Institutional Change and Economic Performance*. Cambridge: Cambridge University Press.
———. (2005). *Understanding the Process of Economic Change*. Princeton and Oxford: Princeton University Press.

Olson, Mancur. (1965) 1971. *The Logic of Collective Action: Public Goods and the Theory of Groups*. Cambridge, MA: Harvard University Press.
Ostrom, Elinor. (1990). *Governing the Commons: The Evolution of Institutions for Collective Action*. Cambridge: Cambridge University Press.
Posner, Richard A. (1973). *Economic Analysis of Law*. Boston: Little, Brown.
———. (1993). "The New Institutional Economics Meets Law and Economics," *Journal of Institutional and Theoretical Economics*, 149 (1), 73–87.
———. (1995). *Overcoming Law*. Cambridge, MA: Harvard University Press.
Ramstad, Yngve. (1996). "Is a Transaction a Transaction?" *Journal of Economic Issues*, 30 (2), 413–425.
Rutherford, Malcolm. (1994). *Institutions in Economics: The Old and the New Institutionalism*. New York: Cambridge University Press.
———. (2001). "Institutional Economics: Then and Now," *Journal of Economic Perspectives*, 15 (3), 173–194.
Veblen, Thorstein B. (1898) 1919. "Why Is Economics Not an Evolutionary Science?" *Quarterly Journal of Economics*, 12 (July). Reprinted in Veblen (1919), 56–81.
———. (1919). *The Place of Science in Modern Civilization and Other Essays*. New York: B. W. Huebusch.
Williamson, Oliver E. (1975). *Markets and Hierarchies: Analysis and Antitrust Implications*. New York: Free Press.
———. (1986). *Economic Organization: Firms, Markets, and Policy Control*. London: Harvester Wheatshelf.

### *Japanese*

Chavance, Bernard. (2007). *L'économie institutionnelle* (Hiroyuki Uni, Takayuki Nakahara, & Hideharu Saito, Trans.). Paris: La Découverte. (Original work published 2007).
Hayashida, Seimei. (1996). *'Hō to Keizaigaku' no Hō Riron* (Legal Theory of 'Law and Economics'). Sapporo: Hokkaido Daigaku Shuppan-kai.
Kobayashi, Hideyuki, & Hideki Kanda. (1986). *'Ho to Keizaigaku' Nyūmon* (Law & Economics). Tokyo: Kōbun-dō.
Matsuo, Hiroshi. (2000). "Shin-Seido-ha Keizaigaku wa Hō to Keizaigaku ka: Coase to Posner no Giron kara" (Is New Institutionalist Economics Law and Economics: From Coase and Posner Debate), *Yokohama Kokusai Shakai-kagaku Kenkyū* (Yokohama Journal of Social Sciences), 5 (1), 1–15.
Moriwaki, Toshimasa. (2000). Shūdan Soshiki (Groups and Organizations). Tokyo: Tokyo Daigaku Shuppan-kai.
Taka, Tetsuo. (1998). "Commons ni okeru 'Hō to Keizaigaku' to Seido-shugi" ('Law and Economics' and Institutionalism on Commons), *Keizaigaku-Ronkyū* (The Journal of Economics of Kwansei Gakuin University), 52 (1), 65–84.

# 9 The potential of Commons' transaction economics

## Cumulative legal causation toward reasonable capitalism

In this chapter, we consider the realization of reasonable capitalism from the institutional economics theory of Commons, especially the concept of transaction. The history of the capitalist economy shows that, in the process of its development, various unfair and unjust transactions have taken place: merchants connected to kings and governments have been given privileges to dominate the market, monopolies have dominated the market with monopoly prices, and inferior quality goods and services have been falsely sold as good quality without disclosing information about the goods and services. Unfortunately, these are part of the result of modern capitalism. Equally unfortunate, these immoral practices have yet to be eliminated in the contemporary capitalist economy, and they persist and regularly disrupt the economic society. How can we prevent unfair and unjust transactions and realize reasonable capitalism? This topic is the problem set for this chapter.

To do this study, we first identify the contemporary significance of the transactional economics of Commons. Next, we focus on "authoritative transactions" in *Legal Foundations of Capitalism* to better understand the methodological feature of applying juristic concepts to economic analysis and grasp the implications of government intervention in the market. We will then examine the similarities between "authoritative transactions" in *Legal Foundations of Capitalism* and "rationing transactions" in *Institutional Economics*, especially "reasonable rationing transactions." And finally, we will examine approaches to reasonable capitalism based on these transactions.

### Contemporary significance of transaction economics

To summarize what we have done so far, the institutional economics of Commons is transaction economics, which analyzes markets and organizations based on transaction concepts, expresses the will and legal relations, and gives them continuous order and freedom. What is the contemporary significance of his transaction economics? This section finds its potential in the "pluralistic economic agents" and the "micro and macro legal interrelation."

DOI: 10.4324/9781032701394-14

### *Pluralistic economic agents*

As we have noted, Commons' conception of economic agents was that of individuals with "willingness," who negotiate with their trading partners by "performing," "avoiding," or "forbearing" their actions. Institutions constrain these individuals, but at the same time, they are given freedom from them. Commons distinguishes between liberty and freedom. We obtain liberty through the working rules of a going concern, an organization of continuous activity, which means release from obligation, whereas freedom has a more positive meaning.

Commons says, "Freedom is power. It belongs to the 'free man,' but not to the mere 'freedman.' It is the power to call on the officials to make one's will effective" (Commons, 1924, p. 119). Thus, the individual who belongs to the going concern has liberty through working rules. At the same time, he also has freedom because he has a willingness that constitutes the going concern. Therefore, individuals have "liberty" and "freedom."

His idea encourages reconsidering the traditional "class" consciousness, which holds that an individual is bound to only one class because he or she belongs to various positions depending on economic interests. Commons argues that "[c]lass conflict may be growing, but it is not inevitable if this third class, which is not a class, is able to determine directly the issues" (Commons, 1913, p. 82). According to his survey, two-thirds of voting adults in early 20th-century America were "spectators" (Commons, 1913, pp. 71–72) who did not belong to a distinct working class or capitalist class. He calls these spectators "the public" (Commons, 1913, p. 72), and in the final part of the paper, he explains that they are "[e]conomically it stands apart as a class of consumers." He also understood that the existing economic classes were established by "class legislation in the past" such as protective tariffs for manufacturers (Commons, 1913, p. 83).

Commons believed it was important for this third "class," the "spectators," to avoid class conflict through legislative activity. This work is purely the work of the legislature and participation in juries and various administrative commissions. Commons says that there is not a "class" but a "classification" of people (Commons, 1925, p. 384). The classification is significant because it represents a pluralistic economic entity in which active individuals with "willingness" and "freedom" can belong to various organizations (going concerns) according to their purposes. It is the foundation of democracy.

### *Micro and macro legal interrelation*

These pluralistic economic agents conduct various transactions depending on the time and place. These are the three types of transactions that we have already described: bargaining, managerial, and rationing. These link the individual to the going concern. The going concern that Commons refers to is not limited to companies. It represents an active organization "with the working rules that keep them agoing, all the way from the family, the corporation, the trade union, the trade association, up to the state itself" (Commons, 1934, p. 69). The going concern refers to the "institutions" themselves, which are "collective action in restraint, liberation, and expansion of individual action" (Commons, 1934, p. 73). Thus, the three transactions link the micro-individual, the mezzo-organization, and the macro-society and give them an interrelation. These ideas have led to an analysis of the interrelation among micro, mezzo, and macro based on reconsidering the institutional understanding of the old institutional school.

By incorporating Commons' evolutionary theory of "artificial selection," transaction economics ensures dynamism. The key is an understanding of the evolution of law. Commons' survey of Supreme Court precedent shows that the law evolves through due process. The court artificially selects customs or working rules through statutes. On the other hand, the court is influenced by past customs that have emerged as common knowledge among people from individual and organizational customs. In other words, the court, as the fifth person in the transaction, directly adjudicates individuals through statutes and, in doing so, grants them liberty. On the other hand, however, the individual with the freedom is the source of power, and the customs arising from it indirectly "forbear" the court's actions and restrain the execution of the compulsory "rationing transactions," especially "autocratic rationing transactions," we have seen in Chapter 7.

Applying to companies, the management class controls employees through articles of incorporation, but the rules give rise to employee business practices, which form business ethics. This process represents the evolution of working rules within the company, where these business ethics ultimately influence the decisions of the management layer. This relation is the micro–macro legal interrelation with explicit and customary law.

Thus, transaction economics of Commons demonstrates its contemporary significance as an economics that analyzes economic and social relations based on legal understanding, as opposed to transaction cost economics, which analyzes laws and organizations based on economic methods. In the following sections, we will examine this cumulative legal causation of transaction economics in detail.

## Authoritative transactions in *Legal Foundations of Capitalism*

In this section, we review the transaction concept and its legal relations in Commons' *Legal Foundations of Capitalism* (Commons, 1924, hereafter LFC). Confirming capitalism's legal foundations will help us understand the necessity of state intervention in the market. In LFC, Commons uses figures of legal relations to explain such collective behavior. In this section, we will use these figures to understand the significance of the concept of transaction in LFC.

### *Unauthorized transactions and authorized transactions*

Commons considered a participant's behavior in a transaction as "performance" if the individual chooses to do a sure thing and "avoidance" if the individual chooses not to do it or to do something else. In addition to these two choices, he added the option of "forbearance" in which the individual restricts their actions depending on the power relations with the other party. The forbearance is an interpretation that restricting one's actions is also a kind of will. Based on the above, Commons argues that:

> [E]conomic determinism arises only from the fact that the will acts in a world of limited resources and that these resources are tied up or loosened up by means of working rules that vouchsafe to the individual certain rights, duties, and liberties of performance, avoidance or forbearance.
> (Commons, 1924, p. 82)

As identified in Chapter 1, Commons argues that "[a]ll rights and duties are relative" (Commons, 1924, p. 84). If they were absolute, one side of a transaction could reflect its will on the other without limit. He understood this situation as a physical action and reaction, not right and duty. Thus, the actual transaction is relative, but if it is immature and not authorized by a third party (the government) other than the parties, what will their legal relations be? Commons states in LFC,

> The wish of one that he had a divine or natural right to a certain behavior of another may not coincide with the fear of the other that he is bound by a divine or natural duty to behave with exactly that amount of performance, avoidance, and self-control.
> (Commons, 1924, p. 85)

This condition is non-correlative relations, as shown in Figure 9.1, where the rights of party A do not correspond to the amount of duty of counterparty B. Therefore, even if a party delivers goods to the counterparty, expecting payment for the goods is not always possible. Moreover, the boundary between the other party's duty and no duty is also ambiguous because the boundary between right and no right, which the rights of Party A do not extend, has not been defined.

Commons states that transactions in such a state are the historical stage of appeals to divine or natural rights and the stage of anarchy, dogmatism, and

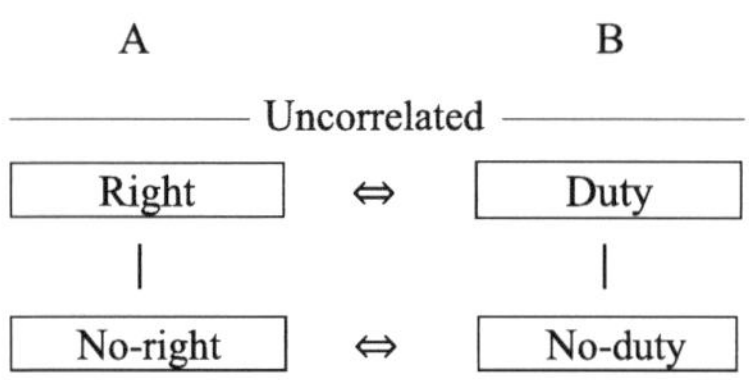


*Figure 9.1* Legal relations for unauthorized transactions (Commons, 1924, p. 86, Figure III, partially revised).

metaphysics (Commons, 1924, p. 86). Therefore, such an unauthorized transaction is a world in which the rights and duties of the parties do not coincide and where many transactions are expected to fail due to disagreement; in this sense, it is a state of unreasonable economy that does not produce reasonable prices. What is an authorized transaction, then, and how does it differ from an unauthorized transaction? In LFC, Commons wrote as follows:

> (T)he correlation of rights and duties is not a conclusion of logic, as is often inferred, but is a command of government. For this reason we pass over from the merely ethical transactions depending on individual interests and beliefs, to authorized transactions where the will of a superior party or parties imposes limits on their transactions by imposing or interpreting a rule of conduct applicable to the dispute.
>
> (Commons, 1924, pp. 86–87)

In other words, through the presence of a third party other than the parties to the transaction or, more precisely, as the fifth party, the rights and duties of the parties to the transaction are correlated. Furthermore, their respective quantities are matched, and at the same time, the boundaries between rights and no rights and duties and no duties are clarified.

As identified in Chapter 1, at LFC, Commons developed his diagram of legal relations based on the analytical diagram of legal relations by Hohfeld. Commons follows his relation between "right" and "duty" but modifies it for the remaining two concepts. In other words, Commons regarded "no right" as a state of "exposure" in which no protection of action is obtained and "privilege" as "liberty" to choose opportunities. In this way, Commons explained the legal relations among economic agents based on the behaviorist aspect. These are connected to the working rules (Commons, 1924, p. 68), which are derived from "can" for right, "must" for duty, "cannot" for exposure, and "may" for liberty. The above is illustrated in Figure 9.2.

This relation makes right and duty correlative, and consequently, for example, when one gives a commodity to a counterparty, one can expect full payment for it. This relation applies not only to transactions of goods but also to

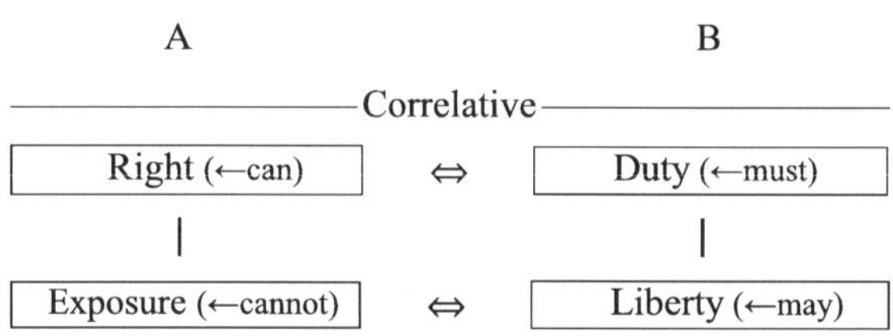


*Figure 9.2* Legal relations for authorized transactions (Commons, 1924, p. 97, Figure IX, partially revised).

credit–debt relations. It thus represents the development of the legal system at the same time that the concept of property evolved from tangible property to incorporeal and intangible property. Commons states that "(a)ll value is expectancy" (Commons, 1924, p. 25), which is closely linked to whether transactions are authorized, that is, whether the legal foundation of capitalism is in place. At the beginning of LFC, he declares that "the aim of this volume is to work out an evolutionary and behavioristic, or rather volitional, theory of value" (Commons, 1924, preface), and these legal diagrams are one way to explain his theory of value.

### *Characteristics of authoritative transactions*

In the words of Commons, the following is a summary of what we have so far:

> We have seen that unauthorized transactions are likely to fail in the two respects of lack of correlation and insecurity of expectations. For this reason a government or judiciary, with its rules regarding transactions, is needed to intervene with the double purpose of correlating rights, exposures, liberties, duties, and of maintaining the correlation even if the parties prove false or change their minds.
>
> (Commons, 1924, p. 100)

This intervention in the rules of the transaction is an "authoritative transaction." Commons describes this transaction as "the official is the state-in-action, and the state-in-action is the authoritative transactions of officials and citizens measured off by the juristic dimensions of reciprocal power, disability, responsibility, and immunity" (Commons, 1924, p. 371). This relation is illustrated in Figure 9.3.

This figure is the one described in Chapter 1,[1] but we will reiterate it below for the sake of confirmation. The figure adds official C to the bilateral (A–B) transaction. "Power" represents a promise to protect the "right" of citizen A. On the other hand, "liability" (responsibility) refers to enforcing citizen B's "duty" when he fails to do so. Moreover, "disability" refers to the inability of official C to assist citizen A when citizen A is in "exposure."

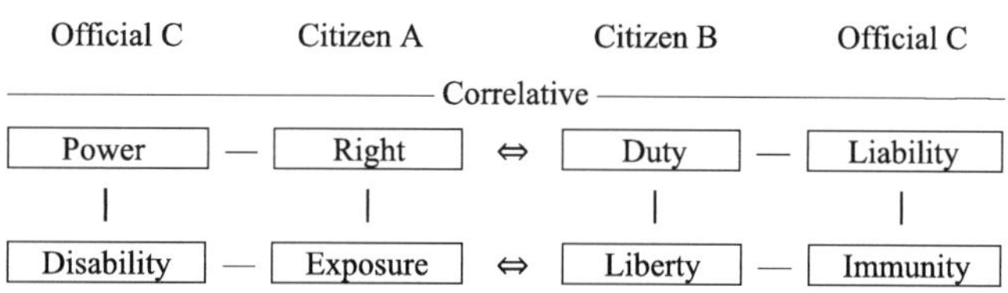


*Figure 9.3* Legal relations between citizens and officials (Commons, 1924, p. 113, Figure XV, partially revised).

Finally, "immunity" refers to the state in which official C does not need to use legal force when citizen B is in "liberty" (Commons, 1924, pp. 117–119). The horizontal link in Figure 9.3 is a correlation such that as the right of citizen A increases, the power of official C also increases, but as the duty of the other party B increases, so does the responsibility of official C. The vertical linkages are mutually limiting so that as "power" increases, "disability" decreases, and as "liability" (responsibility) increases, "immunity" decreases. The problem here is the type of collective power that official C exercises over citizens A and B. The exercise of collective power from official C to citizen A is a positive guarantee of citizen A's right to do something in the "future." In contrast, the exercise of collective power from official C to citizen B is to force citizen B to perform a duty created in the "past." In other words, officials have two types of authority in authoritative transactions: to protect existing rules by enforcing duties and to formulate new rules by guaranteeing rights (Commons, 1924, pp. 114–119). This is the overview identified in Chapter 1.

Commons called the former "remedial powers" and the latter "substantive powers." In this case, "the remedy is simply the power of one set of officials to hold another set of officials responsible for enforcing the remedy" (Commons, 1924, p. 109). Furthermore, according to Commons, the difference between both is as follows.

> The substantive power creates legal relations, and the remedial power enforces them. . . . A substantive power arises out of lawful acts of the principal party creating legal relations for the future. A remedial power arises out of an unlawful act of an opposite party infringing on legal relations created in the past.
>
> (Commons, 1924, p. 115)

As we have identified some of them in the previous section, in LFC, Commons says these two powers are tied to two categories of liberty and freedom.

> Liberty, as such, is only the negative of duty, the absence of restraint or compulsion. But "freedom" is positive. . .. The freedom of the ex-slave was not only that empty immunity from legal subjection to his master provided for in the Thirteenth Amendment of Emancipation from slavery, but also the participation in citizenship provided in the Fourteenth and Fifteenth Amendments.
>
> (Commons, 1924, pp. 118–119)

In other words, when liberty is granted to formerly enslaved people by the 13th Amendment to the Constitution, it is connected to the remedial powers in the sense that if someone tries to make them perform slave labor, it rescues the formerly enslaved person from that illegal act. On the other hand, in the case of granting citizenship, it is a new grant by law of an entity that did not exist before. Thus, "(l)egal power, that is, Freedom, is substantive though inseparable from remedial power" (Commons, 1924, p. 121). An authoritative transaction contains these two powers: the remedial power that leads to liberty and the substantive power that leads to freedom.

Although not explicitly stated by Commons in the LFC, authoritative transactions based on the remedial powers lead to a libertarian market economy in which some of the duties of regulation are removed and, conversely, to a state-controlled economy in which the state ensures that the duties of existing rules are strictly observed. If the transactions between citizens A and B in Figure 9.3 are viewed as market transactions, then official C intervenes in the market to set the rules and, at the same time, enforce the rules. If the transaction between citizens A and B goes well between the two parties, then official C is unnecessary. Even if it does not go well between the two parties, then also official C is unnecessary if it is possible to increase the number of participants on both sides and establish a fair transaction through competition. However, Commons did not believe that the market order could function spontaneously. Hence, in LFC, he developed an explanation for authoritative transactions, which requires the state to intervene in the market. While he stressed the need for the state to intervene in the market, he also indicated that this alone was insufficient and referred to the significance of creating a legal system that would lead to freedom. In the final chapter of LFC, "Public Purpose," he states the following.

> According to this appreciation of relative importance they get the assistance of officials in the form of rights and liberties, and the restraint or neglect of officials in the form of duties and exposures. So that instead of an "organic" theory of the state based on duty, or a "contract" theory of the state based on liberty, we reach what may be distinguished as an economic theory of going concerns based on authoritative proportioning of inducements in a world of limited resources. We may distinguish these as the duty-theory, the liberty-theory and the economic theory of going concerns.
>
> (Commons, 1924, p. 360)

Since LFC analyzes the legal foundations of capitalism, its economic–theoretical analysis is left to the later *Institutional Economics* (IE). LFC also examined the legal changes in the concept of property from American business practices and the changes in corporate forms, such as those seen in joint-stock companies and the accompanying changes in legal provisions – that is, the changing legal foundations of capitalism, using diagrams of legal relations. Therefore, it can be said that, in LFC, Commons sought to realize ideal capitalism by "securing correlations" and "stabilizing expectations" through the authoritative transactions described earlier.

## Authoritative transaction and "reasonable" rationing transactions

### *Commonalities of both transactions and reasonable value*

From our discussion so far, we can confirm a link between authoritative transactions in LFC and rationing transactions in IE, which is essential for creating reasonable value. Commons states about authoritative transactions, "(t)here is no bargaining between citizen and official, no power to withhold service or property, the psychological aspect of the transaction being that of command and obedience" (Commons, 1924, p. 107), which is common to rationing transactions that are based on command and obedience. Furthermore, "in order that these authoritative transactions may be protected against bargaining, the well-known devices of a public hearing, notice of hearing, and related procedure have grown up in practice and been consolidated under the name, 'due process of law'" (Commons, 1924, p. 107). This indicates that among the powers of authoritative transactions, the substantive powers that lead to freedom are consistent with the content of "reasonable" rationing transactions, which is creating reasonable value. This approach ultimately deals with what process we should use to create a legal system. This topic is illustrated in Figure 9.4 as follows.

Suppose we respect the "right" of a private economic agent (e.g., company) A to engage in economic activity freely. In that case, official C ensures that the "right" of the diagram is greatly expanded. In turn, the duty of private economic agents (e.g., consumers and workers) B is similarly expanded, and official C monitors to ensure they are observed. As a result, B's liberty is reduced, while A's exposure is also reduced, thus stabilizing the company's profit-earning. This law is a legal system that prioritizes the profit-earning of a company. However, the result is more likely to be unfair competition and unequal income distribution favoring the companies that have obtained the

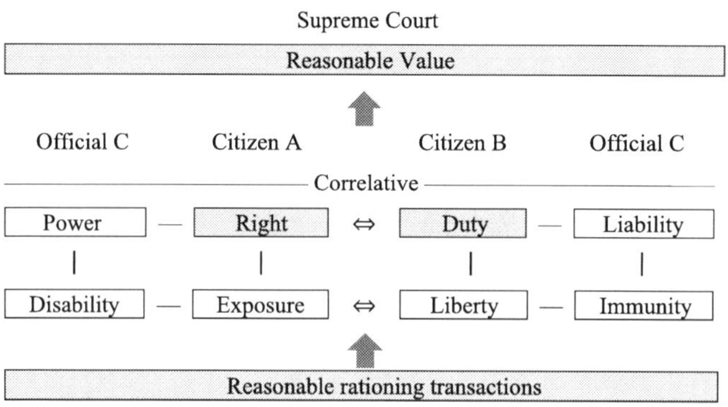


*Figure 9.4* Legal relations and reasonable value (Commons, 1924, p. 113, Figure XV, revised).

rights. Thus, what emerges from this process is neither a reasonable price nor a reasonable value.

Conversely, suppose the state attempts to manage the economy as a whole. In that case, official C is responsible for developing a legal system that expands the "duty" of private economic agent B (company and household). In turn, the right of private economic agent A is expanded, but the right is limited under the legal system established by the state. This approach is the legal system in a dictatorship. The result is a world in which the legal system is likely to change depending on the power struggle among politicians, and the will of private economic agents is not reflected, making it difficult to say that expectations will be stabilized, so a reasonable price and value will be challenging to be created.

The overall impact of the legal system changes depending on where the focus of the legal system is placed. From the discussion of rationing transactions in the previous chapter,[2] we can say that it is necessary to emphasize the process of creating a legal institution and practice rule-making from the middle or the outside in Figure 9.4, not from the "right" or "duty." In short, reasonable value in the broad sense, in line with the LFC of Commons, is realized from a state of complete freedom in authoritative transactions, and in line with IE, it is realized through "reasonable" rationing transactions. Furthermore, the final decision on the reasonableness of the rule is judged by the Supreme Court.

### *Legal relations and creating reasonable value*

The above connections can be recapitulated in Table 9.1. First, the "rights-oriented" legal relations are "democratic" reasonable transactions regarding the macro dimension's classification of rationing transactions. As discussed in Chapter 7, "log-rolling" and "cooperation" apply in this case. If the benefit–burden ratio is implemented without problems by voluntary agreement, then reasonable prices in the market can be achieved. In reality, however, the activities of lobbyists often distort rule-making. In the previous example, the rights of large corporations to profit are prioritized, resulting in capitalism going in the direction of a widening inequality.

Next, "duty-oriented" legal relations are "autocratic" rationing transactions regarding the classification of rationing transactions. As discussed in

*Table 9.1* Legal relations, rationing transactions, and directions of capitalism. Compiled by the author.

| *Legal relations* | *Rationing transactions (macro)* | *Directions* |
|---|---|---|
| Rights-oriented | Democratic | Widening gap |
| Duties-oriented | Autocratic | Dictatorship |
| Rights and Duties–balanced | Reasonable | Reasonable capitalism |

Chapter 7, this is efficient in decision-making, but the duties to the collective organization take precedence over the rights and will of the individual. This approach can easily lead to a dictatorship of the powerful, primarily when the economy is controlled by quantity or price rationing, resulting in the concentration of power in the hands of the central government. While a dictatorship may be able to control the economy successfully, it has the weakness that, depending on the political power struggle, the economy may be adversely affected.

Commons has seen the above two drawbacks up close: profit monopolies by large companies and fascist/communist dictatorships. Therefore, he recommended a third method that balances rights and duties to protect capitalism from these horrors. This involves authoritative transactions that follow due process of law, which are the equivalent of "reasonable" rationing transactions. This is what produces reasonable price and reasonable value. However, the Supreme Court will ultimately decide whether the rule created is reasonable.

## Toward reasonable capitalism

Incorporating the Supreme Court's decisions and customs into the figure described so far, the transaction economics of Commons as a "cumulative legal causation" toward reasonable capitalism can be summarized as follows.[3]

### *Artificial selection by the Supreme Court*

The base is active individuals with willingness and freedom and the going concern they belong to. What is agreed upon through collective bargaining by their representatives, that is, what has gone through the institutional process

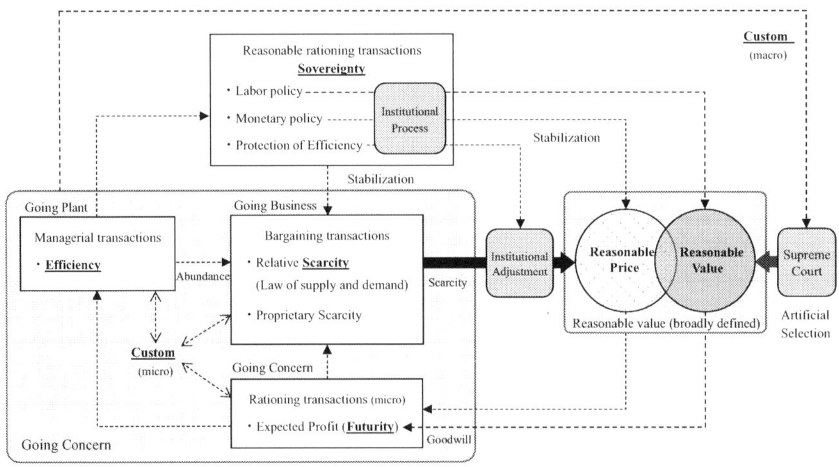


*Figure 9.5* Cumulative legal causation toward reasonable capitalism. Compiled by the author.

or due process of law as a "reasonable" rationing transaction, is made into a rule (stabilization of expectations) by the sovereignty (the state). That would be reasonable value in the narrow sense, but the Supreme Court ultimately determines whether it is reasonable. As we have seen, if the rule favors a particular class at this time, it will be eliminated by an unconstitutional ruling, as was the case with parts of the New Deal.[4] This is the artificial selection of the legal institutions. However, the Supreme Court, influenced by the macro conventions in the diagram, that is, the conventions of the time, will forbear its outbursts and select rules appropriate to the time.

### *Goodwill and efficiency improvement*

The point of the legal cumulative causation of Commons shown in Figure 9.5 is that artificial selection is not the ultimate goal. If it has created reasonable value, the rule subjected to artificial selection will affect the going concern and the next period of economic activity as goodwill, that is, a good rule. Specifically, when rules to prevent workers' accidents and unemployment, such as Wisconsin's workers' compensation and unemployment compensation, are created by labor–management agreement, they are clearly stated as working rules within the going concern. At the same time, goodwill arises from good rules, resulting in an increased efficiency (increased productivity[5]). This is sometimes combined with corporate culture and ethics to generate micro-customs. If this increases the expected profit of the going concern, it becomes an intangible property. This is the "futurity" part of Figure 9.5. If the expected profit rate exceeds the market interest rate, the going concern invests in debt, in which "futurity" is associated with intangible property. In this way, rules subjected to artificial selection affect economic activities such as production and sales activities in the next period.

### *Cumulative legal causation and economic activity*

Artificial selection is not the end goal or an equilibrium. Instead, it is a cumulative causation of legal institutions. A virtuous cycle between institutions and the economy is created if reasonable value is created through "reasonable" rationing transactions, as we have seen in Chapter 7. However, if institutions are created through "autocratic" rationing transactions, the probability of such a virtuous cycle is extremely low, and it may ultimately end up as a political power struggle. On the other hand, if the institution that favors large companies is created through "democratic" rationing transactions, it may end up with unfair competition and unequal income distribution, as we saw in the previous section. These will result in neither a reasonable price nor a reasonable value because expectations will not be stabilized except for the parties who gain from the institution. Finally, if the degree of competition and income distribution is severe, such an institution will be discarded by artificial selection.

Thus, cumulative legal causation means that explicit rules influence the going concern to generate working rules, creating micro-customs, including mezzo level, within the going concern and forming the business ethics of that concern. Together, they form the macro-customs of society as a whole, which ultimately influence the Supreme Court. In other words, customs have a significant impact on economic activity.[6] The work to create reasonable values evolves institutions through trial and error, as seen in the unconstitutional rulings by the New Deal. This is the pragmatic approach that Commons has conceived, the economic evolutional theory of cumulative changes in micro and macro legal relations. Realizing cumulative causation that creates reasonable value through "reasonable" rationing transactions is essential for reasonable capitalism.

This idea differs from Veblen's idea of natural selection, but they share the meaning of "cumulative causation" of institutions. In "Why is Economics Not an Evolutionary Science?" (Veblen, 1898), Veblen said, "[A]n evolutionary economics must be the theory of a process of cultural growth as determined by the economic interest, a theory of a cumulative sequence of economic institutions stated in terms of the process itself" (Veblen, 1898 (1919), p. 77). This is in common with Commons' aforementioned idea and can be characterized as a theoretical pillar of the old institutional school.

## Conclusion

Toward reasonable capitalism, transaction economics of Commons has its potential in cumulative legal causation. In *Legal Foundations of Capitalism*, Commons explored ways to intervene in the market. It eventually emerged in the form of "authoritative transactions." It is characterized by the government having two powers: the substantive power and the remedial power. The substantive power creates legal relations and links freedom. The remedial power enforces legal relations and links liberty. These authoritative transactions and "reasonable" rationing transactions in *Institutional Economics* have commonalities in that they are essential to creating reasonable value. In other words, they can create rules by conforming to rights and duties without being too biased toward rights and increasing inequality or too biased toward duties and falling into dictatorship. Reasonable value in the broad sense, in line with the LFC of Commons, is realized from a state of complete freedom in authoritative transactions, and in line with IE, it is realized through "reasonable" rationing transactions. However, the Supreme Court will ultimately decide whether the rule created is reasonable.

The point of cumulative legal causation is that artificial selection is not the ultimate goal. Rules subjected to artificial selection by the Supreme Court will affect the economic activity of the going concern after that. If they can create narrowly defined reasonable value, they will create goodwill within the going concern, which will lead to improved efficiency and higher expected profits. In the process, it generates cumulative legal causations that generate micro-customs within the concern, lead to the generation of macro-customs throughout society, and ultimately affect the Supreme Court.

In *The Economics of Collective Action*, Commons said,

> I find five assumptions or hypotheses to be primary in interpreting modern economic activity. These five simplified assumptions – sovereignty, scarcity, efficiency, futurity, and custom – are logical assumptions, made for the purpose of attaining systematic interpretation and understanding in a world of diversity. They are devices for investigation.
>
> (Commons, 1950, p. 73)

We can incorporate these five assumptions in the cumulative legal causation in Figure 9.5 and understand the overall view of the transaction economics of Commons.

## Notes

1 Refer to Chapter 1, Institutional economics of Commons as transaction economics.

2 Refer to Chapter 7, Reclassification of rationing transactions and creation of reasonable value.

3 According to Dorfman, Commons initially intended to publish *The Legal Foundations of Capitalism* and *Institutional Economics* in one volume. However, on Mitchell's advice, he published them separately in two volumes (Dorfman, 1958, p. 406). Figure 9.5 is a combination of what Commons was trying to publish in one volume.

4 For example, the Agricultural Adjustment Act (AAA) and the National Industrial Recovery Act (NIRA). See Chapter 7, Reclassification of rationing transactions and creation of reasonable value, especially "Reasonable" rationing transactions and reasonable value.

5 "Productivity" is used in the general sense of efficiency of production. Commons used the term "efficiency" rather than "productivity" to describe labor productivity (Commons, 1934, p. 378). This is because "productivity" would be confused with value-added labor productivity, expressed in monetary terms. He assumed that the monetary notation was a bargaining transaction that represented scarcity. So, when physical labor productivity was ascertained by quantity, he used "man-hours," which represents the amount of work per person per hour, to measure efficiency (Commons, 1934, p. 66). For a literature discussion of efficiency and scarcity, see Uni (2014).

6 Such ideas are still attracting attention in the 21st century. A representative example is Hodgson's idea of "legal institutionalism." In a footnote to his book, he states, "I use it to denote legally grounded approaches to the institutional and economic analysis of capitalism, as envisioned by Commons (1924), Samuels (1989), and others" (Hodgson, 2015, p. 12).

## References

### *English*

Commons, John R. (1913). *Labor and Administration*. New York: Macmillan.

———. (1924) 1995. *Legal Foundations of Capitalism*. New Brunswick and London: Transaction Publishers.

———. (1925) 1996. "Marx Today: Capitalism and Socialism," *Atlantic Monthly*, 136 (November). Reprinted in Commons (1996), 371–385.

———. (1934). *Institutional Economics: Its Place in Political Economy*. New York: Macmillan.

———. (1950). *The Economics of Collective Action*. New York: Macmillan.

———. (1996). *John R. Commons: Selected Essays*, eds. by Rutherford, Malcom, & Warren J. Samuels. London and New York: Routledge.

Dorfman, Joseph. (1958). "The Mutual Influence of Mitchell and Commons," *American Economic Review*, 47 (June), 405–408.

Hodgson, Geoffrey M. (2015). *Conceptualizing Capitalism: Institutions, Evolution, Future*. Chicago and London: University of Chicago Press.

Samuels, Warren J. (1989). "The Legal-Economic Nexus," *George Washington Law Review*, 57 (6), 1556–1578.

Veblen, Thorstein B. (1898) 1919. "Why Is Economics Not an Evolutionary Science?" *Quarterly Journal of Economics*, 12 (July). Reprinted in Veblen (1919), 56–81.

———. (1919). *The Place of Science in Modern Civilization and Other Essays*. New York: B. W. Huebsch.

### *Japanese*

Uni, Hiroyuki. (2014). "J. R. Commons no Ruisekiteki Inga Renkan Ron: *Seido Keizaigaku* to 1927 nen Sōko no Hikaku Bunseki" (J. R. Commons' Theory of Cumulative Causation: A Comparative Analysis of *Institutional Economics* and Its Manuscript in 1927), *Kikan-Keizai-Riron* (Political Economy Quarterly), 51 (2), 77–88.

# Conclusion

## Systematicity of transaction economics

Commons' institutional economics is theoretical and systematic. It can be explained by the concept of transactions in detail. Its theoretical systematics are presented in Chapter 9, Figure 9.5. To summarize the main points again, we began by linking the concept of transactions, consisting of three types, bargaining, managerial, and rationing, to a going concern, which is a collective organization. Then, by considering price determination theory, which has not been pointed out much in the past, we linked it to business cycle theory to enable a dynamic understanding of the institutional economics of Commons. Moreover, we classified the rationing transactions of Commons into three types. We pointed out that "reasonable" rationing transactions create narrowly defined reasonable value through direct discussion and agreement between the parties. In this way, we captured the essence of the theory of reasonable value and made it possible to understand it in terms of cumulative causation.

As seen from Chapter 9, Figure 9.5 and the accompanying explanations, Commons' institutional economics can be understood as "transaction economics," centered on the transaction concept, which he took as the smallest unit of study. If we understand it, Commons' institutional economics is theoretical, comprehensive, systematic, and helpful in explaining real economic society.

## Theoretical connections between Commons' works

The relations between Commons' labor theory and his subsequent writings, especially his institutional economic theories, have rarely been considered. Table 10.1 summarizes what has been mentioned piecemeal in this book. In *Industrial Goodwill* (1919), as we saw in Chapter 6, Commons' labor theory consists of the following four stages, each of which relates to the transaction concept.

The first, the "commodity" theory of labor, states that the value of labor is determined by supply and demand and is related to "bargaining transactions" in the market in *Institutional Economics* (IE). That connects to "going business" in *Legal Foundations of Capitalism* (LFC), and in *The Economics of Collective Action* (ECA), it connects to "scarcity," one of the five simplified

DOI: 10.4324/9781032701394-15

assumptions. The second "machinery" theory of labor is the stage in which the quantity of its product determines the value of labor. That is related to "managerial transactions" in IE within the "going plant" in LFC and production "efficiency" in ECA. The third, "goodwill" theory of labor, is that the beneficial relationship between labor and management affects the value of labor. That is related to "rationing transactions" in micro in IE, within the "going concern" in LFC, and "futurity" as the expected profit in ECA. The fourth, "the public utility" theory of labor, involves government intervention in the market, where labor legislation determines the value of labor. This legislation is related to "rationing transactions" in macro in IE, which create reasonable value to achieve reasonable capitalism. It is also done through authoritative transactions in LFC and sovereignty in ECA. The fifth, "practices," were not keywords in *Industrial Goodwill*. However, it refers to labor practices and common law. These are "institutions," "working rules," and "custom" in IE and can also be understood as "working rules" or "common law" in LFC. It is what is keyworded as "custom" in ECA. This study shows custom (micro) and custom (macro) in Chapter 9, Figure 9.5. As described earlier, Commons' labor theory and institutional economic theory have theoretical connections.

## Characteristics and possibilities of transaction economics

The following three are some of the characteristics and possibilities of transaction economics of Commons.

### *Social science theory integrating economics, law, and ethics*

As we have already seen, transaction economics of Commons is a theory that applies juristic concepts to economic analysis. If the emphasis is on rights and

*Table 10.1* The theoretical transition and commonality of Commons from 1919 to 1950. Compiled by the author.

| | *Industrial Goodwill (1919)* | *Legal Foundations of Capitalism (1924)* | *Institutional Economics (1934)* | *The Economics of Collective Action (1950)* |
|---|---|---|---|---|
| 1 Market and price | Commodity theory | Going business | Bargaining transactions | Scarcity |
| 2 Productivity | Machine theory | Going plant | Managerial transactions | Efficiency |
| 3 Corporate governance | Goodwill theory | Going concern | Rationing transactions (micro) | Futurity |
| 4 Public policy | Public utility theory | Authoritative transaction | Rationing transactions (macro) | Sovereignty |
| 5 Practice and rule | (Labor practice) (common law) | Working rule (common law) | Working rule, institution, custom | Custom |

the abandonment of duties, a market economy based on contracts cannot be maintained. On the other hand, if individual rights are suppressed in favor of duties, democracy will be plunged into crisis. In creating rules based on reasonable rationing transactions, it is crucial to maintain a balance between rights and duties and not be biased in favor of either one or the other. This is also applicable to rule-making in the real world.

On the other hand, whether the rules created are reasonable is a problem of ethics. In the transaction economics of Commons, the artificial selection by the Supreme Court is ultimately determined. The criterion for a reasonable price is whether or not equality of opportunity, fair competition, and equality of bargaining power are ensured. Whether a narrowly defined reasonable value, apart from reasonable price, is reasonable or not depends on "the consensus of opinion of reasonable men – 'reasonable' in that they are men who conform to the dominant practices of the time" (Commons, 1934, pp. 206–207). It refers to due process and not favoring a particular class.

Furthermore, Commons' transaction economics does not deny the market's law of supply and demand, as seen in Table 10.1. Commons himself wrote, "The problem now is not to create a different kind of economics – 'institutional' economics – divorced from preceding schools, but how to give to collective action, in all its varieties, its due place throughout economic theory" (Commons, 1934, p. 5). As he states, he does not reject price theory in the market but incorporates other parts of the theory concerning collective action into the overall framework. And in doing so, he understands the importance of the market, as seen from Commons' study of labor history. In other words, he points out that as markets expand and change, the nature of collective organization also transforms, and rules need to be constructed accordingly. This means that as markets become globalized, international politics must be coordinated, and in doing so, as international laws are enacted, economic activities are affected by them, and new business practices are created, which can be viewed as cumulative causation. Thus, transaction economics is a theory that incorporates law and ethics without denying the core of economics, the price theory of markets.

### *Cumulative legal causation*

As discussed in Chapter 8, Commons' transaction economics differs fundamentally in its economic methodology from Williamson's transaction cost economics and North's new institutionalist economic history. One of these differences is the application of juristic concepts to economic analysis, as noted in the previous section. The other is a dynamic theory based on legal relations, including customs, and their cumulative causation. The causation has been explained in the previous chapters up to Chapter 9. As a supplement to "cumulative," in the case of Commons, "cumulation" of judicial precedents influences subsequent society as case law, as Kitagawa (2014) pointed out.[1]

This book builds on these studies and shows that the cumulation of joint agreements will hopefully strengthen the trust relationship (goodwill) between labor and management. As a micro practice (shared knowledge) within a company, the cumulation of working rules forms the corporate culture and business ethics. Furthermore, the cumulation of goodwill leads to higher efficiency (higher productivity). This is important in the transaction economics of Commons. In addition to the transaction concept, this book includes five keywords to understand economic activity (scarcity, efficiency, futurity, sovereignty, custom) and illustrates them in a figure. As Kitagawa also says, this is not just one circle but a simplified model (Kitagawa, 2014, p. 109), but it is a powerful circle that explains reality.

### *The process to protect capitalism and democracy*

How to determine institutions is ultimately essential in achieving reasonable capitalism that creates reasonable value. As we have seen, ideal institutions are formed through "reasonable" rationing transactions. In cumulative legal causation, this approach affects economic performance in terms of efficiency by forming goodwill. Therefore, a narrow understanding of corporate management as a going concern, in which labor is regarded as a mere cost, is unacceptable. In the transaction economics of Commons, goodwill is an intangible property that increases efficiency and contributes to a virtuous cycle in the economy. Therefore, it is necessary to make policies favorable to proactive companies that make efforts to form goodwill.

In economic activities, even if the profit-seeking activities of companies are not at fault, disparities will arise at the macro level if their rights are prejudiced. Commons' idea is to correct this problem by forming rules through collective bargaining among interested parties, that is, institutional adjustment. Put another way, the solution to the fallacy of composition is creating reasonable value through institutional adjustment and the artificial selection of courts. Their existence is necessary for the preservation of capitalism and democracy as well as for resolving the fallacy of composition. This is because institutional adjustment in transaction economics is not about the "concentration of wealth" through widening inequality and "concentration of power" through increased intervention in the market but about overcoming inequality through a joint agreement through democratic collective bargaining. In this way, capitalism and democracy can be maintained, and reasonable capitalism, which can create reasonable value, can be realized.

## Note

1 In other studies, Ramstad (1990) dealt with the cyclical and cumulative causation between individuals and society and understood economic values within this causation. Kitagawa (2014) also addressed the cumulative causation of institutions and the institutionalized mind. Kitagawa also points out that, unlike Veblen, Commons does not include instincts in the cumulative causation to avoid an "antagonism" (Kitagawa, 2014, p. 103). In addition to these, Uni (2014) independently shows the composition of the cumulative causation of Commons from a manuscript analysis of *Institutional Economics*.

## References


### *English*

Commons, John R. (1919). *Industrial Goodwill.* New York: McGraw-Hill.

———. (1924) 1995. *Legal Foundations of Capitalism.* New Brunswick and London: Transaction Publishers.

———. (1934). *Institutional Economics: Its Place in Political Economy.* New York: Macmillan.

———. (1950). *The Economics of Collective Action.* New York: Macmillan.

Ramstad, Yngve. (1990). "The Institutionalism of John R. Commons: Theoretical Foundations of a Volitional Economics," *Research in the History of Economic Thought and Methodology*, 8, 53–104.

### *Japanese*

Kitagawa, Kota. (2014). "J. R. Commons *Seido-Keizaigaku* ni okeru Tekisei-na Kachi to Shuken" (Reasonable Value and Sovereignty in *Institutional Economics* on J. R. Commons) [Doctoral thesis, Kyoto University]. Kyoto University Repository. https://repository.kulib.kyoto-u.ac.jp/dspace/bitstream/2433/199050/1/ykeik00505.pdf

Uni, Hiroyuki. (2014). "J. R. Commons no Ruisekiteki Inga Renkan Ron: *Seido Keizaigaku* to 1927 nen Sōko no Hikaku Bunseki" (J. R. Commons' Theory of Cumulative Causation: A Comparative Analysis of *Institutional Economics* and Its Manuscript in 1927), *Kikan-Keizai-Riron* (Political Economy Quarterly), 51 (2), 77–88.

# Index

Note: Page numbers in *italics* indicate a figure and page numbers in **bold** indicate a table on the corresponding page.

Made in the USA
Las Vegas, NV
19 September 2026

107f2c63-d032-4da3-b441-817b562be0b4R01